# A Journey through Lancashire

Kenneth Fields

**Published by** Sigma Leisure - an imprint of
Sigma Press, 1 South Oak Lane, Wilmslow, Cheshire SK9 6AR, England.

**British Library Cataloguing in Publication Data**
A CIP record for this book is available from the British Library.

**ISBN:** 1-85058-398-6

**Typesetting and Design by:** Sigma Press, Wilmslow, Cheshire.

**Cover design:** by Martin Mills.

Pictures (clockwise, starting top-left) – Gracie Fields; Silverdale; Wigan Pier; the Lune Estuary. Central picture – Darwen Moor.

**Printed by:** Manchester Free Press

# *PREFACE*

There is a tendency in this age of cheap foreign travel for us to venture to the remote corners of the world, yet to neglect that which lies on our own doorstep. Places and landmarks abroad which we read about in holiday brochures, quite naturally, seem to be more exciting and more inviting than those closer to home. I remember sitting on the balcony of a hotel at Luxor in Egypt, gazing across the waters of the Nile at the pink Theban Hills. A group of fellow Lancastrians was preparing to join a tour which would take them to the Valley of the Kings, then on to Cairo to see the Pyramids and the marvellous treasures of Tutankhamun. I wondered how many of these people, who had ventured over two thousand miles and endured the burning desert heat to look upon the remains of ancient Egypt, could say with honesty that they really had as much knowledge of their native county. Had they ever seen the magnificent view from the summit of Pendle Hill, made that unique walk across the sands of Morecambe Bay, ventured to Anglezarke's remote Bronze Age burial mound or explored England's most haunted house?

To discover what Lancashire is really like in this, the last decade of the twentieth century, I decided to make a journey around the county. In these pages you will find my personal recollections of what I found as I meandered backwards and forwards in a light-hearted fashion. My aim was to both explore and enjoy the many diverse features that give our corner of England its special character. To achieve this aim I have climbed to the top of windswept hills, wandered through ancient towns and sleepy villages, then experienced the contrasting bustle of our noisy cities. I have also attempted to look at our chain of history, to reveal both the saints and the sinners, who have shaped our past.

But it is of course people who have created the present face of Lancashire and its legacy lies with our children. With this in mind I decided that throughout my tour I would attempt to both observe and chat with anyone who could spare the time. To these individuals, many of whom remain anonymous, I give my grateful thanks.

Every journey needs a starting point and it was difficult to decide which was the most appropriate place to begin my tour. However, I then learned that the Ordnance Survey had made a series of calculations to pin-point the exact centre of Great Britain, and quite rightly, they found it lies in Lancashire. The most representative centre of mainland Great Britain together with a total of 401 islands, lies near Whitendale Hanging Stones (Ref: SD 637565) in the Forest of Bowland. Lovely Dunsop Bridge, which stands on the banks of the River Hodder, is now officially the village which lies closest to the centre. So it was from this secluded spot, beneath the towering brown fells, that my journey began one hot June day and continued through autumn and into winter.

I decided to take a circular route, following a haphazardly path to see those places which appealed to me most. With a couple of exceptions, I kept within the borders of the present counties of Lancashire, Merseyside and Greater Manchester.

Finally, although this is not intended as a guidebook, I hope those who read it may be tempted to follow in my footsteps and discover some of the delights that I found on my journey through Lancashire.

*Kenneth Fields*

## *Acknowledgments*

I would like to begin by mentioning my gratitude to the marvellous Tourist Information Centres, which have sprung up in most Lancashire towns. The staff are helpful, their leaflets are highly informative, and importantly, their knowledge and assistance is free! I have found those at Garstang, Lancaster, Burnley, Accrington, Clitheroe, Rochdale and Wigan to be of an extremely high standard.

My special thanks to Mike Ince of Croston who, using his artistic talent, has produced the sketches which are used throughout this book. Also I would like to thank the following museums and individuals, who have kindly allowed me to use photographs from their collection: The Kathleen Ferrier Archive at Blackburn Museum, The Rochdale Museum Service Collection, Bolton Wanderers Football Club, Felix de Wolfe, Betty Wainwright, Ben Barker and Mary Morton. All other photographs and the route map are by the author.

Likewise, I record my appreciation of the prompt and detailed information supplied to me by the Ordnance Survey, whose maps have successfully guided me along the byways and up the hills of Lancashire.

Finally, I would like to thank Jack Prescott of Horwich, who, some thirty years ago, first introduced me to the mountains, moorlands and the wild places of the north. And the late H.V. Morton, whose works will always be an inspiration to those who journey through Britain.

This book is dedicated to my wife Wynne for her patience and support during my journey, and for reading, criticising and suggesting improvements to my manuscript.

What is this life if, full of care,<br>
We have no time to stand and stare.

William Henry Davies (1871–1940)

# *Contents*

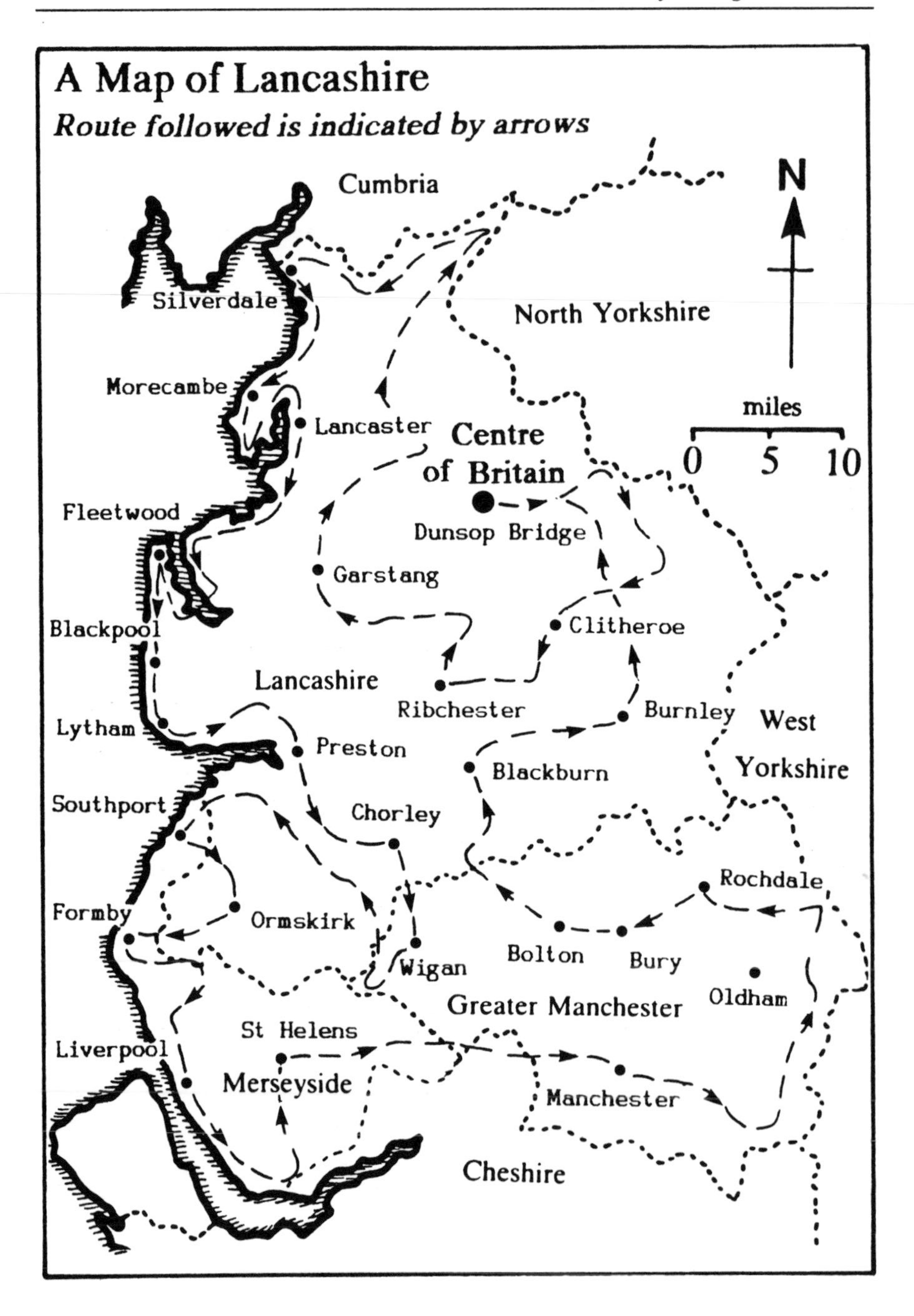
A Map of Lancashire
Route followed is indicated by arrows
Cumbria
N
Silverdale
North Yorkshire
Morecambe
Lancaster
Centre
of Britain
miles
0 5 10
Fleetwood
Dunsop Bridge
Garstang
Blackpool
Clitheroe
Lancashire
Ribchester
Burnley
West
Yorkshire
Lytham
Preston
Blackburn
Southport
Chorley
Rochdale
Formby
Ormskirk
Bolton
Bury
Wigan
Oldham
Greater Manchester
St Helens
Liverpool
Merseyside
Manchester
Cheshire

# *CHAPTER ONE*

# *DUNSOP BRIDGE TO RIBCHESTER*

I begin my journey from the centre of Britain. I wander through Slaidburn and learn about minerals, find the remote site of a drowned village and visit the hiding place of a King. I daydream in Sawley Abbey, saunter through ancient Clitheroe, meet a blacksmith who carves rocking-horses on Whalley Nab and end up in Roman Lancashire.

## *1*

I opened the window of my car on the hottest day of the year and looking up saw the towering green slopes of Beatrix Fell ending in a blue cloudless sky. From the conifer woods, which grow on the lower part of the hillside, echoed the song of a blackbird and with the faint breeze, came the scent of the buttercups and meadowsweet which lined every hedgerow. It was mid-morning in the village of Dunsop Bridge and I was about to begin my journey.

Sauntering from the small car-park into the village street I immediately discovered that the centre of Britain is marked by a public telephone box. An inscription on its glass side relates that it is the 100,000th pay phone to be erected, a map shows the major cities radiating out from Dunsop Bridge. Wooden posts erected outside the box mark the points of the compass and one gives the map reference of SD 66075007. Suddenly I had the feeling that the eyes of London, Edinburgh, Plymouth and Norwich were staring disapprovingly in my direction, so I walked quickly away.

Although Dunsop Bridge is little bigger than a hamlet it has been well known for centuries by travellers. Here lies the gateway to that once dreaded pass, the Trough of Bowland, that winds its way through the high fells, linking the Ribble Valley to Lancaster. It has witnessed a diverse array of humanity over the centuries. Scottish raiders intent on rape and pillage, pilgrims seeking the absolution of their sins at Whalley Abbey, and the Pendle Witches facing death at Lancaster, have all passed through. Today's travellers are much less colourful, mainly Sunday trippers out for a spin in the family car or cyclists eager to test their endurance on the lung-bursting gradients.

*Dunsop Bridge: a tranquil Lancashire village on the banks of the River Hodder at the centre of Britain.*

That lovely Lancashire river, the Dunsop, washes up to the village street before passing beneath a sturdy hump-backed bridge on its journey to join the Ribble. A handful of retired couples were enjoying the hot sun on the river bank, the only sound being that of an anxious female mallard calling to her brood. I walked past Leedham's garage which was once a smithy and continued past the village post office to reach the impressive war memorial which stands sentinel on an elevated corner. From here a breathtaking view of the rising fells could easily be mistaken for a Lakeland scene. Prominent in the foreground, guarding the Trough Road, soars the brown bulk of Mellor Knoll, known affectionately as the Old Man of Bowland.

As I peered into the small garden which surrounds the memorial a sun tanned man of about fifty five, who was busy weeding, looked up. He told me modestly, that he looked after the garden and that the mass of bright yellow and white flowers which were attracting the bees were known as Fried Egg plants. We then spoke of the men of Dunsop Bridge who, almost eighty years ago, left this tranquil spot to end their young lives in the mud of Flanders.

"Nearly every family must have lost a son, for Dunsop Bridge was even smaller in those days. There are two brothers among the fallen", he explained pointing to the roll of honour.

We then talked of the Towneley family who once owned most of the land in the area and of the Roman Catholic church that lies up the road. He told me how a new priest who had once been a police sergeant in Manchester had recently been inducted. The former Chief Constable, Sir James Anderton, who was himself a Roman Catholic convert had also attended the service.

I found St Hubert's church bathed in bright sunshine on the side of the Trough Road, but I had arrived at the wrong time for the interior was being decorated. Tarpaulins covered the pews and a young man was perched high up a ladder, an artist who with great skill was renovating the ornate wall. He did not look around as I stared admiringly at his work, so I tip-toed away, not wanting to disturb this Lancashire Michelangelo.

The benefactors of this church were mainly members of the Towneley family who arranged its construction in 1861 in a mood of elation after their racehorse, Kettledrum, won the Derby. In the small churchyard I disturbed a young rabbit who had been sheltering from the sun under a Towneley tomb. It dashed away through a hedgerow while a huge white marble angel looked down with disdain. This seemed the right time to leave the centre of Britain.

As I drove slowly eastwards along the green valley I could see the silver line of the Hodder below me on the right, while the huge grassy flank of the Bowland Hills overlooked the opposite side. It is along this lane, near to the point were a stream tumbles of the hillside, that a gallows once stood. Here, those who chose to break the strict Forest Laws and were caught, paid with their lives. It is a spot to be avoided on dark stormy nights, so I'm told, for it is said that the moans of tormented souls can still be heard.

The fields beyond Newton were alive with the drone of tractors, the farmers being anxious to gather the first hay of the season. Symmetrical yellow stripes followed their trail over the sloping fields, while here and there the huge cylinders of tightly packed grass littered the landscape. Suddenly, as I came over a rise the stone tower of St Andrew's church came into view, with the tranquil stone cottages of Slaidburn spreading upwards from the river valley.

I managed to obtain the last remaining car space by the river, for Slaidburn had assumed the identity of Cannes. Sun hats, swim-suits and ice cold drinks were the order of the day as toddlers, young couples and octogenarians all mingled together to soak up the sun. I ambled towards the village centre, then stopped in surprise, for I discovered a shop which was not selling cream-cakes and bread as I expected, but rocks and minerals. Intrigued, I decided to investigate.

Neatly laid out and labelled, on shelves, tables and in boxes were hundreds of different pieces of stone from all over the world. Many were polished to reveal their true colourful beauty, reflecting in purples, reds, greens, and translucent gold. Others were mottled, striped or banded in a fascinating blend that had been created when the earth was young. There were pieces so small I could only just make out their shimmering hue, while others were as large as a house-brick. Many of the larger pieces had a dismal dark outer surface, but had been broken to reveal a breathtaking inner Aladdin's cave of glittering crystal. Some bore romantic names like bloodstone, tigers eye, agate, and smoky quartz, while many had academic names which often ended in *ite*, such as rhyolite, andesite and albite.

"Are you an expert on minerals?" I asked the lady who was sat behind the counter.

"No, I must admit that I am not. Over the years I have gained some knowledge, but the more I learn, the less I know."

She went on to tell me that although the shop was in a country area there were few similar outlets in the north, so the business had become well known. Her customers ranged from geology students who wanted samples for their studies, people who loved the sheer beauty of the minerals and were building up a collection, or women who made them into jewellery. Some large specimens could cost between fifty and eighty pounds.

I purchased a small sample of turquoise phosphate that took my eye, then headed in the direction of the 'Hark to Bounty', to quench my thirst.

The inn, which is said to date from the 13th century, was full of serious eaters. Pubs such as this have witnessed a revolution over the last twenty years, drink having become secondary to food. But the aroma of roast beef, pork chop and vegetable lasagne could not tempt me, being in a traditionalist mood I ordered half a pint of real ale.

Up to 1937 the inn also acted as a court-room, it still contains the witness box and jury bench. For over five hundred years travelling justices brought the law to Bowland, Slaidburn having the only court-room between York and Lancaster. Its unique name came about through an incident which happened in 1875, for it had been formerly known as The Dog. The local squire, who was also the parson, owned a pack of hounds. One hot day after hunting on the fells he and his friends called at the inn for a drink. But their talk was disturbed by the loud yapping of the dogs outside. The squire amazed his friends by insisting he could recognise the call of his favourite hound above the din, telling them to "Hark to Bounty".

Slaidburn has been well known to generations of walkers and cyclists for the village has a youth hostel. Like Dunsop Bridge, it is a gateway to the high fells of Bowland and also to the Yorkshire Dales. A single track road, which was once gated to keep in the sheep, leads northwards through a lonely pass that might have been stolen from the Scottish Highlands, to Bentham. A second route only passable on foot, is the Salter Fell track, which crosses the windswept summits to Hornby and the Lune Valley.

As I walked in the direction of my car I could hear a bell calling the reluctant pupils of the primary school back to their classrooms, their excited chattering echoed across the otherwise quiet street. A pair of wicked-eyed jackdaws sat placidly on the top of a stone wall, watching a tall man who was wearing a bright white sun hat amble past.

"England. It's not bad is it?"

I smiled in reply. On a day such as this I knew exactly what he meant.

## 2

The Lancashire sun-worshippers were still paying homage to their deity as I drove away from the riverside across Slaidburn's impressive bridge. This road climbs steeply at first, then quickly levels out to allow extensive views of a patchwork of green fields full of curious lambs, their pathetic calls sounding right across the valley. After five miles the county border into Yorkshire is reached at Tosside, then the road continues to Long Preston and the Dales. But at the cross-roads at Stephen Moor I turned left to make a detour up the quiet lane which leads to the remote banks of Stocks Reservoir on the edge of Gisburn Forest. The only building I passed along this narrow lane was a small church which appears strangely out of place, so far from any human habitation.

Enveloped on its eastern bank by a wall of towering trees the hidden waters of Stocks Reservoir seem to have stepped out of the pages of an Arthurian legend. It is difficult to believe, with its natural lake-like appearance, than this home of black-headed gulls and Canada Geese, is less than seventy years old. But perhaps this atmosphere of age conveyed by these moorland waters results from the ancient ruins of a lost village which lies beneath the waves.

The reservoirs of the Pennines have become an accepted part of our northern landscape, they often enliven a featureless valley with a splash of blue. Over the years they become integrated into the countryside, attracting trees and plant life to their banks which in turn creates a habitat for birds and animals. The oldest of these reservoirs were built at the beginning of the last century to supply clean drinking water to the rapidly expanding towns of

Lancashire and decrease the ever-present threat of diseases, including typhoid. However, like the present day building of the rail-link to the channel tunnel and the growing motorway system, there is a price to pay by any community which lies in their path. The ideal site for any new reservoir is a deep-cut river valley which can be easily dammed, this causes the least expense of construction and it has a guaranteed source of water. But almost always, such valleys contain ancient farms or, as in the case of Stocks Reservoir, a complete village. In 1925 when the Fylde Water Board was given permission to begin work on their new reservoir it spelt the death sentence for the isolated village of Stocks-in-Bolland, or Dalehead as it was known locally. The village was made up of twenty cottages, a post office and shop, a church with a nearby vicarage and a school. The close-knit community was moved out, many to live in Slaidburn, and the demolition men moved in.

The church, which now stands forlornly on the high ground at the forest edge, was rebuilt from stone taken from the old building. The remains of people buried in the old graveyard had also to be taken to new graves. The operation was completed with the damming of the River Hodder, which starts its journey off nearby Lamb Hill Fell, to which was added the waters of Hasgill Beck and Bottom Beck.

They say that in a dry summer the tumbled stones of the old buildings can still be seen protruding from the dark mud. I drove away wondering if any villagers ever return to look upon the drowned homes of their childhood and perhaps dwell on the heartache they had to suffer so that the holiday makers of Blackpool could enjoy a cup of tea.

Strangers to the Ribble Valley need to come armed with an Ordnance Survey map, for a patchwork of lanes spread out across the whole area like a huge spider's web. It is easy to set off with the intention of visiting say, Chipping, then find yourself in Bashall Eaves, Hurst Green or even Waddington. Once this happens you will spot something that takes your interest and your carefully laid out plans will soon be forgotten. I had no intention of this happening to me, Gisburn was where I was heading and Gisburn is where I would go. The rest of the afternoon I spent at Bolton-by-Bowland . . .

I imagine there are exiled Lancastrians walking the streets of Vancouver, sitting in a shady spot in Perth or feeling the soft winds of Wellington on their face, and all dreaming of home. If they have a picture of an English village in their mind, and I'm told even city folk dream of the country, then it must surely be Bolton-by-Bowland on a hot June day. It has all the ingredients that an English village ought to have, attractive stone cottages ablaze with flowers, a village green complete with market cross and stocks, an inviting inn and an ancient church. I wandered up the deserted street watching the house martins soar over the rooftops like Tornado jets, admiring the placid waters of Kirk Beck and thinking how strange that in this quiet backwater I was following in the footsteps of a king.

*The Ribble Valley. This lovely green sweep of unspoilt countryside, which contains almost 50 villages, has been declared an Area of Outstanding Natural Beauty.*

I am quite sure that women find it much easier than men to understand that bewildering period in English history which ended in what we call The War of the Roses, for it reads like a medieval soap opera. It is full of complicated plots, larger than life characters, with power, wealth and the crown of England being the ultimate goal. It is not surprising that Shakespeare took advantage of this ready made canvas to colour with his genius, for no work of fiction could ever live up to such factual intrigue.

It was King Henry VI, once regarded as a royal saint, who was given sanctity at Bolton Hall close to the village, and here perhaps spent one of the happier periods of his tragic life. He was born in 1421 at Windsor, the son of Henry V and great-grandson of John of Gaunt, Duke of Lancaster. His father was a great soldier and diplomat, having been the victor of Agincourt and by marriage heir apparent to the throne of France, which had raised England's prestige to new heights. But sadly the warrior king was destined to die prematurely from dysentery while in France, leaving his nine months old son the legacy of a boiling caldron of problems in two kingdoms.

While the infant king was growing up England was ruled by a council which had his uncle, the Duke of Gloucester at its head, while France was ruled by the Duke of Bedford as Regent. But it proved to be a period of severe unrest in both kingdoms, factions began taking advantage of the lack of a mature king, so that corruption, assassination and private warfare became commonplace. One historian says that his reign 'has strong claims to be the most calamitous in the whole of English history.' Even before he was crowned at the age of eight, an uprising in France had brought about a series of skirmishes including the Siege of Orleans from which the English army had to flee from the forces led by Joan of Arc.

In 1431 Henry was crowned at both Westminster and Paris, then at the age of sixteen he took over the full powers of kingship. He is said to have grown into a gentle, mild mannered youth who was highly religious and fond of the arts. These characteristics were reflected later when he founded Eton College and King's College at Cambridge, with the intention of training poor boys for the priesthood. However his sensitivity was to become regarded in such harsh, blood-thirsty times, as a sign of weakness. Adhering to pacifist principles, he refused to punish those nobles who conspired against him, he stopped the horrific quartering of traitors and he would not fight in battle.

A truce was made with France when he married Margaret, the high-spirited daughter of the Duke of Anjou and Maine in 1444, but peace was short lived. Two years later French soldiers crossed the Loire, they took Rouen then went on to capture all of Normandy. By 1451 the English domination of France had ended, only the single castle at Calais remained under Henry's control. This weakened the crown by cutting off French revenue and caused widespread discontent throughout England. A serious revolt by the men of Kent, headed by a shady character named Jack Cade, followed, causing Henry and his court to flee from London to Kenilworth. Although the revolt was eventually quelled and Cade slain, it had cast a dark shadow over the House of Lancaster, for there was a strong suspicion that the rich and ambitious Duke of York, was behind the plot.

A son, Edward, was born to Henry VI in 1453, but its joy did not offset the many fears of his troubled reign. He suffered, what at the time was described as a 'bout of madness' but may well have been a nervous breakdown. This allowed the Duke of York the opportunity to take over the King's role as Protectorate. By 1455 Henry had recovered and was able to take control once more, but the Duke of York, having tasted power wanted the crown for himself. He gathered together an army of followers under the banner of a white rose, opposing Henry, who was represented by the red rose of Lancaster, beginning the cruel War of the Roses. It grew into a terrible civil war which was to split up the country for the next thirty years.

Six major battles took place during Henry's reign, with most of the king's followers coming from the north. The Yorkists won the early battles, Henry being captured at St Albans then released under a pretence of reconciliation. The fighting was renewed and after a further Yorkist success at Northampton the Duke of York, for the first time, officially laid claim to the throne. The Lancastrians fought on and saw their first, short-lived, success at Wakefield, when the Duke of York was slain. However, his son Edward, immediately succeeded to the title and became claimant to the crown. His followers grew in numbers leading to a council in London proclaiming him to be King Edward IV, stating that Henry had now forfeited the throne. The Battle of Hexham in 1464 brought the decisive defeat of the Lancastrians and saw Henry VI a fugitive in his own country. With the aid of his northern followers he managed to escape from the battlefield with the Yorkists in pursuit. Moving quickly from one safe haven to another he eventually arrived at Bolton Hall, the home of Sir Ralph Pudsey.

I wandered down a footpath on the edge of the village that follows the fast flowing waters of Skirden Beck. Young rabbits played beneath my feet while overhead a pair of oyster catchers, who seemed to have found an inland home, piped angrily at my intrusion on their territory. After a mile the valley levelled out allowing me a panoramic view across the river to the site of Bolton Hall, which was sadly demolished earlier this century. The rising hilltop was shrouded in trees and foliage, the bright red of rhododendrons contrasting vividly with a dozen shades of green.

In the tranquillity of this hidden valley Henry stayed for almost a year, seeking relief from despair for he knew he had lost his crown forever. He is said to have worn plain clothes with thick black farmer's boots, rather than the fine gold cloth and silks displayed by other monarchs. King Henry's Well, which lies close to the former hall, is said to have been discovered by him using a divining rod, during a walk through the estate. He is also said to have influenced the design of the village church which dates from this period. Its tower is unlike any other in the Ribble Valley, being of a type found only in Somerset.

He later moved just six miles to Waddington Hall where he was reputedly betrayed by a Black Monk who was also staying as a guest. He escaped down a ladder and ran across the fields to the Ribble, only to be captured trying to cross the river at Brungerley. There followed his ignominious journey to London and his imprisonment, then yet another temporary restoration in 1470 following a successful battle led by his wife, Margaret. But the whole bloodthirsty episode came to a sad end in 1471 when his son was stabbed to death at Tewkesbury and Henry himself was murdered at the Tower, just hours before Edward IV came triumphant into London. Henry's body was hastily buried at Chertsey Abbey, but over the next fifty years he became revered as a saint, his tomb becoming a place of pilgrimage. His intercession was said to have brought about many miraculous cures, particularly among the very poor and young children. He even began to rival St Thomas of Canterbury in popularity, but his official canonisation was never attained. His remains were later transferred to St George's Chapel at Windsor and the book which lists his miracles is still in existence.

Before leaving Bolton-by-Bowland I went, like all visitors should, to view the remarkable Pudsey Tomb inside the church. It consists of a huge slab of limestone, measuring three metres long by two metres wide. On it are carved the figure of Sir Ralph Pudsey, his three wives and his twenty five children! A later member of this incredible family began minting his own money to avoid bankruptcy. When the Pudsey Shillings came to the notice of the authorities he made his escape on horseback by jumping across a chasm in the Ribble, now known as Pudsey's Leap.

## 3

I have discovered a cure for depression which I am quite sure is finer than any drug available on prescription and it is free. If your girlfriend has left you, or you are living with the threat of redundancy or perhaps just tired of our noisy age, then escape to Sawley. Come on a quiet June afternoon when the hot sun is shining and the sky is blue and there is not a soul about. Sit on a bench in the Abbey grounds, stare across the emerald grass to the weathered ruins and beyond to the hazy blue profile of Pendle Hill. Soon you will be hypnotised by a profound silence, the type of silence that can only be found in places that once knew great religious activity. Although the monks left this spot over four hundred years ago the spirit of their calling can be felt as strong as ever among its crumbling stones, it remains a holy place in which the mundane troubles of our present century fall away.

It was in 1147 that a band of twelve Cistercian Monks together with ten converts first descended on this green river valley. Led by their Abbot,

Benedict, they had been lured from Fountains Abbey in Yorkshire by Baron Percy and other wealthy Lords who had been willing to grant them land. Once established on the site it quickly became apparent what an enormous task lay before them in building a new abbey. The ground was boggy, the winters very cold and disease spread through the community. At times the effort seemed too great for them, they pleaded to return to Fountains Abbey but they were told they must remain at Salley, as it was then known. Very slowly the ornate arches rose into the sky, water was diverted to power their mill and the abbey began at last to take shape. It then quickly grew into a great religious focal point for the Ribble Valley, which it remained for the next four centuries. The most notable monk to come from Sawley was Sir William de Rymington whose great intellect led to him becoming Chancellor of Oxford. He became a worthy opponent of John Wycliffe during the Reformation.

It was, of course, the Reformation that led to the closure of Sawley Abbey, then reduced it to a sad ruin. Its last Abbot, who is believed to have been Thomas Bolton, was among those who opposed Henry VIII at the unsuccessful uprising known as the Pilgrimage of Grace. The king at first granted a pardon to those who had participated, then changed his mind, allowing Abbot Bolton to be hung for treason. The abbey was dissolved, speculators moved in buying up the land, tearing the lead from the roof, smashing the stained glass windows and taking away any useful masonry. In an instant they had destroyed not only a great religious community, but what at the time was the equivalent of a doctor's surgery, a hospital and a hotel.

I reluctantly drove away from the solitude of Sawley, passing the popular Spread Eagle Hotel to cross over the three arched bridge that spans the Ribble. The meandering lane, bounded by hedgerows ablaze with summer foliage, led me through the villages of Grindleton and West Bradford to a tea shop in Waddington. Here among miniature Pendle Witches and jars of home made jam I replenished my energy with a piece of bran-cake and a pot of Lancashire tea before beginning my exploration of the village.

Waddington is an ancient settlement which has become a popular stopping-off point for visitors to the Ribble Valley. An unusual feature is the fast flowing brook which splashes down the main street, crossed here and there by a series of bridges, with manicured lawns and gardens close by. A Saxon chief named Wada is said to have given his name to the village and there is a mention of him in one of our oldest historical documents, the Anglo-Saxon Chronicle. Apparently he was involved in a conspiracy which led to the murder of King Aethelred in 794 A.D., but he later suffered defeat at a battle at Billington near Whalley. However, despite his apparent failure he must have been held in great esteem locally, for his name is also remembered by the windswept fell which rises upwards to the north, separating the Ribble from the Hodder.

As dusk approached I wandered along the quiet streets of Wada's village, looking through the imposing gates of the old hall and thinking of the saintly Henry VI attempted escape; I watched bats skim like pieces of black paper around the tower of St Helen's church as they have done for five hundred years; and I thought of Robert Parker whose charity three centuries ago still houses 'widows and spinsters' in twenty-nine attractive almshouses. Here is a man who must surely sleep soundly in his grave.

## 4

Clitheroe was bustling, for it was Saturday morning, which means market day. The farmer's wives who for six days each week hide away in domestic isolation in homesteads at Downham, Wiswell, or Barley had literally thrown in the towel. They had escaped to what the travel writer, H.V. Morton, once described as the town which is 'half in Fairyland and half in Lancashire'. Although the ancestors of these ladies of the Ribble Valley have been coming each week to Clitheroe for eight hundred years they would not recognise their modern counterparts. What was once a hazardous ten mile journey on foot, carrying eggs, vegetables and perhaps driving a couple of pigs, is now completed in twenty minutes in a Range Rover or BMW. Wearing waxed jackets and green wellies in winter and designer clothes from Vogue in the summer, they no longer come to sell, but to eat lunch in the Swan and Royal or The Apricot Meringue, and of course to chat, as women have always done.

While most towns in England boast about possessing the 'largest, longest or richest' in the land it is refreshing that Clitheroe claims to have one of the smallest. The white-stoned Norman keep, which rises majestically above the town, is the second smallest in England. I climbed up the grassy slope to the lofty walkway which stands 130 feet above the town, here I discovered a breathtaking panoramic view. Below me lay the rooftops of Clitheroe: stone built shops and cottages lying askew along an elevated ridge, leading to a high point on which stands the parish church amidst an elegant row of Georgian houses. The buildings of the town end quite suddenly in a circle of green meadowland from which, to the east, soars the dramatic bulk of Pendle Hill. My eyes followed the steep gulleys and thin black lines of drystone walls ever upwards, till they at last came to rest on the high horizon at the cairn that marks the summit. This is the spot were George Fox once had a vision which led to the foundation of the Quaker movement, but is remembered more for the horrors of witchcraft when the name of Pendle was synonymous with terror.

*Clitheroe, a bustling market town, overlooked by its 800-year-old castle.*

It is appropriate that Clitheroe's small castle, topped with a flag, should still proudly dominate the scene, for around it the town was built. After the Conquest this highly prized hunting area was given to Roger de Poitou, who was probably responsible for building a military stronghold here, which is known to have been in existence in 1102. From necessity, these early castles were quickly constructed from timber, then when they had become established they were rebuilt of stone. The present Keep is believed to date from about 1150, having been built by Robert de Lacy who at this period had taken possession of the area. The castle, which had a chapel, a jail, stables and administration buildings, was the important centre of control for a large isolated tract of wild countryside.

The ownership of the castle and lands, known as the Honour of Clitheroe, has had a chequered history, passing from one family to another as their individual fortunes rose and then declined. Its sturdy walls have also witnessed many colourful and sometimes savage scenes over the past eight hundred years. In the early years of its foundation it was the Scots who were a constant threat, a battle took place at Clitheroe in 1138 in which the English suffered a humiliating defeat. In 1315 it was the scene of a local rebellion when Sir Adam Banaster occupied the castle, disputing the authority of the Earl of Lancaster. Following a battle at Preston the rebellion failed, but the Earl was later executed for treason. King Edward II, a jolly man, but a weak king who was fond of hunting and heavy drinking, paid a visit in 1323, just four years before his horrific murder in Berkeley Castle. The next century saw the brief imprisonment of King Henry VI in the castle jail after his betrayal at Waddington.

Clitheroe had grown into a prosperous small town by the mid-sixteenth century, but the castle itself was in need of repair, some parts of it had completely collapsed. However, it was still able to play a part in the Civil War, for in 1644 Prince Rupert, leader of the Royalist Army, lodged here overnight on his way to a battle at York. A small garrison of troops were left behind to secure the town and make necessary repairs to the castle gateway. Surprisingly, after so many years of bloodshed and intrigue it was a pay dispute which brought an end to its days as a stronghold. After the Civil War had ended a number of county militia regiments, quite rightly, refused to disband because they had not been paid. They secured themselves in the castle in what would be regarded today as a sit-in, refusing to move. General Lambert was sent to negotiate, but the dispute only ended when £4,600 was given to the troops as back-pay. Parliament was alarmed by the success of this rebellion so it decreed that the castle should be disabled to prevent any similar action being repeated in the future. Today a large hole can be seen in the east wall of the Keep which for generations local people have insisted was made by the devil, but perhaps in this case the devil was Cromwell's Parliament.

Today the castle and its grounds, which include a fine local history museum, serves as a unique war memorial. It was purchased by public subscription after the First World War by the people of Clitheroe. As I strolled slowly down the steep footpath back to the town I had the feeling I was walking across some of the most exciting moments in Lancashire's history.

Clitheroe, I found, is a delightful place to explore for it still possesses that rare feature, individuality, that sadly seems to have disappeared in many other towns. Its high street has not become the same monotonous clone that the big national retailers seem to relish, for happily, local shopkeepers are still in control. Looking into the window of Cowmans Famous Sausage Shop I discovered what must surely be the largest selection of bangers in the whole of England! There were pork with tarragon, pork with chives, pork with chestnut, Welsh pork with leek, Edisford Spicy Specials and even some flavoured with wild boar and venison. I counted fifteen different types in the window alone, with even more inside of the shop. My conviction that the residents of the Ribble Valley have a little known taste for the exotic was borne out further down the street when I looked into the window of a greengrocers shop. Not content with stocking the humble potato, pea or apple, I saw guava, rambutan, papaya, kumquat, passion fruit, gourds and star fruit. It seems that meals we ordinary mortals could only hope to sample on a world cruise are commonplace here in Clitheroe.

As I wandered around the town my gaze was constantly drawn to the many inviting alleyways and courtyards fashioned from limestone, which in turn led my eyes upwards to the amphitheatre of surrounding fells. The slopes of Easington, Waddington and Pendle seem to appear in the most unlikely places, framed here by a chimney pot, then peeping over a broken ridge tile, or reflected in a shop window. I stood for several minutes at the corner of Castlegate looking across Moor Lane at this strange contrasting view of the wild and the suburban, which seems to epitomise Lancashire. I also listened to the voices of the locals who walked by, their unique accent I found fascinating, it is a distinct clear tone which always ends a sentence on a high note. To hear it immediately reminded me of that classic film, Whistle Down the Wind, whose characters captured the spirit of this corner of our county so completely.

The spire of St Mary Magdalene church, which overlooks the bustle of Clitheroe, reminded me of the little-known adventures of a former curate's son.

It was to this church in 1743 that James King brought his wife Anne to begin their married life. They settled happily in the town and soon began to raise a family, eventually having five sons. There second son, also named James, had an early fascination for the sea and at the age of twelve he became a midshipman. He later showed an equally brilliant aptitude for mathematics, so he finished his education at Oxford where he studied astronomy.

At this time Captain Cook had completed two voyages of exploration that had astounded the world, but he was intent on finding out if a North West Passage, linking the Atlantic and Pacific Oceans, really existed. James King, with his seafaring and astronomical experience, was invited to join the expedition as Second Lieutenant. Their ship, *Resolution,* left Plymouth in July 1776 to be later joined by a sister ship, *Discovery*. After taking on supplies in Cape Town they discovered, for the first time, the Prince Edward group of islands. James King was the man chosen to land on the main island, planting the Union flag and claiming the territory for Britain. They then continued to Van Dieman's Land, which is now Tasmania, and then on to New Zealand which had been previously charted by Captain Cook. After a fortnights anchorage their journey continued into the Pacific where another uninhabited island was discovered. They named it Christmas Island, and James King together with an astronomer name Bayley, went ashore to observe an eclipse of the sun.

Five weeks later they sighted what was to be their main discovery of the voyage. They sailed past a large mountainous archipelago which Cook named the Sandwich Isles, now known as the Hawaiian Islands. The crews of the two vessels happily managed to establish a good relationship with the islanders, but they had to quickly proceed with their search for the North West Passage. After sailing for a month north-easterly they reached the coast of North America where they encountered severe gales which mercilessly battered the two ships. After landing to repair their damaged masts they continued northwards to Alaska, charting, surveying and naming landmarks as they journeyed on. They crossed the Bering Straits, named a sheltered inlet the Bay of St. Lawrence and then crossed the Arctic Circle. Soon, temperatures had dropped far below zero and they came upon an endless horizon of pack ice which forced them to return hastily to the Sandwich Islands.

William Bligh, later to become the infamous captain of the Bounty, went ashore to see if the bay was suitable for anchorage. James King, in his log book, estimated that at least nine thousand islanders in hundreds of canoes came out to greet the two ships. However, their friendliness was short lived for the visitors proved too costly to feed. Equipment belonging to the ship was later reputedly stolen so Captain Cook went ashore to try to recover the property. He was immediately attacked by an inflamed mob, within a few seconds the world's greatest explorer was savagely cut to pieces. James King, who had always been on good terms with the islanders, bravely went ashore, managing to persuade then to release Cook's body, for burial at sea.

On their return to England the officers of the two ships found themselves the toast of Georgian society. The curate's son from Clitheroe went on to command his own frigate, which saw action during the French Wars. But sadly his health broke down, and he died at Nice in 1784 at the early age of thirty two.

As I drove away from Clitheroe in the direction of Whalley, I decided that this town of many surprises would be a marvellous place in which to live.

# 5

The Calder at Whalley was gushing white beneath the town's ancient bridge, for the days of sunshine had been replaced by an unceasing torrent of rain. But as I climbed the steep pathway up the side of the Nab the weather prospect now seemed more promising. The dark cloud base had begun to break up and shy beams of soft sunlight were beginning to filter through, lighting up the green sweeping river valley. Beyond, the foothills of Pendle appeared a misty blue, rising in tiers to the high point which almost merged with the sky.

"Will you give me a lift?" a voice cried out, as I passed the entrance to a farm. Startled, I looked around to see a middle aged, stocky man beckoning me from outside a barn. A large black and white collie dog stood close by, held firmly by a chain.

"Keep well away from Shep, he's real mean. He copped two burglars breaking in to the farm last week and he took a chunk out of one of their backsides. Police and ambulance were here when I got home and I'll probably be prosecuted," he declared, scathingly.

Carefully avoiding Shep, I put my rucksack down on the floor and followed him into the barn. He walked over to a corner, removed a tarpaulin which to my astonishment revealed a magnificent rocking-horse, intricately carved out of solid wood. It stood about a metre high, perched upon a rectangular base and was still awaiting the addition of a tail and mane. Together we moved it across the barn, then we began to chat.

He told me that he had worked as a blacksmith in Whalley all his life, but his workshop had been in the path of a new road, so it had been demolished, which led to his early retirement. He had only taken up wood carving as a hobby about two years ago and was now intent on carving seven rocking-horses, one for each of his grand-children. He then invited me into his home to look at more superb examples of his new-found talent of which he was justly proud. These included a wall-picture of the Last Supper and a marvel-lously proportioned horse about eight inches long. We then talked of his life as a blacksmith.

"Do you know, the huge Shire horses are really gentle giants and very easy to shoe," he confided, "but Shetland ponies can be devils, they kick and fight and they can really cause some nasty injuries. But come and look at these ... "

We walked into his garden which overlooked a huge sloping field that disappeared over the edge of the hill towards the valley bottom. He began to whistle which within a few seconds brought two galloping miniature horses breathless up to the fence. They stood little higher than his collie dog, with attractive blonde manes and tan coloured bodies.

"I've started breeding these, just for fun. They originate from South Africa and they never grow more than twenty seven inches high. There are eighteen more out over the ridge somewhere," he said, pointing.

We then talked about the history of this secluded hillside. He told me that the area was once the site of a Quaker community and that only the previous week a couple of Americans had arrived on his doorstep, trying to trace their roots. It seemed that their ancestors, who had once lived near to his farm, had emigrated to the USA in 1834. He then spoke of the small hill on the banks of the Calder which was the spot where some of the monks from Whalley Abbey had been reputedly executed following the Pilgrimage of Grace, and of a secret passage that leads to the Abbey. A wreath of flowers is still placed on the hill on the anniversary of their deaths: the residents of the Ribble Valley have long memories.

After spending a further half hour hearing about foxes which roam across his fields and badgers which stare through his window, and of the torrential rain which ruined the Great Harwood Show, I once more continued with my walk. After skirting the wooded hill-top I began the descent to Whalley down narrow Moor Lane, stopping at intervals to admire the commanding view. Traced by a meandering line of green foliage I could follow the route of the Calder as it made its short journey to pour into the Ribble. Beyond, the wide sweeping valley rose gently upwards to reveal the full expanse of Longridge Fell which ends dramatically at the steep, wooded Kemple End. I remembered hearing of how the young Conan Doyle once roamed over this wild moorland ridge when he was a pupil at Stonyhurst College and how its haunting isolation impressed him. It is said that he used it for the setting for his book, *The Hound of the Baskervilles,* but changed the name to the more commercial Dartmoor.

## 6

I walked along King Street in Whalley gazing over the bridge to the river and admiring the stone cottages of this quiet village which, like its neighbour Sawley, is one of Lancashire's holy places. The dismal skies had driven away most of the summer visitors apart from an adventurous party of elderly ladies from Rossendale who were nostalgically looking into a sweet shop window. On display were Coltsfoot Rock, Sarsaparilla Drops, Aniseed Rock, Pear

Drops and even Whalley Rock. They smiled with delight, having re-discovered a little of their childhood.

A marmalade cat with an appealing meow, demanded a stroke before I was allowed into the churchyard to view the village's proud heritage – the three Whalley Crosses. Some locals will tell you that they were carved to commemorate a visit by St Augustine while others say it was St Paulinus. However, the scholars say they date from the 10th century when the Vikings controlled this part of northern England and their inscriptions are half pagan and half Christian.

*The three ancient crosses which stand in Whalley churchyard are believed to date from the 10th century.*

Perhaps it was this reputation that Whalley had for being a holy site that inspired the Cistercian Monks to leave their flooded abbey on the Wirral to come here in 1296. But they quickly regretted this move for it brought them a great deal of trouble. They argued with their fellow monks at Sawley about tithes, they had a dispute with Pontefract Priory concerning land, they also quarrelled with the local vicar and with the Bishop of Lichfield. These initial difficulties were, however, finally overcome and the abbey grew to become a graceful riverside building, a place of prayer, refuge and hospitality. As I explored the serene ruins, where alert blackbirds hunt for worms on the green lawns, I thought of that much maligned character John Paslew, Whalley's last abbot. It is said by some that he enjoyed a 'lavish lifestyle', living and travelling like a lord and that he had broken with the original rules of the monastic order, inferring that he 'got what he deserved'. But, if this was really the case would such a man refuse to take the Oath of Allegiance when Henry VIII suppressed the monasteries and pay with his life for high treason at Lancaster?

Turning by the war memorial at Billington, I joined the narrow lane that leads past Hacking Hall to Old Langho. Overhung with trees it led me along a wide valley coloured with the pale red of willow herb and the pink of foxgloves. The sun was now fighting its way through the grey clouds, lighting the fields and making the Ribble's gushing water sparkle silver beneath Ribchester Bridge. Parking in the centre of Ribchester village I decided that the White Bull would be my first stop. Although it cannot claim to be Lancashire's oldest pub it must surely have the oldest pub entrance, for the 18th century building is supported by two Roman pillars.

Five locals were sat on stools around the bar while an overweight black dog looked on with obvious boredom, as pub dogs always do. I sipped my shandy in the corner listening to the good humoured conversation, the topics discussed ranged from the merits of growing Rape Seed which now festoons the fields of West Lancashire, to the disadvantages of criticising the wife in public. A grey-haired, bearded man who had obviously been guilty of this last sin, put his case forward with passion to his understanding friend.

Students of village architecture would be enchanted with Ribchester for its cottages display an amazing kaleidoscope of features making each one unique. Alleyways, stepped doorways, gables and roofs, have been fashioned by the forgotten builders of the last four centuries to produce a feeling of timeless harmony. I wandered with admiration up the village street which ends at the river, then found a bench on which to sit and take in the view.

The peaceful riverside scene which lay before me would have delighted any landscape artist: below, the wide Ribble turned across a sweeping bend, creating white water as it sped a determined course across hidden stones. Willow trees, bent by the wind, gently touched the water from the nearside bank forming a natural frame for the blue flank of the ever-present Pendle

Hill which filled the distant horizon. On the far bank a tired herd of Friesian cows began to move slowly on to new pastures, while a pair of jet-black crows curiously looking on, gave their approval with a haunting shriek. This summer panorama was made complete by a warm breeze which brought with it the aroma of burning grass: a farmer downstream had built a bonfire.

*The White Bull: one of Lancashire's most famous pubs; its entrance is supported by Roman pillars which were once part of the fort.*

The Ribble's changing course has over the centuries sliced through what was once the important Roman fort of Bremtennacum. It was built about 78 AD by the Roman governor of Britain, Julius Agricola who had been appointed by the Emperor Vespasian. Ribchester was regarded as an ideal site because it lies to the western edge of the valley which cuts right through the Pennines and was accessible by boat from the coast. Five roads converged at the fort, linking it to Manchester, Chester, Hadrian's Wall, Lancaster and York. The original ramparts were constructed of timber and clay, but were later replaced by stone. Four gateways led inside the fort which housed the headquarters, the commander's house, the granaries, the barracks and the bath house. Of these, only the remains of the bath house, the granaries, together with parts of a ditch system can be seen today. The present parish church, Roman Museum and the rectory all lie within what was once the fort. In the marvellous village museum I looked upon Ribchester's greatest treasure, a highly elaborate Roman parade helmet which was found in the river. It is in fact an accurate replica, for the original was claimed by the British Museum to display in London.

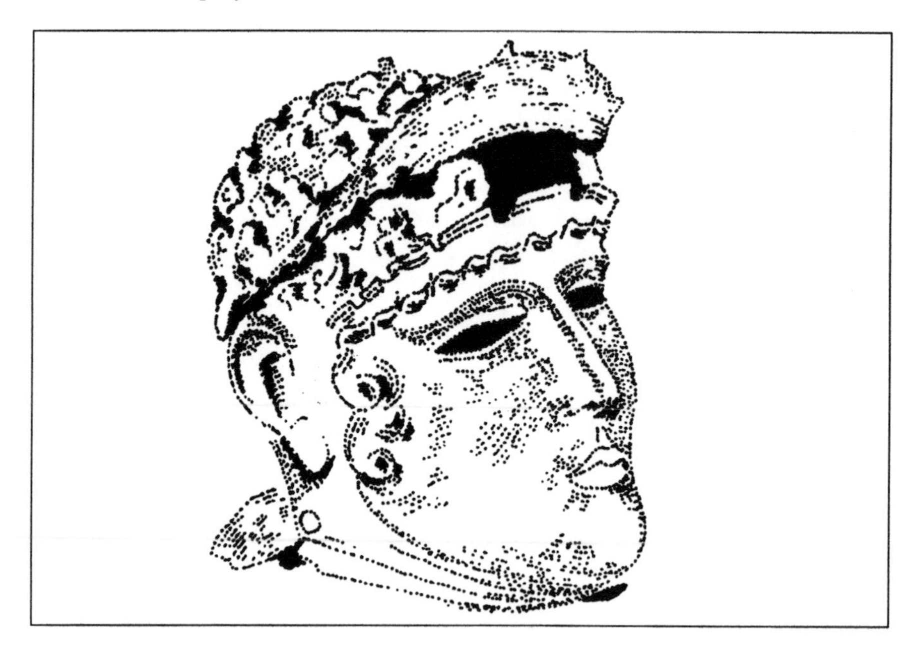

*A replica of the Roman cavalry helmet found at Ribchester and dating from the first century AD.*

As I wandered along the river bank and through the deserted streets of Ribchester I thought of the Roman soldiers of two milleniums ago who would have regarded this patch of Lancashire as home. Among these were the Asturians who were recruited from Spain and the Sarmatians who were brought from Hungary. The fort was later given special status to become a veteran settlement, allowing land to be given to discharged soldiers on which they could permanently settle down. So perhaps it is true to say, that some of Ribchester's farmers have the blood of Rome running through their veins.

# CHAPTER TWO

# RIBCHESTER TO THE LUNE VALLEY

I visit the Lancashire college which began in France, listen to the grouse on Longridge Fell, then end up in England's most haunted house. I discover a hidden shrine, drive over Beacon Fell to see Garstang, climb Nicky Nook then follow Turner into the Lune Valley.

## 1

The rain that had appeared on St Swithin's Day had proved prophetic, for Lancashire had seen the wettest July for half a century. I was hoping that August would change this trend, but as I drove from Ribchester up meandering Gallows Lane the signs were not too promising. In the rich pastureland that rises gently upwards from the Ribble I noticed that half the cows were standing and half were sitting, so the weather outlook, I decided, would remain uncertain.

I turned left near the Shireburn Arms in picturesque Hurst Green, passing the mass of bright flowers which surround the war memorial, and I continued up to the entrance to the grounds of Stonyhurst College. A sign told me that the college was open to visitors, which happens on just thirty days each year, so I drove slowly along the driveway. A sharp right turn near a statue of the Virgin Mary, suddenly revealed, what must surely be the most impressive approach to any school in England. The road, flanked by sweeping green fields ending in woodlands, led my eyes onwards. I could then see two large rectangular lakes which, as I got closer, I found to be brimming with tame ducks and geese. These splashes of silver-grey reflected the striking south front of the college with its twin towered entrance, spreading out on each side in architectural splendour, for this is a school that was once a stately home.

Two smiling, elderly, ladies took my entrance fee then it happened – the fire alarm bell began to reverberate through the building. Visitors began to look at each other perplexed, what should we do? Were we about to witness the dramatic end of a four-hundred-year-old institution? A woman, wearing a lapel badge that said she was a guide, came dashing down a staircase.

"I'm sorry – we need to evacuate the building, regulations you see."

*Stonyhurst College, in the shadow of Longridge Fell.*

Then the bell thankfully stopped ringing. A young man in overalls entered the room and quickly conferred with the anxious guide. She smiled, the crisis was over for it had been a false alarm due to a computer error. We all breathed a sign of relief, we could now begin our tour.

Stonyhurst College, which during the last two centuries has become an important part of life in this corner of the Ribble Valley has a unique and romantic history. It was founded by the Jesuits in 1593, not in Lancashire, but in St Omer in Northern France. Funded by King Philip II of Spain it was established to provide a Roman Catholic education for the children of the English nobility who had escaped from religious persecution in this country. It flourished for 170 years until 1762 when the Jesuits were expelled from France, forcing the school to move to Bruges in the Netherlands. But after eleven years more problems arose, so it was moved yet again to the then independent Principality of Liège.

One of the schoolboys educated at Bruges had been Thomas Weld, who became a rich landowner after inheriting vast estates which included the magnificent mansion of Stonyhurst, which had its origins in the fourteenth century. It had previously been in the possession of the Bayley and the Shireburn families, whose names are remembered in the pub signs in Hurst

Green. The last son of the Shireburns, Richard Francis, had tragically died as the age of eight in 1702, after eating yew berries in the garden at Stonyhurst and his married sister had died childless.

The French Revolution had brought yet more problems to the school, but Thomas Weld came to the rescue by offering the Jesuits asylum at Stonyhurst which was at this time unoccupied. Religious tolerance had largely returned to England in the late 18th century, so they were happy to make the move. After a six weeks journey by boat, canal barge, and finally on foot from Skipton, the weary company of priests, servants and twelve pupils arrived at Stonyhurst in August 1794. The first boy to enter the building was George Lambert Clifford, who beat a rival by climbing in through a window. The building proved to be in a dilapidated state, dismal and dirty, full of cobwebs and in parts, roofless. But through absolute dedication the Jesuits and their staff transformed it back to its former glory and today it is regarded as being one of the leading schools in the country.

Unlike some guides I have met, whose 'patter' can become quite boring, the woman who took our party around the college was both knowledgeable and enthusiastic. Dressed in a bright floral suit, she related with humour the antics of the present pupils and the many curious tales that make up the history of Stonyhurst. Climbing the staircase she pointed out that the steps were covered in small squares of oak which would last for fifty years. The only other place that they are known to be used is on Crewe railway station.

We stopped at the War Memorial at the top of the stairs which lists the former pupils of Stonyhurst who lost their lives in past conflicts. These include Lt. Archer-Shee who died during the First World War. He is remembered as the famous Winslow Boy of Terence Rattigan's play which was first performed in 1946. After being falsely accused of stealing a postal order his family fought courageously to clear his name. It was during this anxious period that he continued his education at Stonyhurst.

Another tragic reminder of an event which hit the world headlines in 1956, is the name of Lieutenant Moorhouse of the West Yorkshire Regiment who was a member of the famous jam making family. During the Suez Crisis he was abducted while driving a jeep through the streets of Port Said. The news that he was alive and well raised the spirits of his parents back home, but sadly the tales were false. It was later discovered that he had died soon after being captured, for he had been accidentally suffocated whilst being hidden from a search party.

Each room has its treasures and memories of the past, for many great and a few infamous men have walked the corridors of Stonyhurst. We were shown the stage where the film star Charles Laughton probably performed for the first time and the desks which were familiar to Sir Arthur Conan Doyle, creator of Sherlock Holmes. Two of his fellow pupils had the surname Moriarty, which he later chose for Holmes's infamous arch enemy.

In the main hall is the table on which Oliver Cromwell is reputed to have slept when he paid an unwelcome visit to the house in 1648. Being well aware of the possibility of assassination he had the table placed in the centre of the room where he lay in full armour on the hard surface with his pistols and swords at his side. Shortly afterwards he was the victor of the decisive Battle of Preston which completely destroyed the Royalist army.

Among the group of visitors on our tour was a small, shabbily dressed man, in his mid-seventies. I noticed him looking closely at one of the large portraits of Stonyhurst's seven VC holders. I walked over to him and we began to chat. He pointed to the striking figure of Colonel Harald Ervine-Andrews of the East Lancashire Regiment, who gained his VC at Dunkirk.

"I was in his battalion at one time. He is a fine man – in his nineties now and I believe he lives in Cornwall. Never reached Dunkirk myself, was taken prisoner on the way to the coast and spent the rest of the war in a prison camp".

One of the surprises, to those who have never attended a public school or an independent school as they are now known, is the rudimentary conditions in which the boys live and sleep. Having, in the main, come from wealthy families who dwell in luxury, the change in lifestyle must at first be quite bewildering. We were shown the stark dormitory in which the younger boys sleep, an uninviting large room with a series of partitioned sleeping quarters. I wondered how many generals, bishops, diplomats and even saints, have as small boys, cried themselves to sleep in such places. However, this is all part of the broad education at Stonyhurst, its aim being not just to provide an academic grounding, but also to give 'a sense of moral values, a social conscience and a sense of fair play'.

Before leaving the house to enjoy a highly recommended strawberry tart and cream in the tearoom, I asked the guide why we had not been shown some of the priceless treasures that I know the college possesses. She told me that, sadly, this was due to the problems of security. So presumably, hidden away in the college strong-room, is the 7th century Gospel of St John found in the coffin of St Cuthbert in Durham, the prayer book which Mary, Queen of Scots held in her hand at her execution, a first folio of Shakespeare's works, a relic of the true cross . . . and many, many more.

## 2

Anyone who wants to cheat by experiencing the splendour of a hilltop viewpoint without suffering any of the exertion need only drive, like I did, over Longridge Fell. On a magical day when the sky was as blue as gentian and the air breathtakingly clear I turned off the B6243 road near to the Hall Arms pub. I found the lane climbs steadily upwards, the pastoral greenness quickly giving way to the soft brown of the high moorland. The high point of this road occurs at Jeffrey Hill which at 938 feet (286m) above sea level, is only slightly lower than the summit of the fell.

*Longridge Fell, covered with the purple of heather in early autumn.*

A young man employed by the county council was busily at work with a hand rake turning the hay on a small elevated field on the northern flank of the hillside. Behind him the land fell steeply away revealing a magnificent sweeping panorama of broad pastures encompassed by hills. Below lay a wide fertile valley watered by the Hodder and the Loud. It was criss-crossed by a maze of lanes and walls which led onwards to the half hidden rooftops of Chipping. Beyond, the rounded slopes of Parlick Fell marked the beginning of the vast range of the Bowland Hills which spread to the far horizon. From my map I identified the soaring expanse of Wolf Fell, Burnslack Fell and Totridge Fell, a few of the host of wild summits which seem to merge with the sky.

Longridge Fell is true to its name, for it is a long narrow hill which rises to the east of the small town of Longridge. It stretches for six miles, climbing gradually over its length to reach its highest and most impressive contours to the east. Like Pendle Hill it stands alone, its towering bulk forming a natural barrier between the Ribble Valley and the lovely green Vale of Chipping. Ablaze with the dense purple of early heather I could hear the piercing call of a red grouse echoing across the isolated slopes. What a dramatic backcloth this wild moorland must have made for the huge Cromwellian army of 8,500 men when they passed this way in August 1648.

The small town of Longridge looked bright and inviting in the hot sunshine, but unfortunately I had not the time to stop, for I was on my way to see England's most haunted house. Up a narrow lane in the former Viking village of Goosnargh, I found in idyllic isolation Chingle Hall. But perhaps I had come on the wrong day for the whitewashed house, surrounded by green fields in which cows were contentedly feeding, looked far too friendly. With visitors in shorts and tee shirts picnicking on the lawns, the sinister, gloomy atmosphere that I had expected was just not apparent. However, as I later learnt, this is part of Chingle's charm, for this fortress of the paranormal is neither menacing nor frightening, but simply mysterious.

Again I was fortunate, for the lady named Vera who guided our group of visitors around the house, related its story with both knowledge and sincerity. She told us that her interest in the ancient hall had begun because of its religious connections. At first she did not believe in the existence of such things as ghosts, but now she has definitely changed her mind.

Chingle Hall is rather a grand name for what is known as a moated manor house, what most people would recognise today as a large ancient farmhouse. It was built by Adam de Singleton, a Lancashire knight, in 1260 and is believed to be the oldest domestic brick building existing in the United Kingdom. The outline of where the moat once stood appears as a slight depression and the drawbridge, which was used until the Tudor period, has been replaced by a small stone bridge. This part of Lancashire has a strong Roman Catholic presence, both the Singletons and later the Wall family who took over Chingle in 1600, were staunch followers of the Old Faith. During the reign of Queen Elizabeth I the house became a secret mass centre and most of the ghostly happenings seem to be associated with this period.

As we walked along the bridge Vera pointed to a large barn on the edge of a field that had recently been converted into a house. She told us how a young man who, in a fit of despair because he could not marry the girl he loved, hung himself from a beam. His ghost, accompanied by terrible moans, has been frequently seen around the site.

"I believe, when his body was found hanging, his father who was the farmer refused to cut it down. He said the rope was too valuable to ruin," said a young man in the group. "I have made a close study of all the tales about Chingle," he continued.

*Chingle Hall, said to be the most haunted house in England.*

The ancient oak door at the entrance to the house, blackened with age, is also closely bound up with the supernatural. It appears to be reluctant to be photographed, often appearing blurred or completely blank. The latch will also suddenly open of its own accord and ghostly footsteps will follow. On one recent occasion a letter, delivered by a friend of the present owners, Mr and Mrs Bruce, was found behind the door. This puzzled them for the solid door does not possess a letter-box. Their friend said she simply posted it through a slot in the door, but when asked to point this out she found it had disappeared.

In the year 1620 the Wall family of Chingle were overjoyed by the birth of their son John, who unknown to them was destined to a life of religious service, martyrdom and finally in this century the mantle of sainthood. Strangely, the man who baptised him into the Catholic faith, Father Edmund Arrowsmith, is also now a saint. John Wall studied his outlawed religion at Douay in France, then went on to the English College in Rome, before becoming a Franciscan Monk in 1651. He came back once more to England to continue his missionary work among the poor, but was captured and arrested by the authorities. Following a swift trial at Worcester in 1679 he was sentenced to be hanged, drawn and quartered, which was duly carried out. His body was buried in St Oswald's churchyard in Worcester, but his head, being regarded as a relic, was secretly taken to a convent in France. However, it is believed that at the time of the French Revolution the head was brought back to England, and it may well be concealed in an unknown hiding place within Chingle Hall. Some people believe that this is the explanation behind the hundreds of supernatural sightings made in the house, many of these being of a cowled monk. It is concluded that not until the head is discovered and given a proper Christian burial, will the hauntings cease.

Our tour of the house continued, we were shown a hidden chapel which was uncovered in 1962, the room in which St John Wall was born, and a priest's hiding hole built by Nicholas Owen. Two ghostly perfumes, we were told, appear occasionally in some rooms, the scent of lavender and the unmistakable smell of incense. At one spot young female visitors frequently feel faint and in another, a strange orange light is often seen. Doors being flung open, strange unexplained sounds, objects jumping across the room and apparitions moving through walls, are now an accepted way of life in the house. Spiritualists, ghost hunters and sceptics from all over the country flock to Chingle, many having an overnight stay. But Vera, who has also spent many nights at Chingle is convinced that in spite of its supernatural reputation it is a lovely home in which to live.

"A house in which a saint was born, can only be good," she remarked.

I walked from Chingle Hall across the old stone bridge, thinking that sometime in the future I would like to spend the night in St John Wall's birthplace. But it would have to be on a cold night in winter, with no leaves on the trees, a cruel wind blowing and rain pattering on the windows. This would be the right atmosphere for me to see a ghost . . .

As I sat soaking up the sunshine among the lawns of Chingle I realised that I had also followed in the footsteps of Oliver Cromwell, for it is said that he called here and climbed the chimney to spy out the Royalist positions.

Although, at this time he was on the brink of taking full control of the country, his success was destined to be short lived. Like St John Wall, he eventually lost his head, but under even stranger circumstances for it occurred three years after he died.

In 1649, the year following the Battle of Preston, a Commonwealth was declared and Cromwell was eventually given the title of Lord Protector. Although he refused the Crown of England he went through an elaborate coronation type ceremony in 1653 and again in 1657, but by this time his health was quickly failing. The premature death of his daughter, Elizabeth, added to his suffering and in September 1658 he finally died. His embalmed body was buried in the chapel of Henry VII in Westminster Abbey and his son, Richard, inherited his position. But the people had become alienated by the bleak austerity of the Commonwealth, Richard was deemed weak, so in 1660 they welcomed back the rightful successor to the throne, King Charles II.

However, in an act of revenge on the anniversary of the execution of King Charles I in 1661, Cromwell's body, together with those of his colleagues, Ireton and Bradshaw were exhumed. They were taken to the gallows at Tyburn, close to the present day Marble Arch, where they were hung. The bodies were then taken down and the public executioner cut off their heads which were placed on pikes on the roof of Westminster Hall. This being the site at which they had condemned King Charles I to death.

These gory relics remained in place until 1685 when a storm blew Cromwell's head down. A sentry who found it lying on the floor decided to steal it. He hid it at his home and did not reveal its presence till he was on his death bed, when he passed it on to his daughter. In 1710 it turned up in a collection of curiosities owned by a Frenchman living in London, named Du Poy. Over the next century it had a succession of owners, it was offered to a Cambridge College, sold to a jeweller, then bought by a syndicate who displayed it at an exhibition in London. Finally, in 1814, it was sold to a doctor's son name Josiah Henry Wilkinson and it has remained with this family ever since. It is kept in an oak casket in a Suffolk manor house, being now known as the Wilkinson Head, it was authenticated in 1935 by two professors from London University.

## 3

She was standing in the garden at Ladyewell House, a young sun-tanned woman, holding a child in her arms with an old dog looking on.

"Can I see the holy well, please."

"Of course. Then, if you go to the house Father Ben will show you the relics."

After driving down a maze of twisting country roads and almost giving up the search, I had finally found Fernyhalgh hidden up a bumpy unmade lane. Here, in a time capsule of woods and meadowland which a motorway has failed to destroy, lies one of England's greatest Marian Shrines. A holy spot that has drawn pilgrims for over six centuries.

In the corner of the garden, shrouded with foliage, and protected by a small fence I discovered the ancient well. It stands at the bottom of a series of stone steps, a square of cool clear water, overlooked by a brown statue of Our Lady which is surrounded with flowers. I opened the small gate and walked down the steps, placing my hands in the water, thinking my action was a link with the time of King Edward IV and perhaps even with pagan times.

We have to thank a priest who lived in the late 17th century, Father Christopher Tootell, for the story of the well. He listened to the tale the local people had told around the firesides of Fernyhalgh for generations, then carefully recorded it in a meticulous script. It begins in 1471 when a merchant, who was sailing across the Irish Sea, was caught in a violent storm. Feared that he would drown he made a vow, stating that if he was saved he would undertake some work of piety. Miraculously the storm abated, and he landed safely on the Lancashire coast. He then heard a voice which ordered him to seek out a place called Fernyhalgh, there he was to build a chapel at a spot where a crabapple tree bears fruit without cores, under which he would find a spring. At first he had difficulty finding Fernyhalgh, but then he heard the name mentioned by a serving girl at Preston. Next day he was led to the parish where he found the crabapple tree and spring, and a statue of the Blessed Virgin Mary. True to his vow he built a chapel which became known as Our Lady's Chapel at Fernyhalgh. The water from the well gained a reputation for curing many different diseases, the shrine growing to become a popular place of pilgrimage.

I wandered around the extensive gardens which surround the well, the hot sun beaming down on the sweeping lawns. White doves fluttered in the still air while a lop-eared rabbit munched its way through a lettuce leaf in the sanctity of its hutch. At the rear of the lawn I discovered a large open-air altar guarded by the statues of St Thomas More and St John Fisher. In a hidden corner lay the Rosary Way laid out in blue and white ceramic tiles, which I later learnt was a gift from Portugal.

Fernyhalgh has gained a reputation for attracting the quiet scholars of the church and this tradition still persists. The small man with white hair and a healthy tanned face, who showed me around the house was Father Benedict Ruscillo, known as Father Ben. He was born in Barrow, the son of an English mother and an Italian father. One of eight children, he took classics at Cambridge, and then studied for the priesthood at Up Holland and in Lisbon where he returned to teach scripture and biblical Greek. With contagious enthusiasm he is now the custodian of the shrine, which has led to an upsurge in interest from all parts of Europe.

In the upper floor of the house as he showed me the modern chapel we spoke of the history of Lancashire and of the northern links that exist with so many foreign countries. He then left me alone to view what must surely be one of the best collection of Christian relics in the land. The centre piece is the Burgess Altar which dates from 1560. It was made by Thomas Burgess for the Towneley family of Towneley Hall to be disguised as an ordinary oak wardrobe. Around the room, neatly labelled in cases, lay many hundreds of unique relics which have for centuries been hidden away. These include vestments worn by saints, part of the hair shirt worn by St Thomas More, dust from the tomb of St Francis, flowers from the Garden of Gethsemane, a measure of Our Lady's foot taken from her sandal kept in Spain and fragments of bone belonging to a score of saints.

Before leaving Fernyhalgh I looked inside the secluded church which lies a quarter mile from the well to see the magnificent fresco style sanctuary which is decorated in breathtaking colour.

## 4

Beacon Fell, I discovered, is a small solitary hill which, snuggling in the shadow of the much higher Bowland Fells, provides a fine all-round vantage point. I was surprised to find as I drove around the winding, one-way road that ends close to the summit, that it is almost completely covered in conifer trees. Here young families from Preston with pet dogs were picnicking in the sunny glades, the children chasing each other among the trees. A grey-haired, elderly couple was quietly ambling side by side along a woodchip pathway, being overtaken by two hardened ramblers in full pack who probably had another five miles to cover before dusk.

Walking from Fell House Car Park, which was once the site of a farmhouse, I took a cobbled path which within ten minutes brought me to the summit. In this elevated clearing on a small mound I came to the trig-point which marks the 873 feet (266m) summit, a low hill by Bowland standards, but due to it being isolated from the main range it provides an unusual viewpoint. A view indicator shows the prominent landmarks but I found it was necessary to take a short walk around the hilltop to identify some of these because, due to the dense tree coverage, they have become obscured. Parlick Pike, Fair Snape Fell and Bleasdale Moors, which lie about three miles to the north, looked magnificent in the bright sunshine. Their huge brown flanks rising steeply upwards into a turquoise sky. Looking eastwards I could see the end of the green Hodder Valley, with Longridge Fell leading on to Waddington Fell and the distant blue profile of Pendle. Beyond, on the far horizon, was the dark uplands of the West Pennine Moors around Chorley. To the west of Beacon Fell the land flattens quickly leading to the Fylde and the curving line of silver which is the coast. I am told that on a clear day both the Isle of Man and the Lakeland mountains are visible, but they were lost to me in a hazy grey mist. In the soft sunlight the whole scene emitted an atmosphere of almost magical splendour. If Lancelot and his fellow knights had suddenly galloped up the lane from Chipping then no one would have raised an eyebrow.

I learnt that Beacon Fell derives its name from being one of those hilltops on which fires were lit to warn the local inhabitants of possible danger. This idea of passing on messages from high-points is ancient, the Romans had signal points along their roads in Lancashire, but it was the persistent raids by the Scots during the 13th Century that really established the system. Rivington Pike, Pendle Hill and Ingleborough were some of the other summits which formed part of this chain. They were lit to warn of the Spanish Armada in 1588, but since then the fires have been used mainly at times of celebration. In 1887 they marked Queen Victoria's Jubilee and following a revival in 1977, their flames pronounced the Silver Jubilee of our present Queen.

Two charming little rivers, the Brock and the Calder, flow to the north-west of Beacon Fell. Their fertile wooded banks are a haven for wild flowers which, I am told, brings a blaze of colour in early spring. Ramblers come from all over Lancashire to walk along narrow riverside paths which are fringed with a huge carpet of bluebells, contrasting vividly with the gleaming gold of gorse. The River Brock begins as a rivulet between Holme House Fell and Fair Snape Fell. It meanders through Brockmill and the small village of Brock, which has the pagan Green Man as an inn sign. It then passes beneath the Lancaster Canal before ending its short journey at St Michael's where it joins the River Wyre. The Calder is also born among the Bowland Fells, it passes through Oakenclough and Calder Vale before joining the Wyre at Catterall. I found the quiet lanes that cross these two river valleys remain largely untouched by our present century. Here, among ancient farms and secluded cottages fat cows happily graze on rich meadows, rabbits run playfully through holes in hedgerows, while huge winged herons return to their home at nearby Claughton, loaded with fish stolen from garden ponds.

## 5

A small group of children had arrived at Garstang in their white school bus which had St Georges High School, Blackpool, written on the side. I watched as they first alighted, then excitedly began to unload canoes, waterproofs and a mountain of other outdoor gear. Under the watchful eye of their instructor, a fit looking tanned-faced man who gave the impression that he could run a marathon before breakfast, they began to dress. Ten minutes later, complete with yellow life jackets and red hard-hats they carried their canoes to the banks of the Wyre. Mallards ducks gazed on at a safe distance as the adventurers were told what to do should their flimsy crafts overturn. Then in nervous silence they took to the water, quickly disappearing around a bend.

The riverside car park, which sits conveniently at the end of the High Street, was unusually empty. Visitors, who normally flock to this lovely little market town had been put off by the weather forecast. A ridge of low pressure, so the weathermen said, was centred over southern England, bringing heavy rain and high winds to all parts. This was not entirely true for the trees, which follow the curving line of the river bank, were only gently swaying and the grey sky had within it a patch of blue.

I quickly found that Garstang is the ideal market town, it has small village-type shops, old pubs, tea rooms and inviting alleyways known as Wiends. It also has flowers: even in the middle of September the hanging baskets and floral tubs were shimmering in blues, oranges and yellows. But of course this is Land Rover and Tractor country, so the residents know quite a bit about growing. To the west lie the wide flat pastures of the Fylde, some of best growing land in Lancashire, while to the east quickly rises the hill-country where only sheep are tough enough to survive. In this contrasting terrain it is possible to drop from 1500 feet (457m) to sea level in just nine miles.

It is believed that in 597 AD a Saxon settlement was established in what is now Garstang. It was a convenient riverside location and crossing point, which was later referred to as Cherestanc in the Domesday Book. The market, which is still held in the High Street each Thursday, was originally granted a charter by King Edward II in 1310. Most of the land and property within the town remained in single ownership from medieval times up to 1919, when it was auctioned in 109 lots. This must have been a fascinating event to witness, hundreds of rural characters descending on the town, each intent on snapping up a bargain.

*Garstang Cross: in a small market town that began as a Saxon settlement.*

I continued my walk up the High Street, passing the sturdy Town Hall which is topped with a small clock tower and weather vane. Nearby, in the centre of the road is the town's most photographed structure, the market cross. It has, what is known as a vertical Tuscan column, which is mounted on a four tier base with a stone orb on the top. The base was bedecked with flowers, adding that sparkle of colour which is the pride of Garstang. I stood for a few minutes at the roadside absorbing the scene as most visitors probably do, thinking of that period in the 18th century when Garstang was an important staging post. The excitement would mount as the sound of the post-horn echoed down the street, then the galloping horses would sweep into the market place, snorting and steaming with the effort of pulling the coach and passengers at breakneck speed from Preston or Lancaster. Seven inns along the High Street provided accommodation for passengers, with stabling for the all-important horses. In 1797 the importance of Garstang increased even more when part of the new Lancaster Canal was opened. The barges, which were pulled along a narrow tow-path by huge shire horses, were used to transport heavy loads of coal, wood and lime. Today this attractive waterway is popular with fishermen who often hold their competitions here, catching roach, tench, bream and sometimes that fresh-water shark – pike. As it is the longest lock-free length of canal in the whole of Britain it also attracts pleasure boats. These are tolerated but often quietly cursed by the fishermen, for their waves disturb the water and frighten the fish.

I walked up a quiet lane, which leaves a curve in the river at the southern end of the town, to look on the solitary ruins of Greenhalgh Castle. Sadly, I found that only a single wall remains, perched precariously on a small hill at the end of a green meadow and guarded by a handful of trees which were swaying in the breeze. When Oliver Cromwell's soldiers came here in 1646 the fortress was reduced to smouldering rubble.

It had been built in 1490 by the first Earl of Derby, the man who placed the crown on the head of Bolingbroke at the Battle of Bosworth Field, thus creating the House of Tudor. The castle was occupied by the Greenhalgh family who became the feudal rulers of this corner of Lancashire. During the Civil War it was staunchly Royalist, Greenhalgh Castle and Lathom House, near Ormskirk, were the last two buildings in the county to fly the Stuart flag. However, after a heroic fight it finally fell and to ensure it could never again be used against Cromwell's forces it was virtually demolished. Much of the stone was carted away to be used by the local farmers, some can still be seen in the walls of Castle Farm which stands nearby.

Walking back down the lane towards Garstang I could hear the excited voices of school children in the classroom of a primary school. I decided to look inside the adjacent Roman Catholic church of St Mary and St Michael where I discovered the relic of a local saint. In a display cabinet I gazed upon an ornate brass container which a sign said contains 'part of the bloodstained garment worn by St John Plessington'. A small silver chalice from the period of the Reformation was nearby together with a series of printed cards which told the saint's life story.

The staunchly Catholic Plessington family had originated at Pleasington near Blackburn, but had later moved to Dimple Hall at Garstang. John Plessington had been born in 1634, his exciting childhood taking place during the Civil War when his father, Robert, was the main defender of Greenhalgh Castle. He was first educated at a small Jesuit school at Scarisbrick Hall, near Ormskirk, then at St Omer in France, which was later to become Stonyhurst College. He then studied to become a priest at Valladolid in Spain, returning to England in 1663 and taking up a position at Holywell near Chester. This had for centuries been a famous place of pilgrimage for it centred around the miraculous St Winifride's Well.

In 1670 he moved on to become the chaplain to the Massey family who lived at Puddington Hall on the Wirral. However, even though the restored monarch, King Charles II, was a crypto-Catholic, to be a practising priest in England was still unlawful. Following a dispute in which he opposed a mixed marriage he was reported to the authorities who arrested him. He stood trial at Chester in 1679, and in the alien atmosphere following the infamous Oates Plot, he was found guilty. On the 19th July he suffered the terrible death of being hung, drawn and quartered at Barrel Well Hill, which overlooks the River Dee at Chester. His body was buried in the churchyard at Burton on the Wirral, then almost three hundred years later in 1970, he became one of seven Lancashire martyrs to be elevated to sainthood.

I paused again near to the Market Place, looking through the small window of Clarkson's Clog and Shoe Shop I could see a cobbler hard at work attempting to put new soles on a pair of farmer's working boots. To my eyes they seemed way past their best, but farmers have a reputation to live up to. They never throw anything away while there is a hint of life in it and they never mend anything that is not broken, which means they do not believe in what is known as preventative maintenance. This reminded me of a walk I once took over the fells above Chipping, the route followed a track which took me near to an isolated farm. In a field lay the remains of six cars, the distant one dated from the 1920s, then progressively they spanned the years up to the most recent, which was about eight years old. The farmer had run each car into the ground, then when it would go no more he had dumped it and bought a new one. This was a system he had successfully adopted for half a century!

Opposite to the riverside car park is an attractive building which dates from 1756, it was once Garstang Grammar School but it is now called the Arts Centre. Looking in I found with joy that tea and refreshments were for sale to visitors. A cheerful lady served me with two home-baked scones and a 'gradely' pot of tea.

"You should look around afterwards, there are some marvellous pictures and photographs on view."

I followed her advice, spending half an hour looking at the work of three very talented Lancashire artists and photographers: Stella Platt, who originates from Bolton, Pam Potter from Preston and Jon Sparks of Scotforth. Each have successfully pioneered their individual style of conveying the beauty of their subjects, skilfully blending light and colour. Being fond of the uplands I was particularly impressed by Jon Sparks's mountain photography, one breathtaking view showed climbers hanging like spiders from Napes Needle in the Lake District.

I continued my journey northwards, crossing the Wyre at Gubberford Bridge to reach the mellow stoned cottages of Scorton, which like Garstang had its walls bedecked with floral hanging baskets. A stranger to Scorton would never guess that the M6 motorway, with its roaring traffic, passes within just a quarter of a mile of the village. For here in quiet oblivion, rooks glide peacefully over the tree tops, grey squirrels launch into startling acrobatic jumps in the churchyard and rabbits saunter unmolested beneath the hedgerows. It also is a place where cyclists, in pied-piper coloured vests, stop at the Priory tea-rooms before making a lung-bursting assault on the Trough Road.

This is the type of village in which I suspect both Lewis Carrol and Beatrix Potter would have felt at home, for overlooking its untouched tranquillity stands a hill with the enchanting name of Nicky Nook. So with thoughts of the Mad Hatter and Peter Rabbit in my mind I decided to walk up to the summit. Within forty minutes I had reached a delightful plateau of gently rolling moorland full of chubby pheasants and black faced sheep. A narrow pathway led me up to a pile of small stones alongside the summit trig-point, then after a further ten minute stroll I reached the Jubilee Cairn. Sitting on a green elevated meadow this rugged stone structure commemorates the first fifty years of Queen Victoria's reign which ended in 1887. It appears as a dark pimple on the top of the hillside to those unfortunate motorists who need to tear down the motorway.

To the west I gazed on the full panorama of the Lancashire coast which unfolded before me like a giant map, from the yellow sand of Morecambe Bay to the hazy blue of the Mersey estuary. On the south side lay half hidden, the deep cut valley of Grizedale, its wooded slopes leading up to the blue waters of two reservoirs. While to the east spread the towering uplands of Bowland, boasting such names as Harrisend Fell, Jonny Pye's Clough Top and Luddock's Fell. The Mad Hatter, sadly did not appear, but there remained a magical atmosphere about this place where the Pennines end and the Fylde begins; yes Nicky Nook is well named.

## 6

The first day of autumn had made an unpromising start, at dawn the rain had poured with grim enthusiasm, but this had slowly eased into a light drizzle. As I drove up the ascending road towards Marshaw the starlings were shaking the water from their wings and the cattle were beginning to feed on the rain soaked grass. In the hidden valley on my left lay the wooded banks of the Wyre around Dolphinholme, the river narrowed by the encroaching hills. On my right lay the brooding uplands, the green meadowland quickly turning to brown, lightened here and there by purple heather which disappeared into a sea of swirling mist. The fields here are wide and uncultivated, cattle grids are the only restriction to the wandering sheep that scale the windy heights, forever on the hunt for food. Had I been shown a painting of this scene I would have said it was the Scottish Highlands, only the Monarch of the Glen was missing.

A sharp bend and a steep ascent brought me up to Lancashire's most renowned pass, the Trough of Bowland. I was now travelling in the footsteps of the Lancashire Witches, for this landscape had been their last glimpse of freedom before they met their fate in the dungeons of Lancaster Castle.

The road made a short dip down towards Abbeystead, part of the huge moorland estate owned by Britain's richest man, the Duke of Westminster. Here converge two rivers, the Tarnbrook Wyre and the Marshaw Wyre, they meet at Abbeystead Reservoir to form a single river. As I was climbing once more and trying to negotiate an awkward bend out dashed a fat pheasant into the road. I pressed my horn, it stopped mesmerised for a few seconds, then after looking at me with disdain it walked slowly into a field. The flattened remains of its less fortunate colleagues I have found to be a sad feature of many Lancashire country roads, rabbits and hedgehogs being the most common victims.

At a high point of 942 feet (287m) on this elevated road stands the Jubilee Tower, a square stone structure which I am sure provides an excellent vantage point – on a clear day! When I climbed the wet steps to the castellated summit the clouds were hanging ominously over the hillside then stretching westwards towards the coast. The Fylde was enveloped in a damp mist, my first glimpse of the River Lune being restricted to a pale snake of white beyond Lancaster's dark skyline. I turned around to look at the hills, a wild wilderness of endless moorland half hidden in the brooding sky. This could only be a north-country scene, a harsh yet magnificent landscape of savage grandeur. For years it has been part of an unlikely battleground, walkers fighting for unlimited access, landowners fighting to retain their vast estates. Today it is only possible to walk lawfully on a small part of these sweeping moorlands, a narrow access strip leads up to Lancashire's second highest summit, Ward's Stone at 1837 feet (560m) above sea level.

I climbed down the tower steps, stopping to read a sign that said 'Local homemade lemon cheese and jam at farm'; a reassuring hint of hospitality in such an isolated spot. Soon I was descending the steep road, watched by a field full of rooks who were foraging among brown rushes. I turned right at Quernmore, passing its solitary parish church of St Peter, then it began to rain with a vengeance. I took shelter in a well designed picnic area near Caton, hoping that my exploration of the Lune Valley would not be marred by this dismal weather.

"Looks like this rain is here for the day", said the man serving steaming mugs of tea at the mobile refreshment bar.

"No, you're wrong, It's just passing over. It'll be sunshining in ten minutes", came the reply from a waterproof covered fisherman who still had his fishing rod in his hand. He had strolled across the road from the river which was barely visible through the trees.

I walked back to my car balancing a mug of tea in one hand and an umbrella in the other wondering who would be correct. Then, like magic it happened; the rain ceased, the clouds vanished, the sky turned a startling blue and out came the sun. The fisherman had won and furthermore this marvellous autumn weather was destined to last for a week.

Every Lancastrian should come on a pilgrimage at least once a year to the River Lune. Not just because its one of England's loveliest rivers, or because it has scores of untouched villages with marvellous pubs, or even because the fishing is the finest in the land. We should come because this is where Lancashire began, for this river gave our county its name. The tribes who lived in this area before the Romans arrived were well aware of the advantages of living here, they called it the 'Lon' which is said to mean 'health giving'. When Hadrian ordered his legions to construct a fort on the river banks they named it Lon Castrum – the fort on the River Lon. This of course, became Lancaster, then the surrounding lands which later came under the jurisdiction of what was now a major town, eventually became known as the county of Lancashire.

*The Lune Valley: one of Lancashire's hidden gems – painted by Turner and visited by poets.*

However, the Lune is born not in Lancashire but in Cumbria, high among the Howgill Fells. A series of streams converge to create the river near the lonely village of Newbiggin-on-Lune, from where it cascades southwards, passing close to Tebay and then Sedbergh. It now presents a wider prospect, being swelled by scores of minor becks it enters Lancashire beyond the 13th century Devil's Bridge near Kirkby Lonsdale. Now in the wide green valley of Lunedale it gently curves its way to the south west, being joined by the River Greta near Tunstall and the River Wenning at Hornby. The famous meander of the Crook-o-Lune is reached near Caton, before it takes the familiar path through Lancaster to meet the Irish Sea beyond Glasson Dock, at Sunderland Point.

The beauty of the Lune Valley is yet to be discovered by many Lancastrians who live towards the south of the county. When heading northwards they tend to be attracted by the splendour of Lakeland, by-passing one of England's hidden gems. But poets and artists of the past knew it well, Thomas Gray wrote with enthusiasm about a visit he made here in 1769, while Ruskin thought the river created one of 'the loveliest scenes in England.' But it is Turner, regarded as one of our greatest artists, who immortalised this delightful river valley.

J.M.W. Turner, the son of a barber, was born in Convent Garden, London, in 1775. From a very early age his unique talent was apparent, by the age of fourteen he was living by the sale of his drawings. He quickly became a one-man industry, working unbelievably hard all his life he turned out thousands of both watercolours and oil paintings. His restless talent drove him ever onwards, he travelled widely throughout Britain and Europe, always seeking new scenes for his canvas.

In 1818 he was commissioned to paint a number of landscapes of Lancashire and Yorkshire to illustrate a new work by the great northern historian Dr Whitaker, entitled *A History of Richmondshire*. While carrying out this project he stayed with a close friend, Walter Fawkes who lived at Farnley near Leeds. One of these scenes, The Crook of Lune, looking towards Hornby Castle, is regarded as one of his finest works. Using mainly blues, browns and greens he has created around one of his favourite subjects, a twisting river, a feeling of both the beauty and the savagery of nature.

As I looked northwards over the glistening water with the first subtle colours of autumn visible in the trees, it was easy to understand what attracted Turner and Ruskin and Grey to this green valley.

# CHAPTER THREE

# THE LUNE VALLEY TO HEYSHAM

I learn about Dr Lingard at Hornby, see where the Brontë sisters went to school then I climb to Lancashire's highest point. I discover llamas near the Lune and bitterns at Leighton Moss, visit an American Connection, explore Morecambe then end up at Half Moon Bay.

## 1

I suspect that the villagers of Hornby were secretly happy that the main road had been closed at Melling, for this meant that the traffic, which normally passes through the village centre on its way from Lancaster to Kirkby Lonsdale, had been diverted.

"Good morning," shouted a friendly middle-aged man from across the street, who was obviously delighted with both the new-found peacefulness and the bright autumn sunshine. I replied with a smile, then turned to read a plaque on the Institute wall which boasted that Hornby was the Best Kept Village in Lancashire in 1989. I continued up the street till I came to the bridge over the River Wenning, here the fast-moving water was gushing over a weir, stained brown by the peat it was bringing down off the fells of Yorkshire. This river, which is joined by the Hindburn just half a mile upstream from this bridge, is a major tributary of the Lune. It is also much favoured by fishermen, two of whom were busy unloading their baskets and rods from a car nearby.

After leaning over the bridge for five minutes (a pastime which I can highly recommend) watching the antics of a dipper comically losing a battle with the current, my eyes were drawn upwards. High on a green hill, its grey turretted walls half covered in red leaves, I saw for the first time Hornby Castle. This marvellous, fairy-tale fortress is the pride of Hornby, dominating the village from its rocky perch it was built by the Norman Montbegons. They had moved to this more defensive site from the motte and bailey Castle Stede which had been built in the valley. In the 15th century it was owned by the Harringtons who became involved in the tragic Wars of the Roses. The female line then married into the dominant Stanley family who became resident in the stronghold. Sir Edward Stanley led the men of Lancashire and Cheshire into a great victory over the Scots at Flodden Field. For his success he was created first Lord Monteagle in 1534 and was later to become immortalised by Walter Scott. The unusual octagonal church tower in Hornby was built by him as a thanksgiving, it contains his badge of an eagle's claw together with the arms of the Isle of Man.

After such success there must have seemed little left for him to conquer in this world, so he decided to prepare for his eternal rest by designing an elaborate tomb for himself. This he commanded, would stand in a new chancel in the church, but sadly his plans went wrong for he died before the chancel was completed. His family had him buried in a temporary grave at Hornby Priory, but they never seemed to get around to moving his body back to the church. As the Priory has now disappeared the exact location of the grave is not known. However Priory Farm stands close to the site and one local character maintains that the hero of Flodden lies buried under a dung heap. Of course, he may well have a Scottish allegiance!

*Hornby*

Crossing the road I continued my stroll, admiring the rows of cosy cottages which look out over the lush Lune Valley. On the front of the imposing Georgian presbytery of St Mary's R.C. church is a heritage plaque which states that Dr Lingard, a historian, lived in the building from 1811 to 1851. Few people today remember John Lingard yet during the early part of the last century he was regarded as one of England's most brilliant men. Great scholars came to this little Lancashire village from all over Europe to consult him, for he was regarded as a world authority on history.

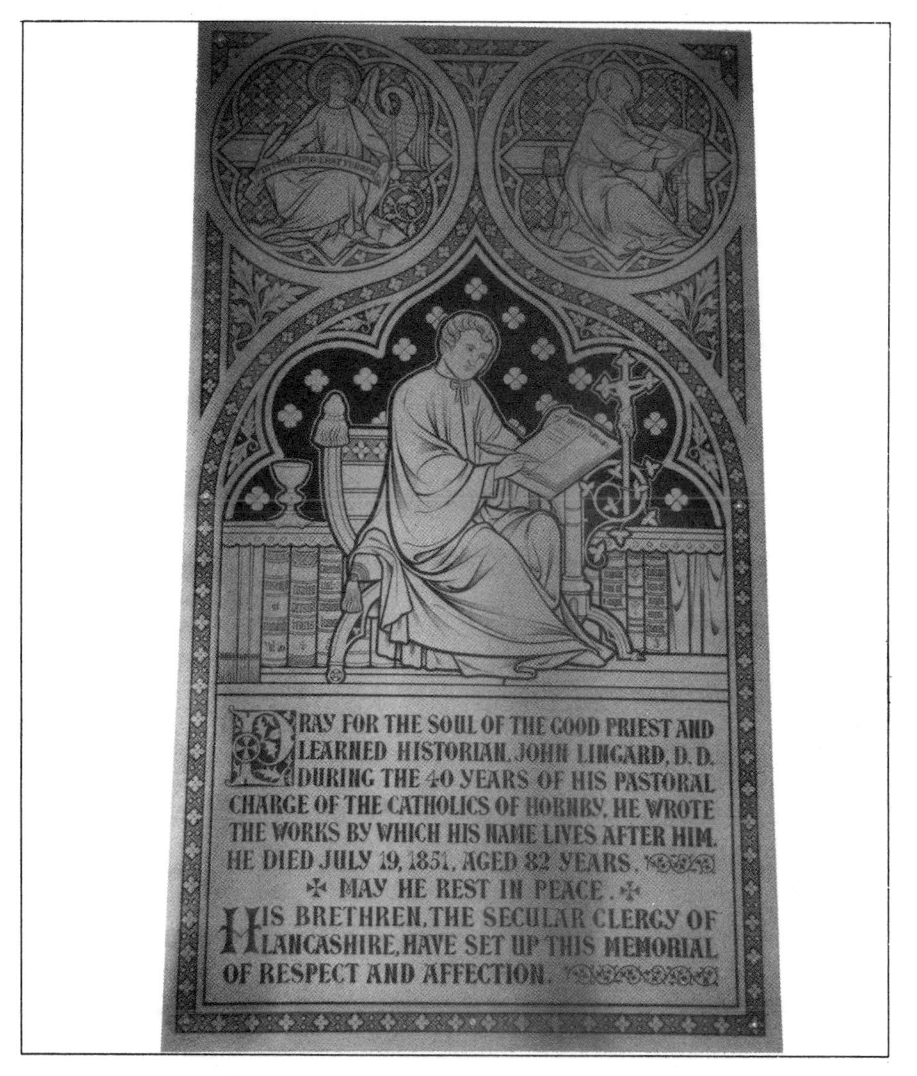


*The Lingard memorial: a plaque in Hornby church.*

He had been born in 1769, the son of a carpenter, who even as a boy was considered to have outstanding talent. He went to Douai in France to study to become a priest, then following the French Revolution he came back to this country to begin his parish work. He was offered high office, there were even rumours that the Pope wanted him to be a Cardinal, but he preferred the peacefulness of Hornby where he lived for forty years. Here he wrote a history of England which was unique, for it was free of any religious bias and it became a work which was universally admired.

Inside the porch of St Mary's church I found a framed print of John Lingard and surprisingly, he looks quite unlike what I expected. Not a serious looking academic, but tall, well built and handsome he stands looking out into the village street he loved, a quill pen poised ready for his next line.

Joining the diverted traffic I took the winding road which contours to the east of Hornby where the fells end and the flat river valley begins. Passing through the secluded village of Wray I remembered the terrible disaster which took place here in 1968 which became newspaper headlines. The two rivers which converge at the village, the Roeburn and the Hindburn, were swelled by a flash flood. The unstoppable water sped down the hillside like a tidal wave completely demolishing one end of the village.

Continuing past the inviting Bridge Inn at Wennington, the first fallen leaves of autumn blowing on the roadside, I headed towards Tunstall. After turning up narrow Church Lane I then came to a sudden halt for the road menders of the Lune Valley were out in force. After a ten minute wait the lorry which was emptying tarmac into a hole, moved on and I was able to reach the secluded church of St John. Surrounded by fields in an unchanging landscape this must have been much the same scene that greeted the Brontë sisters when they came here in 1824. I stood among the gravestones in the churchyard looking up at the room above the porch where, it is said, the girls ate their dinner each Sunday after the service. Charlotte, even at such a young age, remembered all the details of the building which became Brocklebridge Church in her classic novel, *Jane Eyre*.

At Cowan Bridge, a hamlet which sits on the busy A65 road, I found a row of cottages which was once part of the school which the Brontë sisters attended. A plaque on the side of the building states:

*Marie, Elizabeth, Charlotte and Emily Brontë*
*lived here as pupils of the*
*Clergy Daughters School 1824 – 25.*

The school was moved to Castleton in 1833.

*Tunstall: the young Brontë sisters came here each Sunday to attend St John's church.*

What is not stated is how miserable and unhappy the girls were at the school, the details of which are related in Elizabeth Gaskell's fascinating biography, *The Life of Charlotte Brontë*. The school had been started by the Vicar of Tunstall, William Carus Wilson, about 1816 in a former bobbin factory. He seems to have been a forceful character, who was also the editor of England's first penny papers for children, the Children's Friend and the Friendly Visitor. It was the food at the school that was a major upset for the children, the cook was dirty and disorganised and the meals often proved uneatable. The porridge was burnt, the odour of rancid fat filled the air and the milk was described as 'bingy'. The dormitories were also damp and unhealthy, and added to this misery was a two mile walk to church at Tunstall each Sunday. This building was also freezing cold in winter as it had no heating. These appalling conditions led to a deterioration in the delicate health of Marie and Elizabeth who both died from consumption in 1825.

This terrible episode in both Emily and Charlotte's lives, inevitably, left a lasting memory. The school is recorded as Lowood in Jane Eyre, to which Charlotte devotes six chapters.

## 2

To the north east of Cowan Bridge the Lancashire Border juts oddly outwards to embrace a narrow section of wild isolated fells which contains Lancashire's highest point, Gragareth. It is as if the cartographer, after perhaps returning from a Christmas party, decided benevolently to give Lancashire a mountain. However, before the changes to the county border took place in 1974, the county could boast several mountains, but these are now part of Cumbria. At that time the summit of Coniston Old Man was known by almost every Lancastrian as the highest point, but few have even heard of Gragareth today.

I turned off the main road into the secluded village of Leck, then took a single track lane which ascends the hillside to Leck Fell. Below on my left, in a wild and beautiful valley meandered Leck Beck, which is a tributary of the Lune. Here I stopped to watch a buzzard which was giving a magnificent display of its aeronautical techniques, soaring upwards then slowly descending in wide circles.

This lane, which is used mainly by pot-holers and the occasional walker, serves Lancashire's loneliest and highest farm, Leck Fell House. After parking my car off the roadside I went to chat with Alan Middleton, who lives with his wife and children on this rugged mountainside. A lively, healthy looking man in his thirties, Alan was born here, so he feels no sense of isolation.

"My parents came here as tenant farmers in 1949, but they have now retired to Ireby so I have taken over. We have mainly sheep and a few cows."

He went on to tell me about life at Leck Fell House, which is too far from 'civilization' to have any mains supplies. The water is piped to the house from a well on the fellside, but this tends to get blocked with peat. At the moment he has had to by-pass the underground pipe by running a temporary one on the surface.

"It was only trickling from the tap and the wife began to complain!"

But their electricity supply is much more efficient for he has had a modern wind turbine installed. Its small propeller was whirling round very fast in the chill breeze, producing enough power for the family to have both a freezer and a washing machine.

*Leck Fell House: loneliest and highest farm in Lancashire.*

The children go by taxi to the village school in the valley, along the well-made single track road which, when Alan was a child, was full of deep holes. This had been particularly hazardous in wintertime, but in recent years they have had little snow.

"Although there was five inches of snow on the fell last October, which was very early, but it did not last long."

He then told me how this magnificent, unspoilt corner of Lancashire seems to be forgotten, for visitors tend to be attracted by the closeness of both Lakeland and the Yorkshire Dales.

"I think Alfred Wainwright is the only writer who has given us a mention."

Leaving the farm behind I began to ascend the steep fellside, which has no path, only rough boggy grass. The edge of the fell has a series of gritstone screes whose stones have been used by past generations to create a series of guide cairns. The most prominent of these are known as the Three Men of Gragareth, which have become welcome landmarks in this isolated terrain.

*Gragareth: a walker enjoys the view from the Three Men on the approach to Lancashire's highest summit.*

Beyond this point I found that I was on a huge windswept plateau, rising less steeply to the summit which lies half a mile away. Low grey cloud was now swirling across the tussocky grass, reducing the visibility to just a few metres, forcing me to use my compass. At last Trig Point No. S5404 came into sight and I had reached the roof of Lancashire. At 2057 feet (627m) above sea level, Gragareth exceeds the 2000 feet (610m) limit which walkers generally agree separates the hills from the mountains. The next highest points in the county are Ward's Stone at 1837 feet (560m) and Pendle Hill at 1827 feet (557m), which are mere hills!

As I stood at the boggy summit the clouds suddenly began to thin out. Then, miraculously they melted away completely, revealing a breathtaking amphitheatre of rugged hills. Bathed in soft sunlight I could see to the east Yorkshire's famous Three Peaks of Whernside, Ingleborough and Pen-y-ghent. To the north lay the hazy outline of the Howgills Fells leading on to the high mountains of Lakeland, while to the south spread the moors of Bowland. The Lune Valley, green and fertile, was visible far below, with a curve of blue water marking a bend in the river. Walking eastwards for a further half mile I had entered North Yorkshire, below lay lovely Kingsdale with its lonely road which links Ingleton to Dent.

The spirit of that great Lancastrian from Blackburn, Alfred Wainwright, lives on in these isolated, rugged mountains which he loved so much. He had already written his classic guide books to the Lakeland Fells when he came here in 1970. His exploration of Gragareth appears in *Walks in Limestone Country*, one of over fifty books which he wrote about our northern hills. His other works of particular interest to Lancastrians are: *A Lune Sketchbook* (1980), *A Ribble Sketchbook* (1980) and *A Bowland Sketchbook* (1982).

## 3

Leaving the outskirts of Kirkby Lonsdale behind I took the quiet by-road which winds through the gentle countryside on the northern bank of the Lune. It is a rich green landscape, full of small hills, neat hedgerows and distant clusters of trees. After passing through Whittington and Newton I arrived in Arkholme where I stopped at the village pub, the Bay Horse. Here, looked down upon by prints of Old Lancaster and the ancient inns of London, fit-looking men who had taken early retirement were buying their wives chicken and chips in the basket. I took my drink to a secluded table where I overheard snippets of bar-room philosophy. A bearded man called John, who was aged about forty, was listening intently to his lady friend who was relating the problems of office life.

"You get to be like the women you work with if you aren't careful", she confided, "and I don't like it."

As I looked around this friendly pub I tried to picture in my mind the parties which must have taken place here when the First World War came to an end. Arkholme had a special reason to celebrate for it was one of the thirty one Thankful Villages of Britain in which all those local men who went to war returned safely. It sent fifty nine men out of a population of three hundred, this included eight who had emigrated to New Zealand but had returned to fight with the New Zealand forces.

Much of this lovely village, which was once known as Erwhum, is hidden from the passing motorist for it lies down a quiet cul-de-sac which meanders towards the river. I drove slowly past its secluded cottages to reach the village church which dates from the mid-15th century. Inside of this ancient building I saw a copy of the Charter granted to the Lord of the Manor in 1279 allowing a fair to be held on the feast of St John the Baptist together with a weekly market. This, of course, was a good excuse for a village celebration in 1980 to mark the 700th anniversary. The churchyard, I discovered, has the oldest structure in Arkholme which is a mound known as the Chapel Hill Motte. It is a man-made hill which was probably built by the Saxons or the early Normans for defence of their settlement.

As I was leaving the churchyard I stopped to chat with a woman whose husband was a church warden. She told me that they had retired here from Bolton about ten years ago and how they had been welcomed into village life. We talked of the little-known beauty of this part of Lancashire and of the rich history that lies around every corner.

"Arkholme didn't become a parish until 1866", she related. "Up till then all the burials took place at Melling which lies on the other side of the Lune. The river was crossed by a ford, but one day during a flood, a funeral party was swept away by the water. The coffin was lost and two people, I believe, were drowned."

As I began to walk back to my car she called out to me.

"Oh, before you go you must see the llamas. A man who has moved into the village breeds them and at the moment there are some young ones."

I could not resist the invitation. I walked along a pathway which led alongside the church and in less than five minutes discovered one of Lancashire's great surprises. In a lush green meadow about twenty of these magnificent South American animals were happily munching away at the grass. Their thick woollen coats varied in colour, some were almost white, others caramel, while one appeared a dark brown. The innocent looking, wide eyed young llamas, who were about the size of a dog, looked like they might have stepped out of a Walt Disney cartoon. The large adults appeared to be very strong yet placid creatures, with characteristic long necks and small heads. As I watched them peacefully feeding, completely unperturbed by my presence, I wondered why had they been brought from the Andes to the Pennines.

Was it for their wool? Hopefully not for llamas steaks, but maybe just as an unbeatable talking point in the bar of the Bay Horse!

*Arkholme: where llamas, rather than cows, munch the grass!*

I continued along the secluded pathway, the first glorious colours of autumn beginning to show in the hedgerows. The leaves which were turning at their edges from green to pale yellow, contrasted vividly with the glint of red from the rose hips. Soon I was at the water's edge, looking on one of the Lune's finest views. The wide, fast flowing river appeared bright silver in the sun. Healthy cows were busily drinking from the shallows while in the distance a wading fisherman was wrestling with a salmon which had at last taken his bait. I could also picture in my mind the ghost of Turner, setting up his easel once more on the bank of this lovely river.

The lanes around this part of Lancashire are marvellously free from traffic, as if they have been caught in a time-warp of the 1940s. An old man of about eighty, who was slowly cycling through Borwick, was the only person I passed in a dozen miles. Swallows blissfully undisturbed, were lazily stretching their wings on the telephone wires near Priest Hutton, thinking that perhaps, in a few more days they would leave for Africa. While at Yealand Redmayne the only hidden sign of human habitation was the inviting smell of woodsmoke that came in through the open window of my car.

At this point I have a confession to make: I slipped like a refugee over the border for a mile into Cumbria. Unnoticed, I booked into a hotel which overlooks the Kent estuary at Arnside, from where I gazed out on that part of the Lake District which has been stolen from Lancashire: Furness. Then I was relieved to be told that many of the locals regard themselves as adopted Lancastrians. They use Lancashire as their postal address, and with north-country good sense ignore the ancient yet strange county border which splits up this splendid peninsula into two parts.

The wonderful limestone mosaic of this countryside around Arnside and Silverdale is unique: it is as if a giant has plucked the best features of the Yorkshire Dales and placed them on the shores of Morecambe Bay. Here plants, trees, animals and birds which are seldom seen anywhere else in England live in splendid isolation. Naturalists, bird-watchers who are known as twitchers, and walkers who have discovered this untouched countryside jealously guard their secret. I was told that as it is 'not on the road to anywhere' it is seldom discovered by chance; visitors come here only because they wish to do so.

*Silverdale: a spot much loved by Elizabeth Gaskell.*

# 4

I am writing these notes looking out through the high window of a hotel bedroom which I have chosen because it gives me uninterrupted views across the River Kent and beyond to the brown sands of Morecambe Bay. Pigeons are cooing from the rooftop, while far below across a garden filled with flowers of yellow and orange, the quiet life of Arnside moves slowly onwards, seemingly oblivious of the outside world. A bearded cyclist wearing brief shorts stops to anxiously consult his map, then convinced he is on the right road he speeds quickly away. An elderly couple stroll slowly back to their car which is parked on the narrow promenade, reluctantly leaving for home. Two small boys stop to drink from the water fountain, then run up the hill loudly chattering, the sound of their voices die away and then a rich silence returns.

The bright sun, which has continually shone since mid-day, is now beginning to sink behind the hills of Lakeland which stand proudly on the opposite bank of the river. The tide is also beginning to ebb, small patches of shiny sand are appearing on which small wading birds are foraging for food. On my right a two carriage train, looking like a child's toy-town model, passes over the low viaduct which links Arnside to Grange, its reflection moving across the silver water.

I return to the window half an hour later to find that the sun is now sinking fast, turning the cumulus clouds into strings of pale pink. The hills have also changed, first from green to misty blue and now to a silhouette of dense black. Finally, in a triumph of gold, I watch the hush of evening fall over the bay, bringing with it a promise of a continuing Indian Summer.

The people who live around Arnside and Silverdale talk about high or low tides in the same way as the locals of say Oldham, speak of the train or bus times. This is of course, because for many hundreds of years they would take a short cut across the sands of Morecambe Bay to what was the Furness District of Lancashire, saving a long journey inland. The tides were a crucial factor in the 'cross sands route', as it became known, for a miscalculation could easily end in disaster.

A glance at the map of the area reveals the complicated profile of Morecambe Bay whose shallow waters cover around two hundred square miles. Its entrance into the Irish Sea is marked by Barrow in the north and Fleetwood in the south, into which pour four major rivers: the Wyre, Lune, Kent and Leven. Due to this shallowness of the bay, at low tide a huge area of sand is revealed through which only the channels of these rivers flow. So it is easy to see why travellers were first tempted to venture across these sands, which appear to provide a straightforward route. However, time revealed that banks of quick-sand, a powerful tidal bore and the shifting river channels can quickly turn the journey into a nightmare. Strangers wishing to make the crossing sought the assistance of local fishermen who knew the vagaries of the bay and this led to the creation of an official guide system.

It is believed locally that some type of guide system had been established by the early 13th century, but it is in 1501 that the first record of 'Carter upon Kent Sands' was held by a man named Edmonson. He was appointed by the Prior of Cartmel and probably used a cart to take travellers across the river, so became known as a carter. After the Dissolution of the Monasteries in 1539, the Duchy of Lancaster (which is held by the reigning monarch) took over the role of retaining the guides. In 1564 Richard Carter, who probably took the family name from his profession, was appointed and his descendants inherited the job for the next 300 years. The present guide, Cedric Robinson, was appointed by the Duchy in 1963 and lives at Kents Bank.

The Romans, with their general, Agricola, are said to have used the 'cross sands route to reach Cumbria during the 1st century A.D. Then after the establishment of Furness Abbey in 1127, followed by Conishead Priory and Cartmel Priory, the monks were regular travellers across the bay. By the 14th century the route had become firmly established; later, Robert the Bruce, George Fox and John Wesley all came this way. By the late 18th century a regular stage coach service was running across the sands. It began at the Kings Arms in Lancaster, crossed the sands from Hest Bank to Kents Bank, then continued to the Sun Inn at Ulverston; it was recorded by Turner in his watercolour, Lancaster Sands. Only when the Arnside railway viaduct was built over the Kent estuary in 1857 did the 'cross sands route' begin to decline. It now remains as a unique walking experience for parties who must always be led by the official guide.

One hot August day two years ago I joined such a group who met on the small jetty at Arnside. We began by walking along the shoreline path with the sands on our right and the outline of Grange-over-Sands visible across the bay. To my surprise we turned inland for a short distance, cutting across the end of the peninsula known as Blackstone Point before reaching the lovely small bay at White Creek. Taking a deep breath and filled with anxious laughter we then followed the measured footsteps of Cedric Robinson and his assistant – heading over the sands and apparently straight out to the distant glint of the sea. We continued taking a zig-zag path across this Lancashire Sahara, presumably avoiding invisible areas of quicksand which could spell our doom. Being about three miles from the shore in a wilderness of brown sand, was both strange and exhilarating. We also felt vulnerable, for we knew that in a matter of hours the spot on which we were standing would be part of the sea bed. Looking inland the grey line which marked the shore appeared distant and flat, completely overshadowed by the huge expanse of flat sand.

The sand which had initially been quite firm, became soft and oozing as we came nearer to the channel through which the River Kent flows. At this point we removed our shoes, then began to wade across the ever deepening water. The force of the flow grew strong as we reached the deepest point which was above knee level, then thankfully it grew shallower as we ascended the far bank. Another smaller channel remained to be crossed before we strode triumphantly into Kents Bank. Proudly, we accepted a certificate from Cedric Robinson to prove we had walked in the steps of the legions: 'Cross Kent Sands'.

Before leaving from the hotel in the early morning I had a chat with the lady-owner about life in this lovely corner of Morecambe Bay. She spoke of the pleasure of walks along secluded paths on Arnside Knott at dawn, of rare plants and butterflies which hide among the limestone, and of the animals and birds.

"We had a seal on the beach here a couple of weeks ago, it had probably come from the colony which lives on Walney Island. Some of the holiday makers were concerned because it was lounging on the sand, they thought it was ill. But I told them not to worry, for that is just what seals do during the daytime."

## 5

The village of Silverdale was just awakening, a delicious aroma of morning coffee filled the air. Well dressed men in tweed jackets and regimental ties were taking their morning walk to buy a copy of the Daily Telegraph or the Guardian. A van which had stopped outside the Royal was selling Fleetwood fish to local housewives who were busy talking about foreign holidays.

"Hello Doris, glad to see you're back. Did you enjoy yourself."

"It was really nice. We have always loved Malta, but it was very hot this time."

Across the road a family of four were desperately trying to decide which motor coach tour to book. Would it be a day in Morecambe, a drive around Eight Lakes or perhaps a visit to Kirkby Lonsdale?

I walked slowly along the village street then beyond the church I stopped to admire a limestone hill which was shrouded with woodlands. Hidden among this tangle of foliage on Castle Barrow is a conical tower known by the delightful name of the Pepper Box, yet another memorial to Queen Victoria's Jubilee. But then the map of this area is full of such names created to charm the stranger: who could resist visiting the Fairy Steps, Hawes Water, Gibralter or Jack Scout. Unfortunately I would have needed a week to visit them all, but I decided I would go to Jenny Brown's Point.

I drove down a narrow lane which had a harsh warning sign for landlubbers like myself: 'Beware of fast incoming tides and quicksand'. This spot would have been known to both Elizabeth Gaskell and the Brontë sisters for they knew Silverdale well. Mrs Gaskell came each summer to a house named Lindeth Tower to write her novels. While the young Charlotte and Emily came to escape the fever which had broken out at their dreadful school at Cowan Bridge. At that time Silverdale was a port on the River Kent served by steamers from Morecambe. However the constantly shifting Kent Channel is now three miles from the shore.

The residents of Lindeth Road have a problem: wild chickens! It seems that around twenty chickens and two cockerels, which once belonged to a local man, now roam at liberty in the area. They stalk around the gardens, saunter into the woodland and walk nonchalantly across the road, flouting their new-found independence. Reaction is mixed; one lady believes they add interest and character to Silverdale, but others consider them to be a nuisance. The RSPCA and the local health authority are unable to act: the birds are not in distress, they have no owner and are not a health problem. So perhaps in years to come they will become yet another attraction on the tourist map.

I sat on a bench at Jenny Brown's Point, gazing out over the limestone escarpment that leads down to the russet sand and the sea. Rivulets of blue water, reflected by the bright morning sunshine, led my eyes on to the hazy coastline around Morecambe. This lonely shore is guarded by windswept hawthorn trees, their bright red berries having just arrived, were shimmering with dew. I could see a lazy line of cows slowly moving across a distant marshy track, while a hidden curlew piped its approval. Little is known of Jenny Brown who lived here in the 18th century and became immortalised by the map makers, but if this was her home she was lucky indeed.

Sea washed turf was once an important local industry along this north-west coast, but I am told that only one professional producer is now in business – John Brailsford of Silverdale. The turf, which grows on the sea shore and is covered each tide by several feet of water, is much sought after by those who seek the finest lawns. Only the toughest grass can survive this rigourous battering by sea and weather, weeds are killed naturally, leaving a crisp green carpet of fine turf. It is harvested using a special machine which slices it into rectangles of about one inch in depth, for sea-washed turf must never be rolled. It is used throughout Britain on bowling greens and in gardens which are the best in the world, and industries such as Cadburys, British Aerospace and even the Bank of England use it to enhance their headquarters.

I came to the nature reserve at Leighton Moss just as a group of school children were being led along the sunlit lane on a tour that they will probably remember for the rest of their lives. For here, hidden among reeds, in pools or beneath protected hedgerows live in total freedom, what is probably the most diverse collection of rare birds and animals in England. I remember as a small boy listening enthralled to the popular radio program called Romany of the BBC, in which Bramwell Evens took his listeners on enchanting nature walks with his spaniel Raq. I envied him seeing weasels, otters, merlins, woodpeckers and scores of other creatures which somehow never seemed to be around when I went out into the countryside. These children are more lucky, for they will probably see birds which even Romany had never spotted.

Inside the Visitors Centre I spoke to one of the wardens about the nature reserve, which is administered by the RSPB (The Royal Society for the Protection of Birds). He explained that it covers around 320 acres and is really a shallow, reedy marsh which is surrounded on three sides by limestone hills with an outlet to the coast. The area was once farmland which was kept clear of water by pumps, but this was abandoned during the First World War, and the swampy reeds returned. It became a haven for many rare species of birds, particularly the bittern, which was really why the reserve was established in 1964.

I asked, rather shamefaced, would he explain to me what a bittern looked like. Smiling and ignoring my ignorance he pointed to a large coloured photograph of a reed bed which formed part of a display.

" Believe it or not there is actually a bittern on this photo, but it's so well camouflaged that it takes some spotting. It is really a small mottled coloured heron which spends much of its day hidden among the reeds and is seldom seen on the wing. If it is disturbed it will quickly run away on foot, disappearing in seconds. It is also famous for its deep resonant booming which can sometimes be heard over a mile away. This reserve is a main breeding ground for the bittern in this country."

He then told me of the many other rare or unusual species that have made an appearance at Leighton Moss. These include water rails, peregrine falcons, bearded tits, marsh harriers and black-tailed godwits. It is also an excellent place to see otters cavorting among the pools in the reed beds, and red deer which live among the dense woodlands.

As I made my way to the small cafe for morning coffee I read a notice which, no doubt would make the hearts of twitchers start racing: a rare yellow-legged gull had just been spotted . . .

*Leighton Moss: a unique nature reserve.*

## 6

I drove to Warton along a leafy lane passing the entrance to lovely Leighton Hall, which was once the home of Sir George Middleton; he received his knighthood in 1642 for his bravery in fighting for the King during the Civil War. The road meandered past St Bernard's Priory at Hyning to bring me into the deserted village street which was bathed in morning sunshine. The car-park lay hidden beneath the white limestone cliffs of Warton Crag whose crevices were covered in bright pink flowers. Red admirals, peacocks and cabbage white butterflies were sunning themselves undisturbed, their wingtips almost touching as they enjoyed a fleeting moment of pleasure in their short lives.

*Warton: once home to a branch of the Washington family.*

American visitors, so I'm told, make a point of coming here to Warton for the village has important links with their first president, George Washington. I was fortunate, for as I strolled up the pathway to St Oswald's church I met Frank Newman, a local man who helps to look after the 14th century building. I gratefully accepted his offer to show me around, we began by looking inside the tower.

"This is what most visitors like to see, it is a stone on which is carved the original stars and stripes which, of course, became the flag of the USA."

He told me that Robert Washington who lived during the 15th century, had built the church tower on which he had carved his coat of arms. This had been on the outside of the building, which over the centuries had been covered with plaster. Then in 1885 it had been re-discovered and its importance realised. To protect it from the weather a glass panel was placed over it, but this proved largely ineffective so in 1955 it was decided to bring the stone inside of the church.

"This picture of George Washington was sent to us by a lady from America," he said removing it from the wall. "If you look here you can see her name on the back."

We then walked over to a cupboard which Frank opened to show me a large Stars and Stripes flag.

"On the 4th July we fly this from the church tower to celebrate American Independence Day. It was specially sent to us from the USA where it was flown from the Capital Building in Washington in 1966."

Frank then spoke of the colourful village parties which went on for three days during the bicentenary celebrations of 1976. A choir and drama group came from the USA to entertain the locals and the event is now part of the village's history. Before I left the church he showed me a number of newspaper articles concerning the village's American connection which have been carefully preserved together with a family tree. These also tell of a little-known link which exists between the families of George Washington and Sir Winston Churchill. It seems that the local Kitson family who lived at Warton Hall during the 15th century, had two children, Margaret and Thomas. Margaret married into the Washington family, and Thomas's daughter, Katherine, married into the Spencer family who were the ancestors of the Churchills.

Walking out into the slanting sunlight I met a large group of middle-aged ramblers who were preparing to leave for Warton Crag. A ruddy faced man, who I suspect might have known Monty in the Western Desert, had a clip board on which was drawn his plan of campaign. Before leaving Warton I wandered among the ruins of what is now known as the Old Rectory. Its massive walls recapture the memories of the bloodthirsty Scots who for centuries plagued this remote part of Lancashire. It was built during the 14th century by the powerful de Thweng family who at this time ruled the district and appointed the rectors of the church.

## 7

I stood on the promenade at Morecambe looking out over a silver-grey sea, thinking this must be one of the finest views from any English seaside resort. For most holiday towns look out into an empty sky, but Morecambe has the mountains of Lakeland as a backcloth. The view, which extends from Black Combe to Arnside Knott, embraces scores of peaks including the prominent Wetherlam, Helvellyn and Fairfield. For half an hour I watched shimmering white gulls hunt for food on the shoreline, I saw little blue fishing boats bob up and down among the waves and I revelled in the heady aroma of the sea.

It is strange to think that the town of Morecambe, a name that is now so familiar, was only adopted in 1889. Up till this time the resort was made up of three separate villages: Bare, Torrisholme and Poulton-le-Sands. These had for centuries been just a handful of white-washed cottages in which lived fishermen and their families. They took shrimps, cockles and mussels from the bay, grew potatoes in small fields and lived a simple life. However, this was all destined to change, for towards the end of the 18th century sea-bathing had become a fashion. At first steamers from Liverpool and stage coaches from Lancaster brought the visitors to Poulton where they found rough accommodation in local inns. But its popularity as a watering place quickly grew, new houses known as marine villas, began to spring up and the locals became more affluent as the visitors spent their money. Then came the railways, thousands of people from both Lancashire and Yorkshire now had easy access. All manner of new development took place merging the coastal villages into a single town which took the name of the bay which it overlooked.

As well as the locals, known as Sand Grown 'Uns, and the massive influx of visitors, there were those who came to retire in Morecambe. So many came from Yorkshire that it became nicknamed Bradford-by-the-Sea and it boasted a Yorkshire Street. It was granted a Borough Charter in 1901 which led to a colourful celebration the following year at which an ox was roasted and rockets were fired across the bay. The Mayor and his wife presented the town with a chain-of-office and two halberds, and a gift of £400 given by Councillor Birkett was used to erect the famous Clock Tower.

New and grand hotels were built, the promenade was extended and even a tower, intended to compete with that at Blackpool, was erected. However, though this embraced the novelty of a unique design involving an ascent by an electric tramway, it never proved to be a success and was demolished during the First World War.

A feature of Morecambe during the beginning of this century was Ward's Shipbreakers, who had taken over the site of the town's redundant harbour when Heysham Docks were built in 1904. On the face of it the noise and dirt from this site would appear to be out of place in a holiday resort, yet thousands of visitors flocked in to see this graveyard of the sea. About 44 vessels were disposed of over a period of thirty years. These ranged from Victorian sailing ships to German battleships and U-boats taken during the First World War and even a small aircraft-carrier.

Another event which shattered the silence of the resort in 1917 was the sensational explosion at a munitions factory at nearby White Lund. The disaster was played down by the press for it would have provided propaganda for the enemy. It is thought around ten workers were killed and many injured, the locals talked of sabotage but this was never proved.

Morecambe both charmed and attracted the British holiday-maker for over a century. With the crowds came the entertainers, such legends as Vesta Tilly, Florrie Forde, and Dame Nellie Melba were followed by Frank Randle, George Formby and Norman Evans. The resort has also produced a number of home-grown super stars which include the late comedian Eric Morecambe, who adopted the name of the town, and that marvellous actress, Thora Hird. Eric Bartholomew, who was the son of a council workman, was born in 1926 in Buxton Street. His mother, who worked both as a waitress in a cafe on the prom and as an usherette on Morecambe pier, had a show business career mapped out for him from his early childhood. She paid for him to take dancing lessons, then put him in for local talent contests, which he frequently won. In 1939 he was auditioned by the show-business impresario, Jack Hylton, in Manchester where his natural ability became immediately apparent. Another youngster named Ernie Wise, who was already established as a child-star, happened to be watching the audition. Both were booked by Jack Hylton as separate acts, then two years later after becoming friends, they teamed up to form the legendary Morecambe and Wise comedy team. Eric, who in the years just before his tragic death became a keen bird watcher, is remembered at Leighton Moss Nature Reserve where a pool has been named in his honour.

Thora Hird was born in Morecambe in 1911 with show business blood in her veins for both her parents had trod the boards. Her mother, Mary Jane, came from an old Poulton family and her father, who was the director and stage manager of the local Royalty Theatre, had originated from Todmorden. Few can claim to have started a stage career earlier, for as a baby of eight months she took part in one of the plays! She was educated at a small local school then worked in a number of shops, her acting being confined to mainly amateur dramatics. But after her marriage to musician, Jimmy Scott, and the birth of her daughter Janette in 1938, her career really took off. George Formby, who was at the height of his fame, recognised her talent which led to her being introduced to an agent from Ealing Film Studios. A string of film and stage successes quickly followed, and of course still continue half a century later with such TV favourites as *Last of the Summer Wine* and *Praise Be*. Her daughter, Janette, found even earlier fame when at the age of ten she starred in the film *No Place for Jennifer*. She went on to receive international acclaim as a film actress in both Britain and America.

*Thora Hird*

Continuing my stroll around the town I found it to be a fascinating place to explore, its streets echo with memories of departed grandeur. Behind the cheap stalls which sell a dozen varieties of fudge or watches for 50p or where Gipsy Sarah will read your palm for a fiver, hides a marvellous kaleidoscope of the town's past. Neat streets of cottages where fishermen once lived survive hand-in-hand with once smart villas in which Yorkshiremen with a bit 'o brass spoke of wool or steel. A faded plaque tells how George Cartenseu founded the Tivoli Bar in 1843, while the sad face of the Alhambra looks on, mesmerized by the town's decline that has been even more spectacular than its rise. When foreign holidays became available to so many it was inevitable that resorts like Morecambe would suffer. Only now is the town coming to terms with this enforced change, it is in a state of transition, busily transforming the neglect of past decades. Its future role may be that of a residential town more than a holiday resort, for its unrivalled location overlooking England's loveliest bay makes it a splendid place in which to live.

*Morecambe: the town's famous clock tower looks out over the sea towards the lakeland mountains. The resort was so popular with Yorkshire folk, it became known as Bradford-by-the-Sea.*

# 8

I stood on the cliff edge at Heysham looking across lovely Half Moon Bay watching the evening sunlight reflect on the choppy waves. A man was walking his black labrador over a headland path, the animal weighted down by a huge stick which it insisted carrying in its mouth. Two young lovers were sat in a grassy hollow, half hidden by faded gorse bushes. They gently kissed then, starry-eyed, looked out across the water to the spot where some people say St Patrick was shipwrecked. On my right the brown sands of Heysham led my eyes towards the rooftops of Morecambe then across the bay to where the blue Lakeland hills rose up into the September sky. Turning to my left I could see the outline of Heysham Harbour, where people would be leaving for Dublin or Douglas, waiting in the shadow of Lancashire's Nuclear Power Station which stands nearby.

The romantic ruins of St Patrick's Chapel stand on the very edge of a rocky cliff. Only the East Gable and part of the South Wall remain of what experts tell us is a building of Celtic or Saxon origin dating from as early as the 8th century. It was very small, measuring only about 24 feet by 8 feet with walls 30 inches thick, and owes its survival on such an exposed hilltop, to the unique strength of the mortar which binds the stones together.

Close by, I found one of the great curiosities of Heysham; six empty graves. Carved out of the solid rock and partly filled with rainwater, these graves are unique in Britain. They are of different sizes but each is shaped into the form of the human body. Grooves around the tombs indicate where stone covers once fitted and a square hole at the head was perhaps made to hold a cross. Both these graves and the chapel are associated with the tale of St Patrick and many place-names still exist in the north-west which help to substantiate parts of the legend.

Little is known for certain about the early life of the saint before he rose to become the great apostle of Ireland, however tradition does help us to speculate as to how he spent his formative years. It is known that he was born about AD 385 of noble stock at a place called Banavem Tabernise, which was close to the sea. Some experts believe that it was near the Severn estuary close to modern Bristol, while other say it was a Roman fortress on the Clyde near Dunbarton. But the villagers of Bewcastle near Carlisle refute both these suggestions to claim he was born in their village and his mother was a local girl.

It is said that the first sixteen years of his life were spent at home, then following a raid by pirates, he was taken prisoner to Ireland. After six years he managed to escape by ship, but this was hit by a storm which ended with him being shipwrecked. Some historians say that he scrambled ashore in Gaul, but others say that it was here at Heysham that the event occurred, quoting a host of historical evidence to prove their claim. It is his route back to Scotland that provides some clues, for his name is still remembered in many villages. At Hest Bank, just five miles north of Heysham there is St Patrick's Well. Near the small town of Milnthorpe lies Preston Patrick and Lakeland's famous Patterdale was once St Patrick's Dale, where the local church is still dedicated to the saint. Nearby Glenridding has another St Patrick's Well, which is also the name of the village pub at Bampton near Haweswater. Here the local Anglican church which is over 800 years old, is one of only ten in all of England dedicated to him. Finally, to the north of Maryport is Aspatria which is said to mark another place he stopped at on his journey home.

The chapel at Heysham is reputed to have been established by a band of monks who came here from Ireland to revere the saint's memory at the spot where he was shipwrecked. The graves became their final resting place, but may well have been later vandalised by the Vikings who settled in the area. St Patrick's Day was once observed in Heysham, which is borne out by an ancient document preserved in London. It states that in 1272 Adam de Hessayre paid Thomas de Travers an annual tribute of an arrow on St Patrick's Day, which at that time was probably the dedication festival for the village church.

I think the vicar of St Peter's church at Heysham must have a difficult time keeping the attention of his congregation for the church windows look out over one of Lancashire's most inviting views. If the sermon gets just the slightest bit boring then eyes will no doubt wander to admire a passing gull, or to see if the tide has really come in or to listen to the little train trundling its way across the sands from Morecambe. Before leaving the ancient building I ran my hand over a marvellously carved hog-backed stone. It was cut over a thousand years ago by Viking settlers who were changing from paganism to Christianity.

The village street, which tumbles down to the sea like those in Cornwall, was almost deserted. The shops which sell nettle-beer, the man who weighs holiday makers as they sit on a swinging seat and even the souvenir shops had closed. In the half light of dusk the atmosphere of the 17th century seemed to have returned. Were those voices coming from the bar of the Royal really talking about cricket or was it smuggling and wrecking that was on their minds . . .

## CHAPTER FOUR

# *HEYSHAM TO LYTHAM ST ANNE'S*

I explore a village beyond the sea, see Lancashire's oldest church then end up in a dungeon. I attend a Book Fair, drive through Windmill Land to visit Fleetwood and Blackpool, and continue to Lytham St. Anne's where I hear about England's worst lifeboat disaster.

### 1

To reach Sunderland Point involves one of the most exciting journeys in Lancashire, for like Lindisfarne, this isolated village lies across a tidal road. After passing the Ship Inn at Overton, which I am told houses a fine collection of bird's eggs, I read with trepidation a red warning notice: *Do Not Proceed When Posts Are In Water.* I stopped my car, then after convincing myself that the posts were definitely not in the water, I continued along the single track road. Passing gulleys of glistening mud and yachts marooned on sandbanks I cautiously proceeded at a snails pace till at last I reached the shoreline of this unique village. The spot where I parked my car was not exactly designed to give a stranger confidence for a line on the wall above my car roof read: High Water Level. As if to prove this was no joke as I stepped out of the car door I almost stood on a jelly-fish which was very much alive!

Sunderland Point is really a narrow tapering peninsula which has the sea on the western side and the estuary of the River Lune to the east. Dotted along the shoreline is a unique row of houses which have remained largely unchanged since they were first built in the early 18th century. The great charm of this curious village is the way in which the sea and the countryside are brought together, completely unspoilt by any modern development. I got the feeling that if Robert Lawson, who was the father of Sunderland Point, was to return today he would still feel at home.

In one of the cottage windows, which enjoy breathtaking views over the river towards the distant hills, I read a notice which said a book entitled *The Story of Sunderland Point*, was for sale. Here I bought a copy and had a chat with its author, Hugh Cunliffe. He told me how he was first brought here as a child in the thirties for marvellous family holidays, he immediately fell in love with its splendid isolation and now he lives here permanently. His book charts the colourful history of the little port, combining research from local archives with personal memories of both himself and other residents.

*Sunderland Point: a visitor admires the famous Cotton Tree which stands at the centre of this unique 18th century village.*

Up till the 17th century there were only a handful of fisherman's cottage sited on this green peninsula, but then came the Golden Age for Lancaster when the lucrative sea-trade with the West Indies got underway. Robert Lawson, an enterprising Quaker merchant, saw the advantages of creating a landing place to unload his ships on this river estuary. Virtually all the new buildings along the quayside were constructed by him between 1715 and 1720. Here too he brought his family to live at lovely Sunderland Hall which had been built in the West Indian colonial style.

*The Lune Estuary, where the river pours into the Irish Sea; fishing boats lie marooned on the shingle, awaiting the tide.*

Walking in the September sunlight I stopped to look at the village's famous Cotton Tree which is now part of local folklore. It is said to have grown from a seed which was dropped by chance from a cargo landed on the riverside. In summertime, so I'm told, it sprouts fluffy cotton-like seeds, but there have been many arguments about what type of tree it really is. For many years experts said it was a Kapok Tree, but others now say it is a European Black Poplar. There is also a tale that the first bale of cotton ever to reach Lancashire was landed at Sunderland Point. It is said that it remained in one of the warehouses for many years because nobody could find a use for it. Experts sceptically dismiss this splendid story, saying that cotton was well known in Lancashire before this date.

*Sambo's grave. Flowers are still placed on the grave by local children.*

I joined a small group of visitors, who like myself, wanted to see that other attraction on Sunderland Point – Sambo's Grave. We walked along a footpath lined with harebells, nettles, and gorse which is called simply The Lane. On reaching the pebbly shoreline of the west coast we turned left then in the corner of a green meadow we discovered the little white cross on which is written: Sambo R.I.P. A small bunch of flowers, now faded, had been placed nearby and a brass plate on the flat gravestone tells his tale in verse:

*Full sixty years the angry winter's wave,*
*Has thundering dashed this bleak and barren shore,*
*Since Sambo's head laid in this lonely grave,*
*Lies still and ne'er will hear their turmoil more.*
*Full many a sandbird chirps upon the sod,*
*And many a moonlight elfin round him trips,*
*Full many a summer's sunbeam warms the clod,*
*And many a teeming cloud upon him drips.*
*But still he sleeps – till the awakening sounds,*
*Of the Archangel's trump new life impart,*
*Then the Great Judge his approbation founds,*
*Not on man's colour but his worth of heart.*

This poem was written in 1736 by the Rev. James Watson who was the headmaster of Lancaster Grammar School. It relates to a young black cabin boy who was brought over to Lancashire by the captain of one of the sailing ships. He sadly died while in the port, traditionally due to a broken heart because he feared wrongly, that he had been left by his white master. His death is reputed to have taken place in Upsteps Cottage in The Lane, and then he was buried in a field because being a non-Christian, he was not allowed a burial in consecrated ground. His appearance in Sunderland Point highlights Lancashire's involvement in the horrific slave trade which was the basis for many a family fortune. The ships sailed to West Africa where they picked up their human cargo of shackled negroes. They then continued to the West Indies where the slaves were unloaded and a new cargo of rum, sugar, spice or mahogany was taken on board for the return trip to England. Occasionally some coloured people, as in the case of Sambo, were also brought back, as it became a fashion among the wealthy to boast a black servant.

With one eye on the tide, I decided to purchase some local apples which were advertised outside a house, before making a dash for the safety of mainland Lancashire. I walked up to a large shed that as well as containing home grown fruit and vegetables, was festooned with nets, anchors, oars and all the paraphernalia of the sea. A tall sun-tanned man served me with four delicious looking red Discovery apples. I asked him about his island-like existence.

"Well the tides do not effect us as much as you would think. They generally cover the road around noon and midnight. This means that children who go to school and those adults who commute can leave in the morning and return in the evening without any problems."

*Overton: this magnificent Norman doorway leads into what is probably Lancashire's oldest church.*

He then went on to tell me about the joys of living in this unique community with the sea on their doorstep. They get very little snow, but it can become very windy, however its real attraction is the peaceful 18th century atmosphere that prevails without the noise of traffic.

Returning to Overton I decided to make a quick visit to St Helen's Church which I had been told was rather special. A local man, who spoke with an out-of-place Midlands accent saw me admiring the building, so he offered to show me around.

"Is it true that this is the oldest church in Lancashire?" I asked.

He grinned then told me of the friendly rivalry which exists between this church and its neighbour at Heysham, who both claim the title. Pointing to the West Wall he said it was oldest part of the building which dated from Saxon times and was an incredible four feet thick. We then wandered around the church, with an intimate knowledge he pointed out the many interesting features.

"But you must come outside to look at the doorway," he insisted.

In the soft hazy sunshine we both stood silently looking at the marvellous chevron design that Norman hands had carved when the Conquerer was still alive. He then told me how he had exchanged the smog of Staffordshire in the fifties for the fresh air of this corner of Lancashire. He had found a job in Heysham and after forty years he now regarded himself as a northerner, but his accent still labelled him as a newcomer.

I thanked him for the tour, then as he walked away down the lane a curious event took place. As if from nowhere a sparrow hawk took a starling from the air, then fell with outstretched wings just a yard from where he walked. A bloodthirsty struggle took place before our eyes, then the cruel victor zoomed into a nearby tree, the limp body of its prey hanging pathetically from its talons.

## 2

I stood on the balcony of the Ashton Memorial, gazing out over the rooftops of Lancaster and thinking of the wealth which had built such an amazing structure. This marvellous Baroque folly, with its white facade and green dome which dominates the skyline of the city, owes its existence to that most mundane of materials – oilcloth! James Williamson had begun making what was known as American Cloth, in Lancaster about 1830. When his son, also named James, took over forty years later it had grown to be a highly lucrative business. He employed over five thousand people in a model factory which exported linoleum to every part of the world. But being the dominating power in Lancaster he ruled his employees with feudal control, opposing trade-union reforms which might dilute his position. He kept wages low, but was charitable with his money on projects which appealed to him.

*Ashton Memorial, dominating the skyline of Lancaster.*

Williamson Park, in which the memorial stands, had been created by the first James Williamson between 1861-65 to provide work for local people. This was the time of the American Civil War which caused hardship in Lancashire by producing a cotton famine. The site of the park was a quarry from which stone had been taken for many of the fine buildings of the city. In was also the hillside on which public executions had taken place prior to 1800, among those who died on this spot were the Pendle Witches and the Catholic martyr, St Edmund Arrowsmith. The memorial was designed by the unfortunately named architect John Belcher and was built in 1907. It was originally conceived as a memorial to Williamson's wife, but as he was eventually married three times it was diplomatically dedicated to his whole family. By this time James Williamson had the title, Lord Ashton, which many people said he had bought. Although he had been a Liberal MP he left the party following a quarrel with Lloyd George who accused him of betraying its aims. He died in 1936 a virtual recluse, leaving a fortune of £9.5 million and, surprisingly, no will.

I found the view from this high-point quite breathtaking, it is a panorama that sweeps across the full Lancashire coastline, then continues over Morecambe Bay to the mountains of Lakeland and the Bowland Hills. The sky was a clear turquoise, the parkland trees were taking on the gold of autumn yet the sunshine had fooled the birds into singing a spring chorus.

Their songs were awakening the tropical birds and butterflies which are housed in an elegant Edwardian Palm House which lies adjacent to the memorial.

I dipped down the steep hillside into the centre of the city, then drove along St George's Quay where the warehouses of two centuries ago stand waiting for cargoes which never arrive. Some have been made into attractive up-market apartments, one houses antiques and another paper products. Alongside the Wagon and Horses pub which is frequented by writers and rivermen, is the Maritime Museum which houses the remnants of the city's Golden Age. Memories of the time when 364 ships came each year to empty their cargos and pay customs duty, and when Lune-built ships where a common sight from the Mediterranean to the Caribbean.

It was here that mahogany from Cuba, Jamaica and Honduras was unloaded to supply Lancaster's renowned furniture business of Gillows. This firm, which had been started by Robert Gillow in 1730, became one of the most famous in England. It served the sophisticated tastes of the wealthy, being appointed cabinet-makers to Queen Victoria in 1853. In 1901 the firm became Waring and Gillow, and went on to fit out the royal yacht belonging to King

Edward VII and the liner Queen Mary, together with a host of other ships and aircraft. Sadly, trade diminished when for safety reasons, wood was banned in aircraft and ships, and the firm no longer manufactures its once superb furniture.

*Lancaster Priory church, alongside the castle. Among its greatest treasures are the ornately carved choir stalls which reputedly came from Cockersands Abbey.*

Perhaps the best thing to happen to Lancaster in recent times has been the creation of the University, for it has brought to the town the vigour and optimism of youth. Young girls with pale skin and long hair sit on benches in Dalton Square and read Keats. They also walk in groups up Market Street carrying bags of books, staring into health-shop windows wondering whether to buy a Vegetable Lasagne or some Beta-Carotene tablets. These friendships, fostered in the Georgian streets of Lancaster, will bring a lifelong link between the city and many corners of the world.

In the warm still air I wandered leisurely through the streets of Lancaster, looking at the mouth watering display of fish in the covered market, admiring the almshouses built by William Penny in 1720 and seeing the Dukes Playhouse where, I believe, Dickens once read out-loud his own works. In the gardens in Dalton Square I found Lancashire's most impressive statue of Queen Victoria, surrounded by the great men of her reign she has one eye on the Town Hall and the other on the former home of a murderer. It is strange, in an age when murder has become sadly commonplace, that the tale of Dr Buck Ruxton is never forgotten. It was here at No 2 Dalton Square in 1936 that this highly successful Parsee Indian doctor killed then cut up his unfaithful wife, Belle, and their maid, Mary. He scattered their remains off Devil's Bridge at Moffat in Scotland and at a number of places along the A701 road. But these were discovered together with a newspaper, a vital clue which led to his arrest, a sensational trial and his death by hanging at Strangeways Jail in Manchester.

I walked past the Judge's Lodging Museum then ascended the steep cobbled street which leads to where Lancaster really began – Castle Hill. It was here that the Roman war-hero, General Julius Agricola, built a fort in 79 AD to dominate an easy crossing place of the Lune. The Norman invaders decided his choice had been correct, for a thousand years later Roger of Poitou built his castle on the same spot.

As I stood waiting for the castle tour to begin I was joined by a middle-aged couple from Newcastle who were laughing heartily.

"What do you think. We have been queuing for half an hour with a crowd at the front of the castle, then when the doors opened we found they were prison visitors. We nearly ended up in the jug!"

A well-spoken young man with a great knowledge of Lancashire's history proved to be an excellent guide for our tour. He told us that the castle, which is owned by the Queen, is not a dead museum but a living building, for parts of it remain a prison and a court. After its founder, Roger de Poitou, forfeited his lands in 1102 for supporting a rebellion against Henry I, it has been closely associated with royalty. The powerful John of Gaunt, who was the son of Edward III, was created Duke of Lancaster, but he visited the castle only twice. However his son Henry IV, who was the first king from the House of Lancaster, drew up a charter which gave the ownership of the vast estates of the Duchy of Lancaster to the reigning monarch.

We began our tour in the semi-circular Shire Hall, which is a court room built in the Gothic Revival style. On its walls are hung a spectacular array of colourful coats-of-arms of Sovereigns, Constables and High Sheriffs of Lancashire. Some of the more recent High Sheriffs, who do not possess an existing family coat-of-arms, have even designed their own. Moving on to the Crown Court we were shown the unique holdfast and branding-iron which was last used in 1811. The iron was made red-hot then brought into the dock where the prisoner was branded on his hand with the letter M so he could be identified as a malefactor.

It is said that more people have been sentenced to death at Lancaster than in any other court in Britain, but many were reprieved. Records are scant from the early years apart from the well known victims, such as the Pendle Witches and the Catholic Martyrs, but it is recorded that between 1816 and 1819 over 240 persons received the death sentence. In a room covered in horrific instruments of torture which were once used at the castle, we were shown a long length of chain on which were attached shackles.

"These were used to hold prisoners who were being sent for transportation to Australia. Six months ago a lady from Melbourne who was on this tour, told me that her great-great grandmother had actually been transported from Lancaster. She had been sentenced after being found guilty of stealing a handkerchief."

In another room were reminders of when public executions at Lancaster drew in the crowds, local children were given a holiday from school to watch the gory events. A rare noose which had been used at a hanging was on display, few have survived because they were cut up and sold as good-luck charms. Nearby was a surprisingly well-written letter sent by Richard Pedder to his wife in 1853, the day before he met his fate.

"Last year an old man came to the castle to tell me that his grand-mother told him she had walked from Preston to Lancaster in 1865 to see the last public execution."

In one of the oldest parts of the building we were shown a row of forbidding dungeons, with huge thick wooden doors and no windows to the outside. The guide asked for volunteers to go inside while he shut the door. A chirpy small Welshman immediately volunteered, so I somewhat reluctantly followed his example and we were joined by two others. Stepping inside the dank cell the ancient door was slammed heavily behind us followed by the forbidding sound of bolts being made fast. We were encouraged at first by a small amount of light which was filtering through a very small window above the door. But, I suspect, to the silent horror of each of us, we heard a shutter being drawn over this window, leaving us in an inky darkness. Nobody uttered a sound and the darkness was so complete that not even the faintest outline could be seen. We remained there for perhaps only two minutes before the welcomed sound of the door opening met our ears. Yet in dramatic fashion this poignant episode had uniquely illustrated to us the feeling of desolate horror that had once been the fate of many.

Before departing from Lancaster I looked upon the many treasures of the Priory Church which lies adjacent to the castle. These range from the magnificently carved choir stalls which probably came from Cockersands Abbey, to a memorial marking the release of hostage Terry Waite in November 1991. I also discovered with enthusiasm that there is a Priory tea-shop which has saved the life of many an exhausted tourist.

Leaving the city centre behind I drove south, passing the sturdy stone houses of the suburbs along the A6 road. Bright yellow notices attached to the lamp posts were directing me to the university which was the venue for a book fair. A sweeping driveway fringed with neatly trimmed lawns led me past an ornate duck pond to the tranquillity of this success story from the sixties.

The galleried hall was packed with over fifty stalls containing 30,000 second hand books, the once cherished possessions of past owners. Some were neatly stacked in shelves and meticulously labelled, others were thrown into boxes on the floor which had 'Bananas from the Windward Isles' printed on the side. Jeffrey Archer, Danielle Steel and Jackie Collins shamelessly rubbed shoulders with Tibetan philosophy, the poems of Byron and a first edition of Dickens. Auctions, house clearances, church bazaars and car-boot sales had brought together an amazing assortment of volumes. To this treasure house of literature had been drawn, in frenzied anticipation, the bookworms of the north. Making a dawn departure from Kendal, Preston, Blackpool and a score of other towns they had been lured by the hope that all collectors thrive upon. Today's search might at last reveal that long sought after volume that had so far proved elusive.

"Have you anything on watches or musical boxes?" asked a tall, distinguished looking man with greying hair, to one of the stall holders.

"Sorry, nothing at all this week".

Smiling, but failing to hide his feeling of disappointment, he walked away to try his luck at the next stall.

I watched a young girl of about eighteen, wearing blue jeans and a red sweater, scan intently a shelf labelled Classics. Like a kestrel striking a mouse her hand dashed forward and she retrieved a thin blue volume. Her eyes glistened with joy, she opened the book and began to read the title, her mouth slightly apart. She closed the book, for a second she held it close to her bosom, then she paid the stall holder two pounds from her leather purse. As she walked away her face reflected a sense of contentment that only those who love books would understand.

As I wandered around the hall it became apparent that book fairs, unlike perhaps sporting events, attract a wide cross section of humanity with many surprises. Although occasionally I caught a glimpse of everyone's idea of the male academic: middle-aged, bow-tied with glasses and a pipe, most were not so readily identified. An old lady, who I would have expected to read Barbara Cartland romances, was engrossed in a heavy volume concerning American history, while nearby a young man, who looked as if he had several A-levels, was buying a light novel which is known charitably, as holiday reading.

These Lancashire Book Fairs, which have become such a feature of the county, are the brain child of a retired Accrington policeman named Bob Dobson. Driven by a burning desire to record the fast-disappearing traditions of Lancashire he has also written and published several books. These include an authoritative history of Clogs, volumes of dialect verse and books about Blackburn and Accrington.

I found this well-known figure at his stall near the Hall entrance. Tall, balding, with a small moustache he was deeply engrossed in conversation with a smartly dressed man of about thirty.

"You see Bob, my father owned a small shuttle factory at Whitworth but it's closed down now".

They then went on at great lengths to discuss the finer points of shuttle production and their sadness at the demise of the craft. They talked about how, not only each shuttle manufacturer, but each craftsman, had their mark on their own shuttles. Bob then told how he recently met an American tourist who had gladly paid seventy pounds for a particularly rare shuttle.

I walked from the hall, following the contentedly chatting bookworms who had their latest finds wrapped in brown paper bags under their arms. Together with those who, appearing a little morose, had failed to find Lamb's

*Essays of Elia* or that rare Kipling which they so desperately needed to complete their collection.

## 3

I sat in a cafe at Glasson Dock looking across the bow of a moored schooner to where a lorry from Holland was loading a container. Here, where the canal meets the river and the river meets the sea I detected an atmosphere of unfulfilled ambition. For this little port which lies on a corner of the Lune estuary named Fishnet Point, once dreamed of growing to the size of Liverpool.

Building on the decline of Sunderland Point in the mid-eighteenth century its future seemed full of promise. The dock itself was opened in 1788, but the restrictions brought about by the Napoleonic War immediately brought a decrease in trade. Merchant ships were forced by law to travel in convoys for protection, which resulted in a huge amount of cargo arriving in port at the same time leading to low returns. However, when a spur from John Rennie's Lancaster Canal was built in 1836 Glasson's future seemed brighter, for it now had a link with many inland towns. Trade continued to expand up till 1840, and its survival was assured when the railway arrived in 1883. But greater things were never destined to materialise, although still remaining a small commercial port it is now more a rendezvous for weekend sailors or those visitors, like myself, who relish wide skies and salt air.

There is a unique feeling about the Fylde that I began to detect as I took the marsh road beyond Cockerham. It has an atmosphere of fertile remoteness, a place where flat green fields surrounded by trim hedgerows reach down to the sea. Cows and sheep seem to be grazing peacefully, herons and rooks forage undisturbed, yet beneath this tranquillity there is unconfirmed doubt. Is that distant dark shadow really a reed-bed or is it a Viking longboat hidden in the creek? Does that line of grey smoke rising into the clear October sky come from a cottage chimney or from a camp fire? In this secluded landscape once known as Amounderness, where the centuries tumble away, almost anything seems possible.

To my left, hidden among a score of lanes which end at remote white-washed farmhouses, lay Pilling Moss. Here across this swampy land once ran a unique road made of timber which had been constructed by Bronze Age Man; the locals called it Kate's Pad. It was to this rural parish in 1758 that a young curate named George Holden came to preach to its scattered community. Fired also with the 18th century passion for science he began to observe the ebb and flow of the tides. His meticulous records resulted in Holden's Tide Tables which remain an essential guide to all who take to the sea.

I stopped my car on the little bridge that spans Pilling Water to look at the first of many windmills which I was to meet on the Fylde. Only the tower now remains, for like half a dozen others, it owes its survival to being made into a house. Its presence reminded me of the wanderings of prolific writer, Charles Allen Clarke, a Boltonian who settled in Blackpool then grew to love this area so much that he created his own magical name for it, Windmill Land. For this alone he deserves to be remembered.

He was born in what he later termed Steam Engine Land, in 1863, which was the period of the Cotton Famine. Being one of a family of nine children his childhood was very tough, but he was highly talented and was able to escape the monotony of the factory. He worked at first as a reporter on the Bolton Evening News, then later he turned to free-lance writing and publishing. Through his love of the northern countryside, which he explored on his bicycle, he soon became recognised as an authority on all aspects of Lancashire. In 1906 he left Bolton to come and live in Blackpool, where he lived till his death in 1935. He was a prolific writer, using a variety of pen-names for his popular annuals and magazines, Teddy Ashton being the most well known. But he is remembered mainly for his two volumes, *Windmill Land* (1916) and *More Windmill Land* (1917) which capture so completely the spirit of the Fylde in the early years of this century. After his death he was given the most appropriate and unusual memorial of any writer: Marton Windmill, which lies on the approach to Blackpool, was dedicated to his memory.

Windmills, unlike most workshops or factories – for this is what they really are, tend to be looked on with nostalgia. They successfully harmonise with our countryside, a feature which has long been recognised by artists, for many canvases and pieces of porcelain have windmills as their subjects. Two centuries ago the Lancashire coastline from the Mersey to the Lune was a land of whirling windmills. On every convenient hilltop stood a mill ready to grind the corn for the ever increasing population. If Don Quixote had arrived in Liverpool he would have found eight worthy adversaries in the city alone. Manchester had one which is remembered to this day by Windmill Street, while Rochdale, Wigan and Preston boasted several more. But it was the Fylde, as Allen Clarke recognised, that was the centre for windmill power. Here up to a hundred of the friendly giants harvested the fast moving air that blew almost continually from the sea across the flat marshy land. It must have been a wonderful spectacle to look down from the Bowland Fells on to a forest of revolving sails.

The millers, who often both lived and worked in their windmills, were regarded with suspicion by the local farmers for they had a widespread reputation for being wily characters. For the corn they ground they were paid, not in cash, but by taking a percentage of the grain. The farmers often argued that the millers had taken too much and disputes were common. Even Chaucer, so long ago, mistrusted the miller who he said 'was a master hand at stealing the grain.'

However, the millers themselves often suffered at the whims of the local gentry who were the owners of the windmills. At Little Eccleston in the Fylde, an incident happened in 1874 that is still remembered to this day. The local squire at this time was a young man who had gained a reputation for being a prankster and because of his many outrageous escapades he became known as Mad Jack.

It was approaching Guy Fawke's Day when Mad Jack boasted to his many rich friends that he would make the most extraordinary bon-fire ever seen. He sent for a barrel of paraffin to the local store, which he then began to pour on to a pile of wood and straw which he had carefully laid inside Little Eccleston Windmill. The miller, named perhaps appropriately Mr Crook, protested loudly that he had recently fitted new machinery into the mill and that it also contained many sacks of corn. But these protests went unheeded, Mad Jack seized a lighted torch and spurred on by the cheers of his friends, tossed it into the mill. In minutes the ancient structure was ablaze and the revellers began a lively dance around it, shouting and singing. The flames quickly lit up the night sky, being visible at Blackpool, Fleetwood and Preston, as the mill burned for three full days. The incident was later hushed up after the miller was given compensation, but the old windmill was gone forever.

Rather less spectacularly it was steam power which dealt the death blow to windmills, accelerated by the use of steel roller mills. In 1837 there were about twenty working windmills in the Fylde, but by the time of the First World War this was reduced to ten. Today there are around nine remnants of this by-gone age, several have been converted into houses while others, such as Lytham, Marton and Marsh Mill at Thornton, have been carefully restored. Sadly, all of Lancashire's most ancient type of windmill, the post-mill, have disappeared.

The post-mills, or peg-mills, were wooden framed structures which were supported by a single vertical post, around which the whole body of the mill revolved. One of the last example of this type to exist in Lancashire was situated on the banks of the Ribble at Warton in the early years of this century. It was a portable mill which had originated in East Anglia, then was transported to Rufford where it worked for many years before ending its days at Warton. The Fylde windmills which remain today are known as tower mills, being circular in form and built of brick. the sails are attached to a revolving cap which is turned automatically into the wind by means of a fan-tail.

Lytham's famous windmill, which has become the town's trademark, was once lapped by the sea at high tide before the embankment was built. A mill has existed at Lytham for around 800 years, making it the oldest site in Lancashire. The present structure, which was used to produce flour and oatmeal, was built in 1805. It was partially destroyed by fire in 1919, then rebuilt in 1921, and in recent years it has been completely restored. A sad incident occurred at the mill in 1909 when a young boy from Manchester grabbed hold of one of the turning sails. He was carried up to the highest point when he lost his grip and fell to his death.

Marsh Mill at Thornton, is one of Europe's largest windmills, standing 70 feet above the ground. It was built in 1794 and continued working until 1922. During the past few years its machinery has been restored and new sails have been fitted, to preserve it as the centre-piece of a tourist complex.

## 4

Knott End was bathed in bright sunshine but a chill wind which had come from the sea had kept the locals at home. Just one man pulling a reluctant Yorkshire Terrier behind him, was to be seen on the Esplanade. I walked from my car to the low wall which borders the river estuary, scattering a score of snow-white gulls who were spaced symmetrically in a long line. This is where the Wyre, which I had seen as a trickle above Abbeystead, finally empties its clear waters into the sea.

I strolled along a pathway to just beyond the coastguard station where I stopped to shelter from the wind. From near this point a small ferry takes passengers across the river to Fleetwood which lies on the opposite bank, but today there was no business. Up river I could see the docks from which the Douglas boat sails in the summer months, then to the right, the dark sentinel of the lighthouse and the rooftops of the town. Looking seaward a bank of brown sand had penetrated the low water creating a temporary island for a large flock of Oyster-catchers. Some people say this is the remains of Portus Setantiorum, a Roman port of the second century which appears on a map produced by Ptolemy. Evidence of its exact location has yet to be revealed.

The view across the bay is similar to that from Morecambe, for the peaks of Lakeland fill the distant horizon. The cold air was crystal clear, I could see the sun glinting on the buildings of Vickers Shipbuilders at Barrow which house half-built submarines. Beyond towered Black Coombe Hill, contradicting its name it appeared like a pale blue whale almost merging with the sky. There was a time when great things were promised for Knott End, in 1893 it was decided to rename it St. Bernard's-on-Sea, listing this fine view, the sandy beach and unspoilt countryside as some of its many attractions. But the locals were quite happy with its existing name so the attempt to change its image was short lived and it remains Knott End.

I drove south through Preesall, then into the rural villages of Stalmine and Hambleton which border on the salt marshes of the river. Shard Toll Bridge, which since 1864 has provided the first crossing of the Wyre from the coast, has I discovered, now disappeared. It has been replaced by a splendid new road bridge which has been built by Lancashire County Council at a cost of £3 million. Some, I suspect, will mourn the passing away of a picturesque feature of this part of the river. In a similar way, their ancestors probably were dismayed when the man who rowed people across the Wyre in a small boat was once replaced by the Toll Bridge – this is progress so we are told! A ford was in existence at this spot as early as 1330 AD and a Roman ford is reputed to have existed down river near Preesall.

Turning to the west once more, I now followed the bank of the river through Thornton to reach Fleetwood, which a sign told me is twinned with Fleetwood, Pennsylvania. After a journey of around twelve miles by road I was now just half a mile from Knott End, but on the other side of the river. Fleetwood was overflowing with visitors, hardly a parking place was to be found on the promenade. People were flocking into the RNLI car-boot sale at Gullivers Pub, self consciously eating fish and chips near the lighthouse or wondering pensively whether to purchase one or two pairs of kippers. I joined the crowd on a saunter along the 'front', watching the colourful Irish boat from Heysham churn up a white wash as it turned into deep water, while closer in shore, pupils from a local nautical campus took nervously to the waves. I stopped at the impressive memorial to the past fishermen of the town whose descendants continue to face daily hazards in the icy Atlantic waters. It was to help alleviate some of their bronchial discomforts that a local chemist, James Lofthouse, began to experiment with different portions last century. In 1865 he was successful in producing a mixture of liquorice, menthol, capsicum and eucalyptus in a lozenge called Fisherman's Friend which the trawlermen found unbeatable. His descendants now manufacture a range of the famous lozenges in a modern factory using the same formula, and these are exported throughout the world.

*Fleetwood. This memorial to the generations of local fishermen who have faced daily hazards in stormy seas, looks out across the Wyre estuary.*

Looking upon the curving profile of the town's impressive North Euston Hotel is a reminder that much of Fleetwood has not merely evolved, but was carefully planned. The Fleetwood family had lived for generations at local Rossall Hall, but it was one of their daughters who consolidated their dominant position when she married into the powerful Hesketh family of Rufford. A descendant, Peter Hesketh, adopted the names of both families and received a Baronetcy in 1838, becoming Sir Peter Hesketh-Fleetwood.

Inspired by the fervour that possessed many early Victorians he decided that what was his sandy wasteland would make an excellent port and watering place. He employed the designer of London's Regent Street, architect Decimus Burton, to plan the new town and it rapidly took shape. It is said he marked out the lines of streets using a plough. The idea was that the railway would bring passengers to the town, they would stay at the splendid new hotel, then continue on their journey by boat to the Isle of Man and Scotland. Queen Victoria gave a prestigious lead to the project when she came this way on her journey to Balmoral, but then came disaster. In 1847 engineers were successful in pushing a railway line north over notorious Shap Fell, giving direct access to Scotland. This took away much of Fleetwood's potential revenue, putting Sir Peter Hesketh-Fleetwood in such a poor financial state that he was forced to sell his ancestral home. However, his memory lives on in the little town which bears his name which has developed into both a successful fishing port and a popular resort.

I followed the pleasant flat coastal road south, passing rows of smart red-bricked houses which have unrivalled views over the sea. This stretch of coastline between Fleetwood and Blackpool only became developed after 1896 when the tramroad was built. Sir Peter Hesketh-Fleetwood's old home is now famous Rossall School, but little of the original building survives. It numbers among its famous old-boys, the musician Sir Thomas Beecham, whose grandfather invented Beecham's Pills and the author Leslie Charteris who gave us the popular Saint detective novels. Prior to the First World War S.P.B. Mais became a master at the school, he then moved on to Fleet Street where he worked with fellow writer H.V. Morton, before making his reputation as an author of travel books.

## 5

I stood on the sands at Blackpool stroking the head of a donkey named Rosie and thinking that this is surely England's most magical town. Visitors go to Tintagel and to Glastonbury seeking out the romance of the past, but they come to Blackpool to discover present-day magic. For no other town has created such a colourful and bewildering atmosphere, it is a place of enchantment. One glance at the Tower and you are under its spell, scepticism disappears, smiles replace frowns and the laughter of childhood comes flowing back.

It is hard to believe that two centuries ago this astonishing resort was an isolated swampy wilderness. Here a handful of fishermen lived with their families along the green cliffs in the parish of Bispham near the Blacke Poole, an outlet from the marshy Marton Mere.

The mid-18th century saw the first visitors arrive to sample the new fashion of taking the waters, a craze that was to be the mak-

*Blackpool: Europe's most popular holiday town.*

ing of the town. By 1837 its popularity had grown enough for the Rev. William Thornber to write the town's first history, yet he could never have guessed at what lay ahead. The coming of the railway in 1846 was the turning point, for now thousands of people from the highly populated towns of the north had cheap transport to the sea.

Blackpool's expansion was rapid, the sea-front began to take on a new look. Sturdy terraces, three storeys high, were built to accommodate visitors and in 1862, when the construction of the North Pier began, the chairman of the company made a remarkable prophesy. He said that Blackpool would become 'one of the most amazing aggregations of public amusement in the world', and he was right. The pier proved to be so successful that a second one was built in 1867, it was known as the South Pier but later re-named the Central Pier. A third, the present South Pier, which was originally named the Victoria Pier, followed in 1893.

I found it fascinating to wander along the promenade, for beneath the facade of the present, still lurks reminders of Blackpool's Victorian past. The bottom storey of the sea-front hotels are now largely glass conservatories with attractive bars and dining rooms. But above they remain the same stone fronts that visitors of the last century would recognise. I noticed that above one, the Sea Bank Hotel, there remains a stone plaque inscribed 'Tyldesleys Terrace 1880'.

The Winter Gardens, I discovered, perhaps more than any other building displays the splendour of this era. Its ornate tiled entrance, together with the impressive interior is a striking reminder of the optimism of the town. In 1989 Lord Delfont came here to unveil a plaque which commemorates the centenary of the Opera House, a theatre which is part of this complex. For each year since its construction the name of an artist who appeared on its famous stage is listed, remembering some of the world's greatest show-business talent. These begin with Wilson Barrett in 1889, then continue with such great names as, Lily Langtry, Anna Pavlova, Gracie Fields, Stanley Holloway, George Formby, Arthur Askey, Shirley Bassey and ending in 1992 with Paul Nicholas. Surprisingly, in this same building, the destiny of the nation is planned, for here the major political parties hold their annual conferences.

But, of course, it is the Tower which remains the symbol of Blackpool, a unique landmark which lies at the very centre of this special Lancashire Fairyland. I wonder if children still shout with joy, as I did in the forties, when the first distant view of it appeared through the charabanc window? For it signalled our approach to this wonderland of sand castles, donkeys, Punch and Judy, toffee apples, candy floss, dodgem-cars and the laughing-man at the pleasure beach.

In 1891 Blackpool decided to follow the lead given by the Paris Exhibition of 1889 when the Eiffel Tower was built. A company was formed to construct the town's own version of the structure, but at first this met little enthusiasm. However the foresight of the mayor, John Bickerstaffe, won through and the deep pit which was to hold the foundations began to be dug out. The architects for this mammoth project were Maxwell and Tuke, and the engineer was R.J.G. Read. Huge blocks of reinforced concrete, buried in the pit, form the resting place for the four legs of the Tower. Constructed from 2,493 tons of steel and 93 tons of cast iron it rises to a height of 518 feet and eight inches to the top of the flagstaff. After only three years the town's dream was realised when a cheering crowd greeted its official opening on Whit Monday in 1894. Today it forms part of a huge entertainment complex which is called Tower World, which includes the world-famous Tower Ballroom. Here the Mighty Wurlitzer Organ, which is affectionately remembered by generations who have danced the night away, will be forever associated with Reginald Dixon. He came from Sheffield in 1930 to take up the position of organist, then went on to be known as Mr Blackpool, his signature tune *I Do Like to be Beside the Seaside* epitomises the era.

I strolled from Yates Wine Lodge on Talbot Square, where champagne can be bought on draught, to the place where Gipsies once pitched their camp which is now the Pleasure Beach. I watched the green tramcars going to Uncle Tom's Cabin, then saw a laughing young couple self-consciously hire a landau to transport them back to their hotel. Yet in the midst of this colourful funland I spoke to a burly fisherman who told me he was going shrimping as his ancestors had done when this was a sandy wasteland. Yes, Blackpool is still full of surprises.

## 6

I am writing these notes on the sea-front at St Anne's on one of those rare October days which has been stolen from June. The air is still and warm, the sky a hazy blue with a light mist over the sea which has made the horizon an indistinct line of silver-grey. The people of Bolton, Clitheroe, Lancaster and a score of more towns have hurriedly packed up their folding chairs and ice boxes into the boot of their cars and headed here to the coast. But the town does not appear in any way overcrowded, just pleasantly alive with the type of orderly holiday-maker that St Anne's founder, Elijah Hargreaves, would be well pleased. Young couples with children, elderly ladies eating ice-cream cones, grey haired men enjoying the fruits of retirement are all mingling together. They are lying on towels or sat on deck-chairs on the dry yellow sand, sauntering down to the end of the pier or exploring the promenade gardens. But wherever they are taking their pleasure it is in a quiet English way that say, the Italians, the French and the Spanish would find impossible to understand.

*St Anne's, a select resort where holiday-makers can enjoy the sunshine beside the pier.*

This reassuring quietness of the holiday-makers of St Anne's reminded me of a tale that I heard from a cafe owner in Malta a few years ago. He said that from childhood he remembers a vast British army being camped on the beach near his home, following their success in North Africa. It numbered perhaps fifty thousand men, stretching in a line as far as the eye could see. Then one morning he arose, quite bewildered, to find the beach completely empty. The huge army had overnight begun their invasion of Sicily, but he had not heard a single sound. The men, their equipment, the ships that carried them had disappeared as silently as ghosts: an event of fifty years ago that the cafe owner still spoke of in wonder.

*The poignant memorial of England's worst lifeboat disaster.*

After admiring the fine sculpture of a lifeboat-man, which stands in remembrance of a local crew which perished in 1886 going to the aid of the a German ship named Mexico, I continued with my exploration of the town. Unlike many coastal resorts I found that its spacious streets are free from any commercialism that is remotely tawdry, no cheap souvenirs, kiss-me-quick hats or burger bars in St Anne's. Its shops retain an image of underspoken quality that are a successful continuation of the principles on which the town was founded last century. In Wrigley's Chemist shop window for instance, there was no brash advertising for indigestion or constipation pills as I expected, but instead it was laid out like a display from a museum. Remembering the Battle of Britain it displayed a signed photo of the 'Last of the Few', a RAF uniform from the last war, a poem by a Falklands soldier and a copy of the Daily Mail of May 1945 whose headlines read: 'Hitler Dead – Germans Tell World'. Nearby was a plaque which told how the townspeople of Lytham St Anne's had given a Spitfire.

In 1874 Elijah Hargreaves, a rich business man from Lancashire's Rossendale Valley, came to look at the long stretch of sand dunes that is now St Anne's. The development of Blackpool was at this time underway, while nearby Lytham was little more than a small fishing village. The owner of the land was the Clifton Estate whose agent, Thomas Fair, had already considered plans for the creation of a new town on the site. When Hargreaves contacted him he saw the advantages of the finance that the business man could raise, so together they began to plan the town.

Hargreaves invited a group of his rich friends from around Haslingden to join him to fund the scheme and together they formed the St Anne's-on-Sea Land and Building Company Limited, leasing the land for 1100 years from the Clifton Estate. The architects hired for the project were Maxwell and Tuke of Bury, who following this success went on to design Blackpool Tower.

In 1875 the first stone of the future watering place was laid by John Talbot Clifton and the small railway station of Cross Slack was re-named St Anne's. The work began with typical Victorian vigour, many of the buildings using the attractive stone from the Rossendale quarries of William J. Porritt. He was one of the business men who had a great influence on the design of the houses which were laid out in symmetrical rows.

The middle-class mill-owners, solicitors and retired doctors of inland Lancashire began to take up residence in the fashionable new coastal town, creating a Victorian community of discerning affluence. In 1885 the pier was built, followed later by a pavilion, promenade gardens and large sophisticated hotels. Four golf courses were also constructed, including what is now the famous Royal Lytham and St Anne's. Its development continued through the Edwardian period with unusual foresight and imagination, always retaining an atmosphere of spaciousness and greenery. By 1927 it had crept so far towards neighbouring Lytham that the joining of two became inevitable: the Borough of Lytham St Anne's was created.

I drove slowly along the coastal road, stopping briefly on the causeway which separates the placid waters of Fairhaven Lake from the slowly ebbing sea. Colourful boats were bobbing about, the occupants carefully avoiding the wide-eyed gulls which were scavenging on the water. Beyond, on the misty skyline stood the red-roofed detached houses of the thirties, looking as immaculate as if they had been built yesterday. Much favoured by the show business personalities of the north, here have lived George Formby, Violet Carson, Les Dawson and many more. I could see the tower of the White Church which had witnessed Les's recent funeral, his premature death having robbed us of one of our greatest comedians.

Although Lytham and St Anne's are officially one, I found each staunchly defends its own individuality. The shops on Lytham's main street are more intimate than those at St Anne's, the type which might be found in a cathedral town. There is also, of course, the immaculate sweep of the greensward on which stands with gleaming contrast, the white tower of its famous windmill.

When I walked up to Lytham Lifeboat Museum, which lies adjacent to the windmill, it was about to close. However, a tall sallow-faced man, one of the volunteer staff, beckoned me inside to view a fascinating collection of seafaring memorabilia. Here I saw pieces of long-forgotten sailing ships, pictures of the crews of past lifeboats, old posters and newspaper cuttings and a relief map of the treacherous Ribble estuary. Together these nautical odds and ends create a poignant reminder of the high price paid by the tough communities of the Lancashire coast in their unending battle with the sea.

I began to chat with the custodian, we talked about both the successes and the tragedies of Lytham lifeboat crews and also of humorous incidents.

"People often want to donate items to us, which usually we are delighted to receive, but having limited space we also have to be careful. To be given great-grandfather's fisherman's wellies is no great attraction to the museum.

That lady who just came in has offered us a marvellous picture of the Titanic which once belonged to a relative who sailed on the ship. But I told her it would be better to give it to Liverpool – they can restore it and preserve it under the correct conditions."

He then told me that the Lytham inshore boat has been out nineteen times so far this year. Surprisingly, many of the rescues take place in really good weather, people wander across the marshes under the impression that they can walk from Lytham to Southport. They then get into difficulties when they reach the Ribble channel, getting caught in the mud and sometimes in the path of the fast moving tide.

*Lytham: the snow-white tower of this famous windmill has become the symbol of the town, standing in what writer Allen Clarke called Windmill Land.*

I noticed a large display concerning the wreck of the *Mexico* and the loss of the St Anne's boat, whose memorial I had seen earlier, so I asked him the details. He told me that the *Mexico* was an iron barque which, although belonging to the German port of Hamburg, had been originally built in Sunderland. It had left Liverpool on the 9th December 1886 in heavy seas which rapidly worsened into a gale; this led to it being blown on to a sandbank off Southport. The Lytham lifeboat, the *Charles Biggs*, was the first to answer the distress signal, she was a new vessel and this was her first call out. Using oars and sail it took over two hours to reach the Mexico in the appalling conditions of a force seven gale. A lifeline was thrown to the stricken vessel, whose crew had lashed themselves to the rigging, but this broke. A second line was sent aboard and they prepared to abandon their ship. One man almost died as he was crushed between the two vessels and another sustained injuries as he jumped, but finally, after several abortive attempts they were rescued and the proud lifeboat men returned to Lytham, happy with the success of their first mission.

However, unknown to them two neighbouring lifeboats had also been launched into the furious storm: the *Laura Janet* from St Anne's and the *Eliza Fernley* from Southport. Fighting against the enormous breakers the Southport boat took almost three hours before she reached the stricken *Mexico*. On arrival her crew caught a passing glimpse of the Laura Janet which appeared to be moving at a very fast rate further out to sea.

Then disaster struck the Southport boat: a huge wave known by local sailors as a green-back caught her broadside on causing her to capsize. Most of her crew were thrown into the freezing water, others were trapped inside. The boat tried to right herself but failed, the men hung on as long as possible until cold and exhaustion took over.

The *Eliza Fernley* was discovered upturned on Birkdale Beach with three bodies underneath, other bodies were later washed ashore and just two men survived. The Laura Janet had failed to return to St Anne's by daybreak so a search was made, she was finally discovered aground on Ainsdale Beach. Like her sister ship she too contained three bodies but her tale was never fully revealed for her complete crew died.

"Touch wood, we'll never lose as many men again as we did on that terrible day. You see with our modern boats and all this new technology our crews are much smaller."

He smiled a farewell, and locked the door behind me. Alone, I stared across the estuary to the calm silver waves of the Irish sea, a sea which can so easily change into a place of terror.

# CHAPTER FIVE

# LYTHAM St ANNE'S TO WIGAN

I see a severed head at Catforth, a witch's grave at Woodplumpton, and a 12,000-year-old elk in Preston. I hear about the blacksmith who started Leyland Motors and the man from Chorley who sailed on the Mayflower. I meet Ben Barker who is 103 years old, explore Wigan Pier and remember the two George Formbys.

## 1

I left Lytham, driving in the direction of Warton, with the silver waters of the Ribble lying on my right across the marshy fields. This river, which is one of the loveliest in England, is shared by both Lancashire and Yorkshire. It is born on the high fells beyond Ribblehead, a spot well known to walkers who have endured the famous Three Peaks Walk, or those railway enthusiasts who have steamed across the magnificent viaduct which forms part of the Settle to Carlisle railway line.

It cascades from the hills down a splendid limestone valley, passing through Horton-in-Ribblesdale, then over the white-water falls at Stainforth before reaching the old fashioned market town of Settle. Along this stretch it is the home for pied-wagtails, dippers, wrens and many other birds who find food on its banks. After skirting Long Preston and Hellifield, which lie along Ribblesdale, it veers south-west to cross the border into Lancashire. Near this point is Paythorne Bridge, a favourite spot for watching the salmon come up the river to spawn. Now in the Ribble Valley it snakes its way past Gisburn, being joined by the clear waters of Tosside Beck close to Bolton-by-Bowland.

After passing under Edisford Bridge to the west of Clitheroe, it reaches Great Mitton where it is joined by both the River Hodder and the River Calder. Unfortunately the Calder is by modern standards highly polluted, this affects the quality of the Ribble, which up to this point is rated as a class one river. However, it continues its meandering course, widening, moving more slowly and to a degree cleaning itself. It passes through Ribchester and then on to Preston where it is now joined by the River Darwen. Just before it pours into the Irish Sea at its estuary at Lytham it receives the waters of the River Douglas at Hesketh Bank, whose source is on Winter Hill among the high West Pennine Moors.

The Ribble estuary, with its surrounding marshland, is a unique landscape containing many rare plants and it is a haven for birdlife. In wintertime the common Curlews, Snipe and Oyster Catchers can be seen foraging on the shoreline alongside rarer species, such as Black Tailed Godwit, Knots and Sanderling.

Wrea Green looked splendid in the soft morning sunlight, the first visitors had already arrived to feed Lancashire's fattest ducks. The road which I took through Kirkham is said to be part of the original Roman road which linked Ribchester to Portus Setantiorum, near Knott End. After passing the town's once derelict windmill, which has now been restored to form part of an impressive house, I found myself meandering along a maze of secluded lanes in the direction of Catforth.

"Please can I have a look at the Secret Treasure of Chaigley?" I asked Father Hodson who answered the presbytery door of St Robert's church.

Smiling, and looking not the least bit surprised at my request, he told me to walk around to the church door which he would unlock. I suppose after 22 years as a chaplain in the Royal Navy in which he sailed the world in aircraft carriers, becoming the guardian of a severed head is merely routine.

Once inside the church he handed me a booklet written by J.E. Bamber which reads like a classic detective story, telling the amazing tale of the relics which are now housed at Catforth. He then took me to the side of the altar and drew back a purple curtain to reveal a chalice, a missal, an ancient vestment and a 400-year-old human head which remains in a remarkable state of preservation. The flesh and skin have become hardened, the jaw is slightly open, and it can be clearly seen that halfway through the fifth vertebra it was hacked off.

The centuries old traditional story behind the severed head, which up to recent times was believed to be true, begins at Chaigley in the Ribble Valley. It relates that Father Philip Holden was secretly celebrating mass one August morning in 1648. Among the small assembly at Chapel House Farm, was his mother, sister and a few close friends. Suddenly the doors of the farmhouse burst open and in came a band of Cromwell's soldiers. They grabbed the priest and in an instant beheaded him beside the altar.

His head, which had rolled down the altar steps, was retrieved by a soldier and placed on a pike. It was then triumphantly displayed around the room, to the horror of his relatives. The priest's mother begged them to stop, which they eventually did, tossing the head over to her which she caught in her apron.

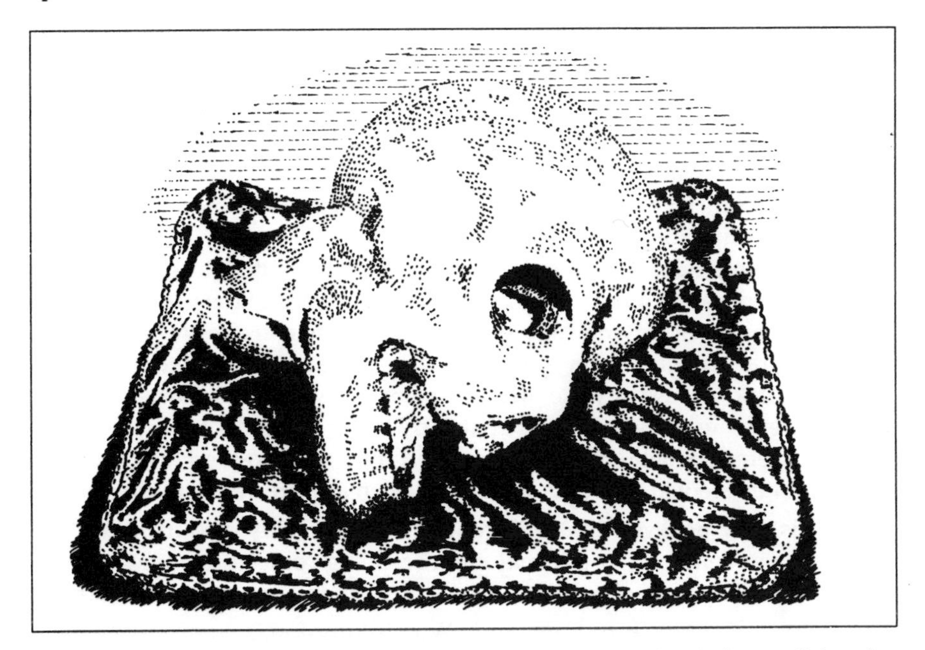

*The mysterious tale behind this severed head has been unravelled in the best tradition of Sherlock Holmes.*

From that day the Holden family secretly kept a number of relics from this last mass, which included the severed head. These were regarded as being sacred, and were handed down from father to son. Only the most senior male member of the family knew of their existence and as he approached death he would reveal the secret to his heir. These relics, which became known as The Secret Treasure of Chaigley, were handed down in this way until 1812. At that time Thomas Holden, who was then head of the family, divulged the tale to a Jesuit priest, Father John Fairclough of Stonyhurst College. He advised that as religious persecution had ended it was safe to reveal the secret. Shortly afterwards the Holden family moved from the Ribble Valley to Catforth Hall and in 1923 they decided to entrust the relics to St Robert's Church.

However, there were elements of this tale which did not seem to ring true, so in classic Sherlock Holmes style, J.E. Bamber began an in depth investigation of which the detective would have been proud. He looked at the history of the Holden family, at all the men from Lancashire who became priests and the conditions which prevailed during the period when priests were hunted. He then submitted the severed head to a number of forensic experts who, like all experts, disagreed on some points, one even suggesting that the head may be that of a woman.

He was then left with a host of historical and scientific data which he examined using the principle, 'When the impossible has been eliminated whatever remains, however improbable, must be the truth.' After sifting through all this evidence he came to the conclusion that the head, which was found to be much older than that recorded in the traditional tale, did not belong to Philip Holden for no such person ever existed! By eliminating all other possible candidates the only known person that fitted the evidence was a man named Miles Gerard. He had been a late entrant to the priesthood due to the disability of having only one eye, which had made the authorities reluctant to accept him. After training at Douay he arrived in England in 1590, but was quickly caught by the priest-hunters. A swift trial followed at Rochester in Kent, and he was then executed by being hanged, drawn and quartered. It seems probable that his sister had married into the Holden family and that she received the relics which had been acquired after his death.

So it is now believed that the traditional and highly colourful tale had evolved over centuries in a casual manner, being conjecture based on half-truths which were mixed with known facts. Elementary my dear Watson!

A couple of miles from Catforth is Woodplumpton, a rural village well-known to fishermen and week-end sailors who frequent the nearby Lancaster Canal. I went there to look at the grave of Meg Shelton, a reputed witch who they say was buried upside down. I found her grave in the quietness of St Anne's churchyard, marked by a boulder alongside a pathway. It is said that anyone who walks three times around her resting place will have their wish granted, provided it is kept as a secret.

Also known as Margaret Hilton, she is said to have lived alone at Singleton during the late 17th Century. Unlike the Pendle Witches, her escapades were relatively innocent, being confined mainly to stealing from the local farmers, aided of course, by magical powers. One tale tells how a miller saw her enter his mill, with the alleged intention of stealing some corn. He quickly followed, but was amazed to find she had disappeared. However he noticed that he now had seven sacks of corn, where he had previously had only six. A quick prod with a pitch-fork followed into each sack, then from the last sack came a shriek. Meg suddenly appeared, apparently from nowhere, with her arm pouring with blood. She quickly hopped onto her broomstick and zoomed off into the night sky!

*Woodplumpton. Fylde witch Meg Shelto is said to be buried upside down beneath this boulder.*

There are many fanciful tales told about this Fylde witch, but she fared better than most, dying in her bed. The church records say that Margaret Hilton was buried on May 2nd 1706, but no mention is made about her attempt to escape death. Local people say that after her first burial she scratched her way out of the grave. Luckily, she was caught, but this time she was re-buried head downwards with a boulder on top.

Carefully scanning the churchyard to ensure that I was alone, I began to self-consciously make the three circuit walk around the boulder. However, I've no intention of revealing my wish . . .

## 2

I could see the Jewel of Preston but I could not reach it, one minute I was almost there, the next I was speeding away in the wrong direction; but perhaps I should explain. Whoever approaches the town from the west will see a towering white rapier of a church steeple rising into the sky, in fact rising 309 feet and six inches into the sky, to be precise. I had been told that only the steeples of Norwich and Salisbury cathedrals are higher, so I decided that St

Walburge's church I ought to see, then my problems began. The new roads of Preston confused me for they have been designed to get the traffic away from the town as quickly as possible, they allow few escapes, saunterers like myself are not wanted. If you wish to speed to Blackpool, Liverpool or Lancaster there is no problem, but if you wish to find St Walburge's Church beware. However, with resolute determination I battled on through a maze of terraced streets, then at last, in frenzied disbelief I turned into the church car park.

I wandered slowly around the exterior of the building, which like York Minster, is festooned in a labyrinth of scaffolding, for a massive restoration is underway. I gazed up with wonder at the glistening white spire, I explored the interior which is huge like a cathedral, then I listened in silence as a young couple exchanged wedding vows, their nervous faces lit by the sunshine which poured in through the Gothic windows. However, the miracle of St Walburge's is not its fine architecture, impressive and beautiful as it surely is, but how it came to be built. For it was the poor of Victorian Preston; men, women and children who laboured intensely hard and lived in squalor, who gave up their pennies to build this church.

The middle of the last century had seen a massive rise in the Catholic population of the town, putting pressure on the small, overcrowded churches that then existed. The tough priests of the Jesuit order, who at that time administered both the educational and spiritual needs of the Catholics, decided to launch an appeal to build a new church. When £15,000 had been raised they commissioned one of England's most talented architects, Joseph Hansom who is remembered as the designer of the Hansom Cab, to carry out the work. In 1854 the church was consecrated in what must have been a breathtaking and colourful service, for it brought together four bishops, 120 priests and over 2000 other worshippers. But the building only took on its present imposing splendour in 1866 when the spire was at last completed. Today the church, which is insured for £4 million, is no longer looked upon as the exclusive domain of Catholics but has grown to be a proud possession of all Prestonians. Its spire has become a symbol of Proud Preston, when the restoration is completed not only will religious services continue to be held but it will become a unique venue for exhibitions, concerts and much more.

"Have you seen the Talbot Library?" a young man asked as I walked out of the church door. I told him that I had not, trying to cover up my ignorance for I had never even heard of the Talbot Library. He insisted that I should look in and he was quite right, for in a simple but beautiful building that was once the church school I discovered one of the Lancashire's best kept secrets.

I walked into this scholarly yet cosy world of books, soon becoming engrossed in one of the most fascinating collections of historical and religious documents that I have ever seen. Huge old volumes, like Whitaker's History of Whalley, stood side by side with thin pamphlets about little known chapels, published just last year. I wandered alone among the shelving, taking out any book that took my eye: an academic treatise on Calvinism, a highly readable volume about the English Martyrs and a fascinating account of the life of George Fox.

A small, healthy looking lady with bright sparkling eyes was busily at work categorising some new arrivals which were piled high on a table. She left her volumes for a few minutes and we began to chat.

"It's very exciting", she told me, "to be in at the beginning of this project, for I believe it will grow to become the best of its type in the country."

She went on to tell me that the library, surprisingly, is of recent origin, being named after a major benefactor of the church, William Talbot. Under the direction of Bishop Foley of Lancaster it has been created to bring together under one roof the wealth of Christian literature that exists concerning Lancashire and Cumbria. Unbelievably, for the collection is already huge, all the volumes have been donated and more are being given each week. It is intended to serve the whole community as a unique reference library, complementing the works which exist in the Lancashire Record Office which is also in Preston.

I asked her which is the oldest volume the library possesses, in reply she took me with a smile, over to a large cabinet in the corner of the room.

"This collection, which is in date order, is our pride and joy. It came from Ladyewell at Fernyhalgh and the oldest book dates from 1499. Many of the missals were carried by people who faced death if they had been caught, so they are of both academic and historical significance."

Some day, when the scaffolding has been removed and the road to St Walburge's has been adequately signposted, I will return to this marvellous academic wonderland that is springing up among the terraces of Preston. But no doubt, by that time others will have discovered its fascination so I will probably have to book a seat.

Winckley Square looked splendid in the bright autumn sunshine, framed with trees whose bronze coloured leaves were cascading downwards, it brings a gracious city feel to Preston. I walked along its quiet pavements, gazing at the grand Georgian houses in which suffragette Edith Rigby and poet Francis Thompson were born last century and thinking of the many other 'greats' this town has fostered. Men like Sir Richard Arkwright, who invented his spinning machine called the Water Frame, then went on to create a business empire; Joseph Livesey who fought poverty and founded the Teetotal Movement and Edwin Booth, a Victorian grocer who came here from Bury to become the father of a modern supermarket chain. Literary figures have also found inspiration here, writers such as Robert Service who penned *The Shooting of Dan McGrew* and Angela Brazil, whose popular school-girl books have become highly collectable.

I walked along Fishergate where the shoppers were spilling off the pavement, so I retreated to the more serene atmosphere of the Miller Arcade with its late Victorian tiles of green and pale orange. Nearby stands the Bull and Royal Pub, and an intriguing alleyway named the Old Cock Yard which hints of 18th century footpads. Round the corner I found a shop which must attract all the connoisseurs of tea in the north. The specialities which I saw on display included Assam, Jasmine Flower, Rose Congau, Russian Caravan and one which only the most daring would try, named Green Gunpowder.

But Preston's pride is, quite rightly, the Harris Museum which is regarded as the best example of a Neo-Greco building in Britain. I sat in the museum cafe sipping a cup of coffee and looking at a replica of the Doors of Paradise. They brought back to me memories of a holiday spent in Florence when I followed a tourist guide at break-neck speed to see the original doors in the cathedral baptistry. In the burning heat she explained how the panels, which date from the early 15th century, depict stories from the Old Testament. At the time I was unaware that I could have studied this same masterpiece in relative comfort here in Preston!

After looking at the impressive Foucalt Pendulum, which swings from the top of the building to prove that the earth really rotates, I went upstairs to see the Poulton Elk. Among a fascinating exhibition which charts the history of the area, I found this huge brown skeleton which even in death looks strangely arrogant. It was unearthed by a mechanical digger in the peat just three feet below the surface, and later research proved it to be a find of great importance. The animal, which dates from 10,000 BC, had drowned in swampy land which is now the Fylde. But before dying it had been badly wounded by spears thrown by human hunters, the bone spearpoints being found nearby. This is the earliest evidence we have of man living in our corner of the north-west, the very first Lancastrians.

I could have easily spent a couple of days looking at this marvellous collection of treasures housed in a building given to Preston by the son of a vicar. Viking coins from the fabulous Cuerdale Hoard found in 1840, thirty human skulls and two dug-out canoes found when Preston Dock was being built and mementos of when the Jacobite Army passed through the town, are just a few of the many unique objects I found on display.

As I strolled back to my car I remembered the phrase which the town has given to the English language, Every Preston Guild, which has come to mean any event which happens infrequently. The last Guild which was celebrated in 1992, is a link with the unique institution which began in 1179. It was established during the reign of King Henry II as a means of controlling all trade and commerce in what was rapidly becoming an important market town. In the early days it was an exclusive club which developed its own colourful ceremony at which members had their names listed in the Guild Roll. Since 1542 this event, at which the officers and members of the Guild form a procession through the town, has occurred every twenty years, being only interrupted once by the Second World War. The power of the Guild in controlling trade has long since disappeared, but it survives in a modern role as a splendid social event bringing visitors from all over the world to enjoy a spectacular carnival.

## 3

I continued my journey south on a day of grey skies and chill winds, the bright sunshine of the past two weeks had ended. The part of central Lancashire through which I was passing is known as South Ribble, it embraces such places as Bamber Bridge, Walton-le-Dale, Penwortham and Longton. Among this collection of rural villages and small towns is a name that is well known in every country in the world. In the desert regions of Africa, in the grasslands of South America, or among the foothills of the Himalayas, where residents might shake their heads when asked if they know the names Manchester or Liverpool, they would almost certainly have heard of Leyland. The rugged trucks and buses which carry the name of this small town have penetrated the remotest parts of the world, some are still in service half a century after they were first built.

This remarkable enterprise began when a local blacksmith, James Sumner, had the vision to see that the era of horse-driven transport was coming to an end. In 1884 he designed and built a five-ton steam wagon for transporting coal, then he continued his motive experiments by fitting an oil-fired boiler and a two-cylinder engine to a tricycle. But real success came with his steam-driven lawn mower which won him a prize at the Royal Lancashire Agricultural Show. His smithy had now grown to become a small factory known as the Sumner Works, and his reputation as a brilliant engineer had spread throughout Lancashire. In 1895 he fitted his lawn-mower engine to a three-wheeler car which was then purchased by the biscuit manufacturer Theodore Carr. The following year he joined forces with Henry Spurrier of Preston, who had the necessary finance, and together they created The Lancashire Steam Motor Company.

Their steam vans which were produced during the next few years became best-sellers, their workforce having grown to almost two hundred by the time the new North Works was being built in 1902. The Edwardian period brought even faster expansion, petrol engines were replacing steam engines and their range of products now embraced vans, trucks, buses and even fire-engines. At the beginning of the Great War the company took on its familiar name of Leyland Motors Limited, with Henry Spurrier at its helm, employing a workforce of 1500 people. The Leyland blacksmith, James Sumner, whose dream had become a reality, retired from the company in 1919. But his brain-child continued to expand, in spite of the many recessions, take-overs and mergers which have become a way of life in the automotive world. Up till about thirty years ago the company was the biggest truck manufacturer in the world, then it merged with the car group to form British Leyland, which proved to be a disaster. In 1970 the local workforce numbered a huge 12,000, but this had declined to around 2,200 by 1990. In 1987 the Dutch vehicle manufacturers DAF bought Leyland Vehicles, to form Leyland DAF, a marriage that seemed at first to succeed. However, due to the present recession truck sales plummeted and in February 1993 the receivers moved in to take over the running of the company. After months of frantic activity a management buy-out has now created Leyland Trucks, the latest episode in the story of this amazing company.

Leyland, in spite of its reputation for being a place of business, has a surprisingly rural feel about it. I wandered into the old village, which is centred around the ancient cross which is reputed to have been broken by the Puritans then later used as a base for two gas lamps. A Heritage Trail leaflet guided me past weaver's cottages, old inns, almshouses and into the ancient church of St Andrew, which dates from the 13th Century. Nearby I discovered lovely Worden Park: in this former home of the Farrington family, I saw local craftsmen who, in the tradition of James Sumner, were hard at work.

## 4

In spite of the sombre skies Chorley was bustling, for it was Tuesday which means the Flat-Iron market was in full session.

"What is England's favourite meal Madam? You don't need to tell me, we all know – chips. And here I have a solution to all your cooking problems, a highly efficient chip-maker . . ."

A good humoured crowd had gathered around a serious faced young man who was demonstrating his highly efficient device. Nearby, another stall-holder was looking on enviously for his flameless lighters did not seem to be selling too well.

Chorley can trace the origins of its famous market back to 1498 when the town lay in the hundred of Leyland. It probably started as a venue for the buying and selling of farm produce, a time when the rural villagers of Wheelton, Adlington, Coppull and Charnock Richard would converge on the town to take in provisions and exchange the latest gossip. Last century it was largely a cattle-market but today over a hundred stall-holders sell an amazing variety of goods, here it is possible to buy clothes, hardware, pet-foods, audio tapes and a thousand other items. It's odd name is said to have evolved from the time when goods were displayed for sale, not on a stall, but directly on the ground, which included the sale of flat-irons. However the town is not content with this huge array of stalls, for just around the corner I discovered there is another covered market!

I stood outside Thornley's famous butchers shop in Chapel Street looking up at one of the strangest locations for a statue to be found in Lancashire. For looking down from a corner of the roof of an opticians, forever watching the people of Chorley, is Lord Beaconsfield, better known as Benjamin Disraeli. Perhaps he is thanking the people of this bustling Lancashire town for their contribution to the arts of this country, for it was a local man who founded London's Tate Gallery. Terrace Mount, which I found on a small hill on busy Market Street, is where Sir Henry Tate was born in 1819. He started work as a humble grocer's assistant, then he moved to Liverpool to work in a sugar refinery where he was rapidly promoted. In 1852 he acquired a new machine for making sugar cubes which he took to London and made his fortune. He then decided to spend his money on a new home for British art. The Government provided the river side site where the old Mill-Bank prison once stood and Henry Tate supplied the marvellous building which now bears his name.

Across the road from Terrace Mount I found the lovely church of St Lawrence, a building that ought to be on the itinerary of every American tourist. For here, so it is said, is where Miles Standish was baptised at the end of the 16th Century. He had been born at nearby Duxbury Hall, which has now been demolished. In 1620 he sailed to America in the Mayflower, where he was appointed Military Governor of the new colony that would evolve into the most powerful country in the world. The small band of settlers suffered terribly during the early years, and his wife was the first to die. His personal tragedy is recorded in Longfellow's poem, *The Courtship of Miles Standish*, which was written in 1858.

Before leaving Chorley I went to look at impressive Astley Hall, which stands in a huge green park that has become the venue for the Royal Lancashire Show. Here, in this survival from Tudor England, I looked upon the magnificence of oak panels and ornate plaster ceilings; I saw a twenty-four feet long shovelboard in the remarkable Long Gallery and the bed in which Cromwell might have slept; but the most moving memories of the town's past lie in those sad mementos of the Chorley Pals who died in the mud of the First World War.

## 5

I went to Aspull, which lies just three miles from the centre of Wigan, to talk to a remarkable Lancastrian named Ben Barker. His daughter, Margaret, invited me inside her attractive modern house and introduced me to her father. I was half expecting to meet a frail old man who would, perhaps, be deaf, wrinkled and hardly able to speak – how wrong can you be! Ben, I discovered, has a clear healthy skin, bright eyes, an engaging sense of humour with a mind as alert as a forty-year-old. What makes these attributes quite astonishing is that he was born on 14th December 1890, just three years after Queen Victoria celebrated her Golden Jubilee, which made him a remarkable 103 years old when I met him in 1994.

As we began to chat over a cup of tea, Ben proudly showed me the Wigan Rugby Club tie and the Barrow Rugby Club sweater he was wearing which were presented to him on his one hundredth birthday. He then began to tell me of his early life, memories of Lancashire a century ago. He had been born at Rainford near St Helens, his father having moved there from Staffordshire to work as a collier where he married Ben's mother who was a local girl. One of his first recollections is of joining other small children at a soup kitchen.

"You see the colliers had gone on strike and we had no food, so the kitchen had been set up to feed their children. They gave us Lob Scouse, which tasted really good. I was only about three years old, which would make it 1893."

The family moved to Adlington, near Chorley, shortly afterwards where his father began work in another mine. Then in 1896 they came to Westhoughton, which is close to where Ben still lives.

*Ben Barker*

"I remember my sister shouting to me to come and look at a carriage that was moving without a horse. This was the first car we had ever seen."

He told me how all the colliers wore clogs for work and how he sometimes helped an uncle who owned a clog shop. He worked into the early hours of the night, for as most of the colliers only owned one pair of clogs, fast repairing was essential. Women who worked in the mills nearly all had shawls and the few street gas-lamps, which gave a dismal light, were lit by the local lamp-lighter using a candle on a stick.

During the Boer War, Ben recalled, that children like himself collected badges on which were painted portraits of the British Generals, such as Baden-Powell and Roberts. Two years after the death of Queen Victoria and in the same year that Orville Wright flew the first aeroplane, he began work in a local textile mill, having refused to follow his father down the mine. Here he became interested in engineering, so he decided to attend night-classes to further his skills. These he attended for almost ten years.

Working during the elegant Edwardian period he remembers some of the world events which made the headlines. In 1909 Bleriot made the first flight from France to England, the day after Ben's 21st birthday in 1911 Amundsen planted the Norwegian flag at the South Pole and in the following year the ill-fated *Titanic* sank to the bottom of the ocean. But it was the start of the First World War that affected his life the most. His work in the mill was low paid, he received just nine shillings for working a fifty five hour week and he was desperate to find a better job. Ben then heard that munition-workers were required at Vickers in Barrow-in-Furness, so he applied for a position and due to his night-school qualifications, was offered a new job. Travelling on a free railway pass from Bolton he quickly settled into the important war work of manufacturing large shells which were urgently needed at the front.

"I worked on a capstan-lathe turning the front profile of the shells and also producing very accurate screw-threads."

He stayed for the duration of the war in Barrow, where he worked a thirteen hour day which enabled him, for the first time to save a little money. He was also able to pursue his life-long interest in Rugby, which he says, "I would much rather watch than soccer. It has much faster action."

In 1917 he returned home and married a girl from Daisy Hill, near Westhoughton. His new engineering job, which was to last for 17 years, was with Wigan Coal at Ince. This was during the period of the General Strike and around the time that George Orwell came to the area to write his celebrated book, The Road to Wigan Pier.

A temporary job at Trafford Park in Manchester in 1937 brought with it the problems of travel which Ben solved by buying a bicycle. Together with a friend he would make a round trip of twenty six miles to work, which introduced him to a pastime he grew to love. When war came yet again in 1939 he found employment in charge of the boiler-house at the De Havilland propeller factory at nearby Lostock. There he stayed until his retirement in 1957 when he was 67 years old.

Much of his incredible thirty six years of retirement have been spent watching Rugby and touring around Lancashire on his bike. In 1924 Tom Hughes of Wigan, known affectionately as Owd Tom, began the famous Autumn Tints cycling club of which Ben is now the oldest member.

"I can't see anyone overtaking me as long as I live," he told me with a smile.

He was still cycling on his worthy Raleigh Wayfarer, at the age of ninety when he calculated he had ridden about 70,000 miles. At this time he made a tour of the Wye Valley and North Wales with an octogenarian friend. He was sadly forced to give up cycling about twelve years ago, but he is still able to walk with the aid of a stick. Three years ago on his one hundredth birthday he received well-deserved VIP treatment which included a telegram of congratulations from both the Queen and the Secretary of State. As part of the celebrations he was invited to return to Barrow seventy-three years after he finished his war-work at Vickers. The mayor gave him a civic reception and arranged for him to revisit the sites he had first known so long ago. But his proudest moment came when two of Wigan's top rugby players came to his home, for they brought with them the coveted Rugby League Cup which they had won at Wembley and they presented Ben with a club tie.

Ben, quite rightly, has become a living legend in this part of Lancashire. When his local doctor calls it is not to administer treatment, but like all Ben's other visitors, to gain inspiration. No smoking, little drinking of alcohol and plenty of fresh air he told me is part of his secret for a long life.

I found it utterly fascinating to speak with this marvellous Lancastrian who has lived through the greatest period of change the world has ever known, yet taking it all in his stride, remains a man of today.

## *6*

If George Orwell was to return to Wigan to day he would be bewildered by the changes which have taken place. He would look in vain for the squalor and the poverty which he recorded during his celebrated visit, for the Wigan of 1936 is as remote from today's world, as that of medieval times. I strolled through a superbly designed new shopping complex known as The Galleries, looking in windows which displayed perfumes from Paris and leather bags from Rome. A dozen different types of bread was on sale in another window, while nearby the vegetables of Tarlton stood alongside the fruits of Israel and Spain. Pies with a large variety of fillings are also a local speciality, including one which contains cauliflower cheese. Nowhere in the world can better the remarkable quality and choice of produce now available in Lancashire. However one thing I found which remains thankfully unchanged since Orwell's visit is the good humour and friendliness of Wiganers. In a letter to fellow author Cyril Connolly, Orwell wrote 'The miners here are very nice people, very warm hearted and willing to take me for granted. I would like to stay a good long time in the north, 6 months or a year.'

*Wigan: once a Roman settlement, now on the tourist trail.*

I walked up Wallgate to the impressive Parish Church which sits, with dignity, on a small hill overlooking the new face of Wigan. Here a plaque told me that on the 1st April 1643 eighty six Royalist sharpshooters climbed to the top of the tower and bravely held out against the Parliamentary Army. It was in a battle along Wigan Lane eight years later that the Earl of Derby barely escaped with his life, while his less fortunate colleague, Sir Thomas Tyldesley, was ferociously killed. The town suffered badly for following the Royalist cause during the Civil War, a fact appreciated later by King Charles II who gave it a new motto to enhance its coat of arms, Ancient and Loyal. But of course Wigan has a fascinating history stretching back to when the Roman Legions first pitched their camps here and established a settlement named Coccium. Legends also mention the town as a possible site for some of King Arthur's battles, and they tell the famous tale of Mabs Cross which lies up Standishgate in the grounds of a school. During the 14th Century, Lady Mabel Bradshaw of Haigh Hall paid a penance for her unwitting bigamy by walking barefooted to this cross from her home each week. She had been misled into believing her husband had been slain at Bannockburn, and then tricked into marrying a Welsh knight.

Wigan Pier is surprisingly badly signposted from the centre of the town, considering that it attracts up to half a million visitors each year. However, after asking directions from a local woman on the St Helens road I at last reached the fascinating development. To renew my flagging energy I immediately bought a bowl of delicious lentil soup in the cafe and for a cabaret I was entertained by watching the antics of a group of school children. They had been dressed in Owd Lancashire clothes for their visit, the girls wore mop-caps, white shawls and long dresses, while the more self-conscious boys sported flat-caps, mufflers and boots. One young extrovert had been chosen as the dandy of the pack, he wore a bowler hat and multi-coloured waistcoat, and was sporting a cane handled walking stick. A teacher tried ineffectively to control their excitement by shouting orders.

"I am making it clear. We have only fifty minutes before the coach leaves, so if you wish to buy gifts for home or lollipops to eat on the journey, you must do so now."

With spectacular success Wigan Council have proved yet again, the old adage that there is no such thing as bad publicity. When George Orwell wrote *The Road to Wigan Pier* his title gave fuel to the fire begun by the music hall jokes of George Formby Senior. Piers, of course, were associated with the sea-side and Wigan being inland and reputedly having a pier, became the butt of the joke. However the town does have a canal wharf which, with a loading bay which is a bit like a pier, and a number of mills and warehouses it has magnificently transformed fiction into fact.

Here in an Venetian atmosphere of bridges and water buses I wandered along the footpaths which link up a score of different attractions. A bright red van was appropriately delivering the weeks supply of Uncle Joe's Mint Balls to the gift shop in which the children were swarming to spend their pocket money. Some visitors were busy eating lunch in the Orwell Pub, while others were stepping back in time to the year 1900 in a live display named The Way We Were. As I walked back to my car Trencherfield Mill's mighty steam engine was giving a nostalgic hoot. I thought, that this town of Rugby League champions, Wigan Wasps swimmers and Olympic medallists need no longer worry about an image problem.

## 7

The Simple Lad from Wigan or The Wigan Nightingale was how George Formby Senior was described on the bill boards, but really he was an adopted son of the town for he had been born at Ashton-under-Lyne in 1878. James Henry Booth, which was his real name, was illegitimate and his early years were spent living in terrible poverty. He began work at the age of twelve as a blacksmith's striker but his real joy was singing comic songs to the accompaniment of an old banjo. While on holiday at Blackpool he decided to have a go at singing with a minstrel troupe who were performing on the sands and he found his act went down well. At the same time he met another performer named Barney Parsons who became a close friend, they later decided to form a team known as The Brothers Glenroy, to tour the Music Hall circuits.

After a few years the duo broke up, but James Booth continued a solo act around the pubs and halls of Manchester. It was during one of these performances that he was spotted by the owner of Birkenhead's Argyle Theatre, Danny Clarke, who offered him a place at the hall for a week. But Clarke thought the name James Booth sounded too formal for a comedian so he persuaded him to change it to George Formby, reputedly after seeing Formby written on the side of a railway truck. Other work quickly followed at halls throughout the country, and it was while he was appearing at Wigan Empire that he met Eliza Hoy who he later married.

George Formby Senior, with the help of his new wife, refined his act to embrace the best of North Country humour and as his confidence grew he quickly became one of the big names in show business. Dressed in outrageous ill-fitting clothes he used his acute bronchial condition as part of his act. "Coughing better tonight" or "I'll cough you for a shilling", always brought a laugh. He followed with a string of jokes, many referring to Wigan where he now lived, then he continued his act with catchy, foot-tapping songs. It was during a performance at Birkenhead in 1904 that he heard his wife had given birth to their first child, a son who was also to be named George, and was destined for even greater success.

*George Formby.*

There was sadness at first when George Formby Junior was born for he was blind. But happily this was found to be due to a caul which was obstructing his eyes, it came free a few weeks later restoring his sight. His childhood was happy, his father earned up to £300 a week which was an enormous sum at the time, so the family were part of Wigan's middle class. George Formby Senior was determined that his son would not enter show business, so when he reached ten years old he arranged for him to become an apprentice jockey, which had been the profession of his maternal grandfather. It was later, during a period at Ayr Stables in Scotland that young George first met Beryl Ingham, a girl from Darwen who was part of a dancing duo.

At this time George's soaring weight was beginning to rule out a career as a jockey, so in spite of his father's wishes he began to look to show business for his future. A talk with Beryl convinced him to make the change, he took the plunge in 1921 as a solo act, making his first appearance at the age of sixteen at Earlestown Hippodrome. On the advice of the legendary performer, Harry Lauder, who was a family friend, he used his mother's maiden name appearing as George Hoy. Sadly, this same year saw the premature death of his father at the age of forty-three.

At first his comedy act which was based on the style of his late father, was not well received which led to him becoming despondent. However, he continued to persevere, and with the help of a friend, Sam Paul, he greatly improved his performance, adding the music of his famous ukulele which he bought for fifty shillings. It was when he starred in a revue at Castleford in 1923 that he again met up with Beryl, who with her sister May, had a clog-dancing act. Their friendship quickly blossomed, this led to an impetuous proposal of marriage and the ceremony took place the following year. It was under Beryl's guidance that his career really took off. She advised him to adopt the well-known Formby name and to wear smart clothes, using the ukulele as the main feature of his act. It was while appearing at London's prestigious Alhambra that he perfected what was to become his famous catch-phrase, "It's turned out nice again, hasn't it."

George Formby's rise to fame was phenomenal, he was to become the biggest box-office draw of the thirties and forties. His gramophone records sold by the thousand with such legendary hits as *Cleaning Windows, Leaning on a Lamp Post, Chinese Laundry Blues* and *My Little Stick of Blackpool Rock.* He appeared in his first talking film, Boots, in 1934, which was followed by twenty more in which he starred with many leading ladies. These box-office successes included *Let George Do It* (1940) with Phyllis Calvert, *Come on George* (1941) with Pat Kirkwood and *No Limit* with Florence Desmond. He appeared in three Royal Variety Shows, then when the war started he began a series of morale boosting tours in both the Far-East and Europe. His popularity continued after the war with appearances in such shows as the spectacular West End musical *Zip Goes a Million* in 1951 and later in television shows.

*George Formby's grave*

Tales of the possessiveness of Beryl became legendary in the show business world. George, who was reputed to be a frustrated Casanova, had to have his every move approved by his clever but dominant wife. To steer him away from temptation she ensured that each film had a different leading lady, and of all the stars he worked with only one, Googie Withers, got a full screen kiss!

Sadly, in the early fifties he suffered a heart attack which began a decline in his health. This was aggravated by the strain of secretly knowing that Beryl was ill with cancer, which resulted in her death on Christmas Day 1960. Two months later a surprised public learned that he was going to marry Pat Howson, a 36-year-old school teacher whom he had known since her childhood. However, the publicity and excitement of his engagement proved too much, his coronary condition worsened and he died on 6th March 1961 at Preston. More than 100,000 people lined the streets of Warrington to pay their last respects to this much-loved Lancastrian, as he was put to rest alongside his famous father in the local cemetery. But a dispute was to continue for another decade when his family learnt that his fiancee was to receive the bulk of his fortune of £135,000.

But George Formby, the Lancashire Lad from Wigan who rose to become one of England's most talented stars, has never really left us. His films appear at regular intervals on television, his hit songs are played on the radio, and the hugely popular George Formby Society continues to flourish. Some people also believe that he had psychic healing powers. One fan says he has found relief from severe back pain by looking at the haunting eyes of the star that stare out from a photograph on his bedroom wall.

The Wigan area has also produced other well-known entertainers. These include Frank Randle of 'Baa Ah've supped some ale toneet' fame, who was born at Higher Ince and Ted Ray who made his stage debut at Prescot.

# CHAPTER SIX

# WIGAN TO LYDIATE

I visit the Lancashire Lourdes, learn about the Transit of Venus, and see where Southport really began. I cross the mere that has disappeared, look on Cromwell's Stone at Lathom, see a wedding at Ormskirk, the dunes at Formby, then end with a drink in Lancashire's oldest pub

## 1

Visitors who come to Ashton-in-Makerfield fall into two groups. There are those who come intent on enjoying a splendid day watching the horse racing at nearby Haydock Park, and there are those who come to venerate one of England's most remarkable Christian relics: the Holy Hand of St Edmund Arrowsmith.

When I drove through the small town centre, on my way to the church of St Oswald, it was bustling with early morning shoppers. The church building itself is striking in appearance for the design is based on that of the medieval churches which are found south of the River Loire in France. It is the work of a local architect and was built in 1930 using local labour, being constructed in alternating blocks of Parbold and Darley Dale stone. Inside of the lofty building I walked down a dark aisle to discover the saint's shrine. Here, preserved in a special glass container is his Holy Hand, which was secured after his bloody execution more than 300 years ago. The story of his life is one of complete devotion to his religion set against a Lancashire background full of hatred and intrigue, and ending with his death at Lancaster.

It was during the reign of Elizabeth I in the year 1585 that Brian Arrowsmith (later confirmed Edmund) was born in the village of Haydock. Both his father, Robert, who was a farmer and his mother Margery were strict Roman Catholics who had suffered for their allegiance to the outlawed faith. Brian, being brought up in this pious religious atmosphere, first attended a local school which still stands at Garswood, then left for Douay in France to study for the priesthood. In 1612 he was ordained at Arras and the next year saw his secret arrival back in England. A small man of 'mean appearance' was how he was described, but behind his small stature lay a personality of great charm and wit, and of remarkable zeal.

His mission, centred in the village of Brindle, near Chorley, covered a large rural area which stretched up to the outskirts of Preston. Here in secret, for ten years he administered to his congregation. Celebrating Mass in tiny isolated cottages, baptising new-born babies and marrying young couples. He was forced to carry out his work like a secret-agent in his own country, for always there was the threat of discovery by the dreaded priest-hunters.

Following the example of many of his closest colleagues he became a Jesuit, then he carried on his clandestine work from a base in the thatched Blue Anchor Inn at Brindle. At this time twenty priests were working throughout Lancashire and they had devised elaborate codes to communicate with each other to avoid discovery. They kept changing their names and became masters of disguise, never staying too long in one house and always looking over their shoulder.

However, in spite of all these precautions Edmund Arrowsmith was betrayed to the authorities. Being warned of the impending danger he managed to make a hasty retreat on horse back towards Preston. He galloped away down a narrow lane with the priest hunters in hot pursuit. Continuing across a large open field he hoped to clear a wide ditch which lay at the far end, but this proved too much for his steed who refused to jump. The delay was enough for his pursuers to catch him up and after a brisk fight he was overpowered. He was then dragged off to the Boar's Head Inn, which still exists at Hoghton, where he was locked in the cow-shed before being transported to the dungeons of Lancaster Castle.

On August 26th 1628 Edmund Arrowsmith stood trial at Lancaster, accused of being a priest, a Jesuit and of reconciling Roman Catholics of which he was found guilty and sentenced to death. During the reign of Charles I no one in England had been executed for their religious beliefs, so many hoped that a reprieve might be forthcoming, but sadly this did not happen. Two days later he was carried across the castle yard, and gazing upwards he saw the face of fellow priest John Southworth of Salmesbury Hall, who had also been imprisoned. Edmund Arrowsmith raised his arm and received absolution from his pale faced colleague; both men were destined to become saints.

He was next tied to a hurdle, then dragged through the streets of Lancaster to the place of execution which is now the hilltop on which the Ashton Memorial stands. The barbaric sentence was then carried out. He was first hanged, then cast down, dismembered, disembowelled and cut into quarters. His heart was ripped out, his head cut off and his quarters boiled in a caldron.

His blood was then mixed with sand and thrown on to a fire. Finally his head and quarters were taken away to be displayed on the castle wall.

Following the execution several relics were secured by his followers including the famous Holy Hand. This came into the possession of the Gerard family who were relatives of his mother. They kept it secretly for many generations before giving it to St Oswald's Church. The veneration of this relic has continued down the centuries, with many miraculous cures being attributed to it. Each Sunday the Holy Hand is displayed and the congregation blessed, and many people make an annual pilgrimage here, to the church which has become known as the Lancashire Lourdes.

Passing through Billinge and Orrell I descended to the green Douglas Valley to look at another human relic which lies in the village of Appley Bridge. In appropriately named, Skull House, a marvellous 400-year-old building full of mysterious odd corners, is kept a large polished skull which is known as Charlie. But who Charlie was is open to speculation. One legend suggests that he was one of King Arthur's knights who perished in a battle close to the Douglas, while another tale says he was a monk killed by Cromwell's soldiers. However, the skull is treated with great respect by the owners, for it is considered bad luck to even move it and it must always remain in the house.

Another famous resident of this village is that great Lancashire artist, Theodore Major. A man, in the tradition of Lowry, who paints not for gain but because of the love of his craft. His works number so many that he has bought a second house in which to a hang them, but he refuses to sell a single one.

## 2

Anyone who wishes to experience the full splendour of West Lancashire should drive like I did, on a bright clear day, to the top of Parbold Hill. By the standards of the Bowland Hills this summit rates as a mere pimple, standing only about 394 feet (120m) above sea level. However, in this area of rich flat fields it seems to be almost a mountain, rising upwards it provides a fine vantage point. I walked along a short pathway which leads to what is known as the Bottle Beacon, a bee-hived shaped structure which remembers the Reform Act of 1832. Below me, in a sweep of green, the plain unfolded to reveal the church spires of Parbold village, the curve of the Douglas Valley and the dark needle of Ashurst Beacon. My eyes were then led onwards to the silver line that marked the chill waters of the Irish Sea.

I returned once more to the flatlands, crossing the hump-backed bridge over the canal at Parbold village. It was here in 1991, that an exciting find was made at Holly House Farm. Ken Linsley, a joiner from Skelmersdale, was helping to renovate the building when he discovered a sword lying in the loft. It was later identified as a Cromwellian Rapier which had lay hidden for an incredible three hundred years!

My journey continued through the lovely village of Newburgh then through quiet Mawdesley to reach Croston. Parking my car in the winding main street I crossed the road to admire the impressive single arched bridge which spans the Yarrow. This little-known but attractive river begins its short journey high on Anglezarke Moor. After taking a wide curve around Chorley it continues westward, passing Eccleston and then Croston before joining the River Douglas. Croston, unfortunately, cannot enjoy to the full its waterside aspect because to protect the houses from flooding the river is hemmed in by a deep stone embankment. The bridge which carries a datestone of 1682, forms part of a narrow lane named The Hillocks which leads to Croston Moss. This is the beginning of West Lancashire's flatlands which stretch unending till they reach the sea.

*Newburgh, with its splended post office, is typical of the rural tranquillity of West Lancashire.*

A long line of school children, led by two woman teachers, suddenly appeared on the bridge, their excited chatter breaking the silence of the village. Expertly guided across the roadway they quickly disappeared around the corner in the direction of the primary school and quietness returned. It is recorded that a school existed in Croston in 1347, but their classrooms, which were once part of a grammar school only date back to 1660. This is regarded locally as almost yesterday, for there have been people living on this spot for well over a thousand years.

Landscape photographers from the north eventually find their way to Croston, intent on capturing on film Lancashire's best example of a traditional village street. Church Street is cobbled, has the village cross at one end, the ancient church of St Michael and All Angels at the other, and is lined with immaculate cottages from the 18th century. In fact it would be perfect except for the curse of our century – parked cars, which distract from the character of the scene.

The well manicured grass which fringes the flat gravestones of the churchyard appeared emerald in the bright sunlight, while the gold of autumn was visible in the fallen horse-chestnut leaves. This beautiful church, so I am told, wielded a lot of ecclesiastical clout in the old days and to a more limited extent, still does. Its rectors, who have always been men of spirit, ensure that such newcomers as Chorley and Tarleton do not step out of line. Indeed the church wardens of St Laurence in Chorley still have to pay a levy of 50p to Croston (but they tend to keep this quiet). And still the vicars of both Bretherton and Mawdesley are appointed by Croston's rector. Among those rectors of the past who are still remembered are Steynsham Master, who died in 1864 at the age of 97, after serving for an astonishing 66 years, and James Hiet who refused to comply with the Act of Uniformity. He had been rector for 37 years, but was buried without 'ceremony or book', having remained true to his conscience.

As I walked back to my car along Croston's famous street, I had the feeling that this is the kind of village that can take almost anything in its stride. Drowned in noonday quietness its houses sleep in the sure knowledge that they remain, while many a dynasty has risen and then fallen.

## 3

The day began grey, overcast and dismal, the clouds were touching the summits of the distant Pennine hills bringing inevitably rain. For two hours it poured with grim enthusiasm as if it would continue forever then, as if by magic, everything changed. The clouds scurried away, the grey sky turned to silver, then blue patches eased their way inland from the coast, so that when I reached Much Hoole at mid-day I was greeted by bright sunshine.

Anyone who is interested in what the newspapers once called the space race, should make a pilgrimage to this village which lies three miles to the north of Croston. I arrived at the quaint church of St Michael on one of those rare occasions when it was possible to tell the time by the sundial which is painted on the church tower. Two elderly men were looking at me from the far end of the churchyard as I read the inscription over the door: Prepare to meet thy God. Believe, Love, Obey.

It was here in 1639 that a young curate from Liverpool named Jeremiah Horrocks worked, serving the religious needs of the village for £40 a year. He was also a naturally brilliant scholar who had taught himself the rudiments of astronomy, having studied the works of Kepler. Fascinated by the movements of the planets he became a keen observer which led him to make some original calculations. From these he became convinced that Venus would pass across the face of the sun, an event that had never been seen. To try to prove his theory he set up his telescope in a darkened room in Carr House, a fine gabled building with mullioned windows which still stands about a mile from the church. The telescope was used to project the image of the sun on to a sheet of paper.

It was a cold winters day when according to his calculations, the Transit of Venus would occur. Unfortunately it was also a Sunday, his busiest day, when he had to carry out a number of religious services, so he had to keep dashing in anxious anticipation from the church to Carr House. At last, at quarter past three, a black spot was seen passing across the bright yellow image of the sun; his predictions had been correct. The only other person to witness the event was his friend, William Crabtree, and it was another 130 years before anyone saw it again.

Undoubtedly this Lancashire curate, who was a genius of his time, would have gone on to even greater discoveries. But sadly, shortly after his first major success his health failed and he died at the early age of only twenty three. He lies buried in Toxteth Chapel in Liverpool and a window is dedicated to his memory at this little church in Much Hoole. Later his work was acknowledged by that other British genius, Sir Isaac Newton, which led to him being honoured by a memorial in Westminster Abbey.

As I waited for the heavy traffic to clear from the busy trunk road that links Preston to Liverpool, I could see the mellowed gables of Carr House; a place few would suspect of having such scientific links.

Tarleton lies among those rich fertile fields that lead on to Hesketh Bank and beyond to the marshy estuary of the Ribble. Motorists, perhaps fortunately for the residents, seldom pass through the village itself, leaving it in rural seclusion. Although, in past centuries it was a welcome stopping-place for travellers as it stands on an ancient route which led northwards crossing the shallows of the river. Today it is the towering spire of the parish church, standing proudly above the flat landscape, which is a familiar landmark for those on route to Southport.

Parking my car in the impressive new shopping centre I walked down Plox Brow, passing a 17th century cottage, to reach the banks of both the canal and the River Douglas which flow side by side. About a dozen ducks were noisily splashing in the water, the only other sound being the drone of traffic from the distant trunk road. Much of this green fertile terrain which spreads outwards from the river once formed part of the ever changing estuary. It was a land subjected to the whim of tide and weather, flooding was commonplace and tales are still told of journeys being made to local villages, such as Croston, not by cart but by boat. After the swampy land of Martin Mere was drained two centuries ago, it was followed by the Hesketh family reclaiming these coastal marshes which ended the annual flooding and created Tarleton's present face.

Records of its early history are scant, although the plough occasionally uncovers relics of the Bronze and Iron Age. By the 13th century a small settlement was in existence which later came into the ownership of Cockersand Abbey, near Lancaster. It was then known as the Island of Tarleton, due to it being almost surrounded by a watery wasteland. Its closeness to the River Douglas, known by the celts as the Dark River, gave the villagers an affinity with the sea, many of the older families having seafarers among their ancestors. As early as the 15th Century cargo boats were using the Douglas and in later years a regular trade route was established to France. Ship building became an important local industry, together with rope-making for many miles of rope were required by the early schooners.

Originally Tarleton, together with Bretherton and Hesketh Bank, formed part of Croston Parish. In wintertime the journey to Croston church was often hazardous so the villagers sometimes held their own open-air service alongside an ancient holy well. The waters from this well were said to have miraculous properties, and like many other such sites, was dedicated to St Ellyn (St Helen). Surprisingly, the location of the well has been forgotten, but it is probably close to the old church.

In 1872 the village was insensitively described by a visitor as 'rough and ready, primitive, with one bewildering street and all sizes of houses which looked in need of shaking up and putting in order again'. If he was to return today he would be happily surprised for Tarleton has indeed been shaken up. It has a fine modern shopping centre with a landscaped car-park, which won an award, an impressive public library and a welcoming hostelry, the Lord Lilford pub.

I drove across Tarleton Moss in bright sunshine, a place of wide skies and distant horizons. Fields of huge lush cabbages stood alongside the final crop of hay, enormous cylinders which were ready for storage. I came upon romantic road signs like Hunters Lane and Hundred End; lonely little by-ways which disappear towards the marshes. There was of course the ever present greenhouses, huge constructions which dwarf the isolated houses which stand nearby. Here the market-gardeners of Tarleton grow tomatoes, lettuces and a host of other vegetables which are regarded as the finest in Britain. It all began last century when shipping began to decline. A number of local men returned, by necessity, to work on the land. Unknown to them, when they invested in their first green-house, they were beginning what was to become a highly successful industry.

## *4*

There is a strangeness about Churchtown for although it retains the quiet atmosphere of an 18th century village it also forms part of the red-bricked suburbia of Southport; it is where Southport really began and now it is where it ends. When Southport was merely an uninhabited stretch of sea-washed sand dunes this was the main village in the township of North Meols, a name that is now almost forgotten. But the miracle of Churchtown is that it has managed to survive at all, for here I discovered what must surely be the largest cluster of thatched cottages in Lancashire. In fact, it has a perfect village layout: a dignified church dedicated to St Cuthbert, two village pubs dedicated to the local gentry, cosy cottages for the villagers and nearby, the former home of the Lords of the Manor, Meols Hall.

I wandered through the curving streets and up the quiet alleyways of the village, admiring the whitewashed cottages and occasionally catching a glimpse of the flat open countryside that lies to the east. These much sought after residences, as the estate agents would say, were once the simple homes of fishermen, weavers and farmers. Shrimping and cockling employed most of the men until about two centuries ago when some locals turned to cotton weaving and later to silk weaving. A popular spot to rake in the cockles on the ebbing tide, was a sandbank off the coast at Lytham. Shrimps were netted from a horse drawn cart driven into the sea known as cart-shanking, or by boat-shanking or simply by putting, which involved using a large hand net. A century ago almost four hundred fishermen made their living around this coast but today only a handful remain.

*Churchtown: the largest cluster of thatched cottages in Lancashire remain in the village where Southport really began.*

"Well Edna, I've never seen anything so luvly."

"You're right Joan, breathtaking they are."

I was intrigued by these comments which I overheard coming from two elderly ladies. They were contentedly sitting in the sunshine in the Botanic Gardens at Churchtown, eating delicious looking ice cream cones. As I wandered up a pathway I soon became aware of the centre of their admiration: huge flowerbeds, still remaining from summer, spread out before me in a feast of spectacular colour. Reds, yellows, oranges and blues merged with a score of other subtle hues to produce an array which must be the envy of many an amateur gardener. I spent a pleasant hour, wandering among these shrubs and trees, watching the antics of the birds in the aviary and drinking tea in the conservatory tea-room. But when I decided to visit the museum it was almost too late:

"I'm sorry but we close in twenty minutes, but you might have time for a quick look around."

Deciding to miss the exhibition of Liverpool Porcelain I was directed upstairs to the Local History Room. Here I found a fascinating hoard of objects and curiosities. Coming together in a haphazard fashion, they vividly chart the growth of Southport from a windswept fishing village to a fashionable resort. Here I saw old photographs showing newly erected Victorian buildings, well dressed Edwardians sauntering in the sun and donkey carts riding over cobbled streets. A horn from 1869 was once used to warn shrimpers that fog was sweeping in and a portrait of a handsome young man turned out to be that of a local hero. John Perry Frederick Hooper was a member of Captain Scott's ill-fated expedition to the Antarctic. He was one of the lucky survivors who returned home, ending his days in Southport as the keeper of the Town Hall. But the saddest mementos relate to the tragic lifeboat disaster which I had learned of at Lytham. In forlorn remembrance stands the rowlock of the Eliza Fernley, a sou'wester and line used by the crew, and a lifebelt from the Mexico.

"We're closing now – sorry."

Reluctantly I left Churchtown.

## 5

I sat in the sunshine in one of the many public gardens at Southport, gazing along what is perhaps England's most impressive street and thinking from what an unlikely beginning this town began. For it was neither the gentry nor the middle-class who created Southport, but the miners of Wigan. They first came here towards the end of the 18th century by barge when a section of the Leeds-Liverpool canal had been completed which came within five miles of the coast. They were at first drawn by Churchtown's annual fair in August, which developed into an event known as Big Bathing Sunday. Simple accommodation was found with the cottagers at Churchtown, from which they would walk, or take a cart along the dunes for two miles to South Hawes. Here they would take to the water, for hydrotherapy had become the fashion, drink their ale and recuperate from fifty one weeks underground. In 1792 a local innkeeper from Churchtown named William 'Duke' Sutton, who was one of the village 'characters', decided to exploit the situation. He built a crude bathing hut from driftwood at South Hawes, then six years later a simple hotel. Many of the locals did not take his effort seriously, they nick-named it the Duke's Folly and then later, during a high spirited party the South Port Hotel, so Southport eventually it became. William Sutton had unwittingly become the founder of what was to become a high class resort, but he gained little financial reward, for he ended up in Lancaster jail for debt.

*A visitor reads the inscribed tablets at the end of Lord Street, Southport, which remember the founder of the town: the 'Old Duke'.*

When the High Sheriff of Lancashire, Bold Fleetwood Hesketh, moved to Meols Hall in 1797 his position attracted many visitors of rank. Some of these were pleasantly surprised by the attractive countryside which spread down to the sea: they decided to build new homes. These began to spring up along the rough lane which led from Churchtown to the beach, becoming first known as Lords Street, named after the two Lords who owned the land, then later shortened to Lord Street. So the town from its early beginnings developed in two separate ways: as a place of residence for the wealthy and as a holiday resort for the not so wealthy, which to a less marked degree it remains to this day.

Set in the balustrade at the southern end of the gardens which mark the beginning of Lord Street I found a series of inscribed tablets. These are a memorial to the Dukes Folly which stood nearby. Retracing the path the Wigan miners took two centuries ago it is incredible to think that this grand avenue of up-market stores, four-star hotels, ornate gardens and fine churches was once a sandy wasteland. I walked up a side street where donkey carts once passed and found a showroom displaying hand-built Morgan sports cars. Affluent elegance and refinement is at every corner, fine clothes, solid mahogany furniture, silverware and antiquarian books prevail. In the spacious Edwardian atmosphere of the Wayfarers Arcade is a faded sign which indicates that Parisian Novelties were once sold here. But today it is the bronze statue of local racehorse Red Rum, three times winner of the Grand National, which gets all the attention.

No buckets and spades, hamburger stalls or slot machines, dare intrude one inch into Lord Street and few are allowed on the sea front. To discover the holiday face of Southport I needed to walk down a side street to the Promenade, then beyond to the marine drive. A company formed by Peter Hesketh Fleetwood in 1835 began this development, he first built a sea wall and a marine promenade which was financed by a penny toll. There followed a rapid expansion which has left a superb legacy of Victorian buildings, gardens, pathways and a marine lake, all appropriately looked over by a statue of Queen Victoria. This once stood in the Municipal Gardens on Lord Street, but was moved to its present site in 1912. I learnt that Sefton Council together with the local business community have begun a Southport Seafront Strategy. Their aim is to restore and preserve these fine Victorian structures which are an important part of Southport's heritage.

A bracing salt breeze and the shrieking cry of gulls accompanied me on my walk to the end of the pier. The sun was reflecting brightly from the vast expanse of pale yellow sand, the slate grey sea finally making an appearance as I reached my goal. This pier was first opened in 1860 when it was 1200 yards long, but eight years later it was extended to 1460 yards, which made it the longest in the country. In 1933 a fire destroyed the Pier head which led to it being reconstructed and shortened, so today at 1200 yards, it has been relegated to become the second longest.

A band was playing a rousing march in the municipal gardens, Japanese, French and Polish visitors were collecting leaflets from the tourist office, and Lord Street was overflowing with affluent shoppers intent on parting with their money. I could almost see the ghost of the Old Duke, half grinning as he looked out from his shanty hotel along a sandy track saying, "I told them so . . ."

*Wayfarers Arcade*

*A Morgan sports car in a Southport Street, where donkey carts once took visitors to the sea.*

## 6

As I took the quiet lane at Mere Brow it was as if I had suddenly arrived in Lincolnshire. The fields seemed even larger and even flatter than those around Tarleton, they stretch to a far horizon where they meet the sky. Dark figures were bent here and there, taking up cabbages and leeks whose pungent aroma began to fill my car. It reminded me of those far-off days when school children reserved their autumn holidays to make extra pocket-money by going 'tatoe pickin', an event which disappeared when high-tech farm machinery arrived.

This land of solitary windmills and isolated farms is still referred to as Martin Mere, though the mere has long since drained away. The rich black earth which remains, covers an area of about twenty square miles, lying to the west of Rufford and Burscough Bridge. The curious freshwater lake which once lapped over these farmlands varied in size according to the season, but is said to have had a circumference of about eighteen miles. It drained into the sea at Crossens and into the River Douglas at Rufford, from which the latter derived its name for it was a ford over this drainage channel. There were plenty of fish in the shallow waters, but up to the Dissolution of the Monasteries only the Cannons of Burscough Priory were officially allowed to remove them. However in this rural marshland, where poaching was once a way of life, it is unlikely that the locals took much notice of such laws. At this time the mere was contained in a slight natural bowl with farms built around the rim. It is said that the surname Rimmer, which is common around Southport, was derived from this area..

In 1692 a proposal was made by Mr Fleetwood of Bank Hall to other owners of the mere, that a scheme should be devised to drain the water and reclaim the land. The incentive to do this was the rising population of Liverpool, who would provide a ready market for any vegetables which could be grown. A plan was accepted and work began on a drainage canal. It was twenty four feet wide and stretched for a mile and a half, linking the mere to the Ribble estuary. A pair of floodgates were built to prevent the sea entering the canal at high tide, but unfortunately they proved to be the weak point of the plan, for they were constantly being silted up with mud and sand.

For the next sixty years various methods of overcoming this choking up of the canal was tried, but with little success. In 1778 a Mr Eccleston obtained the services of Mr Gilbert, who was the designer of the Duke of Bridgewater's famous canal system, to see if he could solve the problem. He put forward a solution which involved a flushing action using the outgoing sea, to help to clear the channel. It also involved the construction of a hundred miles of extra draining ditches. These were dug out using an enormous plough pulled by a huge team of ten horses, and in 1784 the first few acres of this newly reclaimed land yielded a crop.

In 1813 the floodgates were swept away by a high tide, but these were quickly replaced by a mechanical valve system. This too was prone to becoming choked up, but new technology came to the rescue. In 1850 Sir Thomas Hesketh brought in a steam engine to pump away the water and the last remaining part of the mere was finally drained.

As I drove slowly across this fascinating terrain I noticed lonely by-roads named Curlew Lane, Crab Tree Lane and Sugar Stubbs Lane, which lead to the heart of these remote flatlands. It is easy to see why this area was once avoided by strangers, for one wrong step along these marshy paths could end in death in a cold black bog. Here smugglers, wreckers and priests, could remain for years in a hidden refuge. Martin Hall, which was once on the waters edge, is said to be one of the places which burnt a light in its window to guide illicit travellers. Legend tells us also, that it was in this secluded lake that Sir Belvidere tossed King Arthur's sword, Excalibur, which still remains hidden.

But it is to what is now known as the Martin Mere Wildfowl and Wetlands Centre, that most visitors come. Founded by the late Sir Peter Scott, who was the son of the famous Antarctic explorer, the reserve is now one of the best of its kind in England. Up to 132 different kinds of waterfowl feed among pools and in the fields, watched by twitchers whose cameras sport huge telephoto lenses. In wintertime a massive influx of geese and swans takes place, filling the orange skies with one magnificent chevron after another, all intent on getting free food and lodgings on the Lancashire Plain.

The lovely half-timbered Rufford Old Hall, which is administered by the National Trust, was once the home of the powerful Hesketh family. It was built in the early 15th century and became the centre for controlling these marshy lands. In 1580 a young actor named William Shakeshaft, better known as William Shakespeare, is said to have performed in the Great Hall.

*Rufford Old Hall*

I continued through Burscough, where the farm shops were selling potatoes at £2.50 a bag, eggs at 99p for two and a half dozen, and bright orange pumpkins for Hallowe'en. As I passed between the two octagonal gatehouses into Lathom Park a solitary jogger ran by, exercising in his lunchbreak from the nearby Pilkington Technology Centre.

I stopped at a boulder which lies alongside the pathway leading to Lathom Park Chapel. Known as Cromwell's Stone, a plaque told me it had been used during the Civil War for casting shot to break the siege of Lathom House. I ran my fingers over the two circular-ended holes which have been carved in its surface, in which molten lead had once been poured by men of the Model Army.

*Cromwell's Stone*

This lovely little Chapel, with its adjacent almshouses, deserves to be better known for it is one of the hidden gems of Lancashire. It was built to commemorate the good fortune that the decisive Battle of Bosworth Field brought to Lord Stanley, who was created the first Earl of Derby for supporting the winning side. In was in August 1485, that King Richard III faced his opponent, Henry, Earl of Richmond, close to the Leicestershire village of Market Bosworth. Richard had 12,000 soldiers, whilst Henry had only half that number, so whoever gained the strong support of the powerful Lord Stanley would reap victory. Richard had taken Stanley's son as a hostage to try to force his hand, so Stanley stood aloof during the fighting. But Richard, reputedly hated as a cruel tyrant, was eventually killed. Stanley then showing his true allegiance, placed the Crown of England on the head of Henry VII, who became the first king of the House of Tudor.

It was in 1500 that the second Earl of Derby had this secluded chapel consecrated, dedicating it to St John-the-Divine. The architecture contains some original features, with work of Georgian and Victorian origin. Of particular interest is the marvellous carved screen and lectern which came from Burscough Priory; the damage sustained by the bullets of the Civil War can still be seen. When the building was first erected it served as both a chantry and as a church for tenants who worked on what was the Earl of Derby's estate. In the eight almshouses lived the bede-men who would pray in the chapel, administered by a priest who lived nearby.

*Lathom Chapel and Almshouses.*

I walked back down the pathway, looking across a field to where cows were grazing contentedly, disturbed only by the raucous chatter of magpies. On a small green hill, overlooked by sombre skies, I could see the neglected ruins of the third Lathom House. This was built during the 17th Century on the site of the most tragic house in England; a place of romance, tears and bloodshed.

Lord Strange, who was to become the 7th Earl of Derby, was married in July 1626 at The Hague to Charlotte de la Tremoille, who came from a wealthy french family. The couple came to England the next month to take up residence here at Lathom House where they lived happily for the next sixteen years. The only problems they seem to have had were financial ones created by running such a large estate. In the middle of the last century a large number of letters written by Lord Strange's wife to her mother and sister-in-law were found in a cellar in France and they give a fascinating glimpse into this early part of their married life.

In 1642 Lord Strange's father died and he inherited the title and the estates. At this time also, the troubles which Charles I had been having with parliament were reaching a climax and armed conflict seemed inevitable. The Earl raised 3000 men from his estates and he took them to York to meet the King. After persuading Charles to raise his standard at Warrington he immediately returned to Lancashire to prepare for the event. However, the Earl had many enemies among the Royalist ranks who conspired against him. They convinced the King that he could not be trusted, so Charles decided to raise his standard at Nottingham instead of Warrington, and to relieve him of the Lieutenancy of Chester and North Wales.

This came as a great blow to Derby, because at heart he was a fervent Royalist. But the Parliamentarians, having heard of the rift, sent a messenger asking him to join their ranks. This he refused to do, and to try to re-establish his position with the King he continued to muster men from his estate. He also took the precaution of fortifying his home at Lathom and stocking up with provisions.

Still not really trusting Derby, Charles ordered him to sail to the Isle of Man on the pretence of preventing it falling to Cromwell's forces. Derby realized this was just a ploy to get him out of the way, but had he not conformed to it he would have been labelled an enemy. But his absence was seized upon by the parliamentary army; the Governor of Manchester, a Mr Holland, immediately sent a message to Lady Derby asking her to surrender Lathom House. She replied that 'it did not suit her to either humbly to give up her house or to purchase repose at the price of honour'. This was the beginning of the haggling which she was able to carry on for seven months before the siege really began. It cleverly allowed her to build up forces within the house and to stockpile more food and supplies, hoping that her husband would meanwhile return.

Finally time ran out, Sir Thomas Fairfax marched to Lathom with 3000 soldiers and ordered her to surrender. She received two officers into her home, but while refusing their terms she made sure they saw her formidable forces and arms, a tactic aimed at undermining their confidence. The siege then began in earnest, after fourteen days she again refused to give in. Fairfax, frustrated, left the scene for another 'more important' place of war, leaving the battle to other officers. The soldiers became greatly harassed for the defenders were able to secretly escape from the house, kill unsuspecting Roundheads, then return to the security of their fortress.

Colonel Rigby, who eventually took command of the soldiers, was convinced success would come when he introduced a giant mortar. This at first caused the defenders some alarm, but under the cover of darkness they managed to capture it, which led to great elation. This famous siege lasted for four months until the Earl returned from the Isle of Man with his reputation restored. He was joined by Prince Rupert, head of the King's forces, which caused Rigby's men to flee. The Earl and the Prince jubilantly marched into this green parkland to greet the Countess, proudly sporting the colours of a Roundhead regiment they had captured.

Sadly, tragedy was to quickly follow this profound moment of triumph. During the next year whilst the couple were away, the house was again attacked but this time it was forced to surrender. It was demolished and burnt, for it had been a symbol which Cromwell could not tolerate. Seven years later after the disastrous Battle of Worcester at which Charles II was lucky to escape with his life, the Earl was captured and taken to Chester. There he was tried, sentenced to death, then beheaded in Churchgate at Bolton.

But the heroine of Lathom House was never forgotten. Her exploits were immortalised by Sir Walter Scott in his novel, Peveril of the Peak, and her life and letters are recorded in *The Lady of Lathom* which was written by Madame Guizot de Witt.

## 7

I found that Ormskirk has two aspects which make it particularly inviting to strangers: the local people are unusually friendly and the town is an easy place to explore. Sitting inside a cafe a middle aged man nodded 'hello' and immediately began to converse, walking down the street a young woman smiled and said 'Good morning'. All around the town I was made to feel that instead of having arrived just half an hour ago I had lived there all my life. Perhaps this is due to the Celtic influence, for I am told that more than a little Irish blood flows in the veins of many of the residents.

*Ormskirk: The Town Crier and his assistant welcome visitors to the town.*

At the centre of the town is a tall square clock tower which is still referred to as the market cross, which it has replaced. It was built in 1875 by the orders of the medieval Court Leet which had survived up till this time. Around this focal point the colourful street market, happily free from traffic, lives on. It all began in 1286 when King Edward I granted a market charter to the Canons of Burscough Priory.

The four main thoroughfares of Ormskirk: Moor Street, Burscough Street, Aughton Street and Church Street, all converge at the clock tower and each is worthy of exploration. Around the tower itself followers of Animal Rights, surrounded by a weary eyed bulldog, a sleeping Alsatian and a frisky poodle, were collecting money. Saturday shoppers, enjoying the warm sunshine, meandered along the rows of market stalls. A chubby lady was looking with disappointment at a sweater she dearly wanted but which was too small, while a child was skilfully directed away from a toy-stall which he had not even seen.

In Burscough Street, which is part of the ancient highway that once linked Preston and Liverpool, I noticed one of a number of inviting alleyways is curiously named Mystic Mews. Close by is the Buck i' th' Vine, one of Ormkskirk's oldest coaching inns. Here travellers who had crossed the icy, windswept plain, which was often a black quagmire in wintertime, could find much welcomed food and warmth. At one time it boasted its own malt house and a theatre complete with minstrels gallery.

At the end of Moor Street, hemmed in disrespectfully by tall traffic signals, I discovered a ghost-like statue of Benjamin Disraeli who became Lord Beaconsfield. I learnt that it had been purchased second hand in 1884 by the Ormskirk Primrose League, from another Lancashire town. I wonder who this former prime minister had upset, for having once erected a statue to him, they were then happy to sell it off?

Suddenly the bells of Ormskirk Parish Church began to loudly boom out over the rooftops of the town; there was about to be a wedding, so I decided to go and watch. Joining the crowd that had gathered outside the Plough pub which faces the church, I could see a notice which read, with ecclesiastical humour: Thou Shalt Not Even Think Of Parking Here. Shimmering in the bright sunshine and framed in a cloudless blue sky, this sturdy historic building looked particularly impressive. It is said to be one of only three churches in England which possess both a steeple and a tower; the latter was added about 1540 when it acquired the bells of Burscough Priory. Among the 7,000 bodies which are said to lie beneath the church floor, are the remains of the ill-fated seventh Earl of Derby. After he was beheaded at Bolton in 1651 his body was placed here in a short coffin with his head alongside, in a separate casket.

My daydreaming about the history of the church was disturbed by a movement from the pub door, then out dashed the bridegroom and the best man who had been seeking some last minute liquid courage. No sooner had they entered the church than two gleaming white Rolls Royces arrived with four bridesmaids. The two older girls wore splendid turquoise crinolines of satin and the younger two wore white. Anxious relatives rushed forward to direct them into the churchyard. The photographer began to position them with a professional eye, beneath the branches of an overhanging tree, then both the video and still cameras began to roll.

Five minutes later, marked by a loud cheer from the crowd, the big moment came with the arrival of the bride. Looking radiant, as all brides are, in a traditional white dress of glittering diamante, she was transfixed by the photographer halfway out of the Rolls while he took his important picture. She then stood up, looking across to the crowd, she waved and smiled, then began the short walk on the arm of her father to the church door and an unknown future. She is the most recent of a chain of young girls who have been walking with apprehension up to this same church altar for at least six centuries.

## *8*

My journey now continued westwards. When I crossed the Leeds and Liverpool Canal at Downholland Cross the roar of traffic was left behind for I was entering the rural seclusion of Downholland Moss. Like Martin Mere, this is a flat landscape dotted here and there with thatched-cottages and secluded farms. Shrieking gulls were feeding in large flocks on the thick black earth which the plough had recently uncovered, while other fields remained pale yellow with the stubble of last season's crop. Few hedgerows break the expanse of this sweeping land, instead more discreet ditches criss-cross the fields, providing a hiding place for coot and mallard.

It is surprising to discover that this patchwork of freckled fields almost developed into a Lancashire Texas, for this is oil country! As long ago as the early 17th century the locals were well aware of its existence, for Camden recorded that they were using the oil-impregnated turf for both fuel and light. But it was after oil nationalisation came into force in 1934 that the search for our own supply of black gold really got underway in what was known confidently as the Formby Field. The first drilling proved disappointing, but on the second attempt a rich flow of the liquid was brought to the surface. It was hoped that a huge oil field might lie hidden beneath the earth, but this proved not to be the case. However, over a period of thirty years, sixty wells were sunk from which almost three million gallons of the precious liquid was extracted. In the mid-sixties the venture finally ended, but it now continues in Liverpool Bay. The Hamilton Oil Company are in the process of constructing platforms and pipelines to extract both gas and oil from four off-shore fields.

*Lancashire's flat lands create a landscape of wide skies and distant horizons.*

I parked my car in the centre of Formby and walked down the wide avenue of modern shops in which the ladies of Great Altcar, Hightown and Ince Blundell were busily chatting. For although there are around 30,000 people living in what is now a town, Formby is still at heart a village. In pre-war days it was a quiet place of small cottages, family-run shops and ancient farms. It was in the thatch of one of these homes that a Victorian workman uncovered a pigs bladder containing a coin hoard. It had lain unnoticed for over two centuries and was found to contain shillings from the time of Elizabeth I, James I and Charles I. But by local standards this is just yesterday, for this land where sea, marsh and forest meet, is really Viking country. They came here in their longboats from Scandinavia during the 10th Century to settle in what the Domesday Book records as Fornebei. This forges a link with Oslo Airport, for the two have almost identical names.

By more good luck that confident navigation, for signposts are in short supply around Formby, I reached Lifeboat Road which leads down to the sea. In a bumpy car-park which shelters beneath the sand dunes an ice-cream van waited in anxious anticipation for an influx of visitors, only three cars had so far arrived. In a corner of the car-park a poster, aimed at the many naturalists who come to Formby, told of a forthcoming lecture by a bat expert named Phil Richardson.

I strolled up a wide path which ascends the sand dunes till at last I reached a high-point which reveals the glinting silver sea. This marvellous unspoilt stretch of duneland is a rarity in Britain, only a handful of similar places now remain. A series of nature reserves, which link woodlands of Scots Pines to the dunes, stretch from Hightown to Southport. This unusual terrain is home to many types of animal and plant life which is rarely found elsewhere. These include sand lizards, natterjack toads, a continental variety of red squirrel, together with such plants as the Dune Helleborine and the Round Leafed Wintergreen.

I walked for an hour along this unique sandy wilderness, which creates a feeling of desert-island isolation. It seemed quite unbelievable that the bustle of Liverpool is only ten miles away. With a chill wind blowing in my face I watched the dark form of container ships glide like ghosts across the sea, I heard the cry of gulls fighting for food along the shoreline and I heard the laughter of children who were ignoring the cold. I turned my back on the wind and the sea, walking to the shelter of the dunes I was thinking of the warmth that hopefully awaited me in Lancashire's oldest pub.

Soon I was sitting in one of the small rooms of the Scotch Piper Inn at Lydiate, drinking a half pint of bitter in front of a roaring coal fire. This amazing building was here in 1320 when the Plantagenet kings still ruled England, men were sitting here drinking ale when news of the battles of Crecy and Agincourt arrived. Their descendants would joke about King Harry and his six wives, they would argue about the end of the monasteries and live in hope when the first Elizabeth came to the throne. For almost five hundred years, up till 1945, the Moorcroft family were the innkeepers. In 1715 a wounded Highlander took refuge here after the disastrous Jacobite Rebellion and with compassion, which is a normal part of life in Merseyside, the family tended his injuries. The handsome Scot, which I am sure he must have been, fell in love with their daughter. The couple were later married, which led to the inn name being changed from the Royal Oak to the Scotch Piper as a permanent reminder of the colourful event.

*The Scotch Piper, Lydiate.*

"How much is coal a bag now, Charlie?" a plump woman asked the landlord as he stoked up the fire.

"It's about £5.50. Too cheap really."

His reply brought laughter to the room, which led all of Charlie's customers to discuss the merits of the open fire. We talked of the unequalled warmth of coal, of dancing firelight and sadly, of Lancashire's last coal-mine that had recently closed. Our conversation was then halted by the sound of a small motor-coach which had turned into the car park: a party of American tourists had arrived.

I stood at the back of the group as the landlord's wife gave the visitors a talk about the history of the pub. She told how the inn is built around a massive tree which supports parts of the roof and how the thatch could be a fire hazard. Two fires have occurred at the inn in recent years, but it is much safer now, being covered with the long lasting Norfolk Reed. Smiles came when she told of the toilet which once stood outside, for it had twin seats, side by side!

# CHAPTER SEVEN

# LYDIATE TO ASHTON-UNDER-LYNE

I reach the Mersey, explore Liverpool's waterfront, see the Liver Birds and two cathedrals, then learn about a giant. In St Helens I visit the church of Three Saints, then I stand on the spot where Manchester began. I look at Lowry's masterpieces in Salford, then end in the hometown of Britain's best-loved travel writer.

## 1

The residents of Maghull were walking fast along the pavements and dashing for shelter inside any convenient shop, for a ridge of low pressure had brought with it a bitter cold wind. This small residential town, which was known at the time of the Conquest as Magele, has happily managed to keep independent from the creeping suburbs of Liverpool. Built on rising ground above the little River Alt it stands defiant, surrounded by rich flat fields which sweep outwards to Rainford, Ormskirk, Formby and Crosby. But its proudest boast is that it gave the world its greatest horse race, for it is here, not Aintree, where the Grand National began.

It was in 1837, the year in which Queen Victoria came to the throne, that the race was first run. A local publican named William Lynn, organised the event which was then called the Liverpool Steeplechase. Two years later the race was moved to Aintree from which it has developed into the colourful spectacle of today, which attracts visitors from all over the world. During the first race at Aintree Captain Becher fell off his horse at one of the jumps and ended up in the water, which resulted in the famous Becher's Brook.

The race, which covers a distance of 4 miles and 856 yards, contains thirty jumps and is run in March or April. Except for the war years of 1916-18 and 1941-45, when it was moved to Gatwick, it has remained at Aintree. Among the many great horses which have become part of the Aintree legend are Grundan who romped home in a blizzard in 1901, Tipperary Tim who was the only finisher in 1929 and Devon Loch who collapsed just 100 yards from the winning post in 1956. But appropriately, it is that marvellous Lancashire horse, Red Rum, which will always be associated with the excitement of the event. He won a record three times, in 1973, 1974 and 1976 and came second in 1975 and 1976.

The most disappointing year for the Grand National was 1993, when a series of false starts which followed problems with the starting tape resulted in the race being abandoned. But a new starting gate, which has been developed by the Jockey Club, is to be employed at future races. This new gate is said to raise the tape five times faster than the old system.

I continued my journey along the busy A59 trunk road which was full of heavy lorries and endless hold-ups at traffic signals, the type of road which is sadly typical of the approach to all major cities. After passing through Walton, Anfield and Everton, I at last reached the centre of Liverpool, to happily discover a free car park at the Albert Dock.

*Liverpool: this impressive vaterfront, with its legendary Mersey ferries, is regarded with affection by sailors from all over the world.*

Muffled in a heavy coat with a woolly hat pulled down over my ears I stood at the Pier Head, watching the sight which is guaranteed to bring a lump to the throats of all exiled Liverpudlians, the ferry which crosses the Mersey. No other river in Britain is held in such affection as this, for together with the

Liver Birds it is the symbol of not so much a city, but of a way of life. The Mersey looked almost savage in the strong chill wind, its metallic grey waves being turned to silver by the bright sunlight as they bounced off the stone wharf. Although the sky was clear and blue, the buildings and cranes of Birkenhead, which lie on the opposite bank, were void of detail. Bathed in hazy shades of purple, russet and blue-black they looked unreal, as if they were part of an impressionist painting.

This is a boundary river, for 'Maerse', from which its name is derived, once separated Northumbria from Mercia. It rises in Cheshire above Stalybridge, then is joined by a host of tributaries which include, the Irwell, Tame, Medlock, Weaver and Bollin. The main reason that Liverpool developed into a great port is because of the shape of the river, for it widens from one mile at Pier Head to three miles up-river at Upper Pool. This means that the outgoing tide, together with the river water, has to pour through a narrow strait. This rush of water flushes away any silt and produces a permanent deep estuary which is never shallower than fifty feet, creating an ideal natural dock.

*The mythical Liver Birds, based on a cormorant with a sprig of laver in its beak, has become the symbol of Liverpool.*

The relationship which Liverpudlians have with their river can be traced back to 1150 when the first ferries began operating, having been organised by the Benedictine Monks of Birkenhead Priory. This service was officially recognised in 1330 when Edward III gave the Prior a charter allowing him to carry passengers and charge a payment. After the Dissolution of the Monasteries these rights were bought by Ralph Worsley, then over the next three centuries they had a series of owners until 1842 when they were purchased by Birkenhead Council. In 1886 a rail tunnel was built beneath the river which took business from the ferry service, but it continued carrying both vehicles and passengers until 1934 when the first road tunnel was opened. This marvellous engineering feat named Queensway, was the longest underwater tunnel in the world, and a second tunnel, Kingsway, was opened in 1971. The Mersey's most famous two ferry boats are the Royal Iris and the Royal Daffodil. The prefix Royal was first added to the name of two earlier boats as a reward, for they were used to transport troops from Belgium during the First World War.

At the time of the Conquest this corner of the Mersey was a quiet backwater, being part of a series of rural manors which were given to lesser knights. However by the beginning of the 13th Century, due to the wars in Ireland, its strategic position had become recognised. King John granted Liverpool a charter in 1207 and used the small settlement as an embarkation point for his troops and their supplies. Although it was now known as a port, being thought worthy of a visit by Edward II in 1323, its growth was slow over the next three centuries. By the time of the Stuarts only a thousand people lived here, but this had grown four fold by the end of the 17th century.

But it was the 18th Century which brought the golden years to Liverpool, the highly lucrative American trade was opening up with fortunes to be made. Wealthy merchants took goods made in Lancashire to West Africa, which they exchanged for slaves. This human cargo was then transported to Virginia and the West Indies to fill the needs of the plantation owners. The vessels then returned to Liverpool laden with rum, sugar and cotton, having taken a year for the round trip. The end of this horrific slave trade came in 1838, but by this time Liverpool had become well established as a flourishing port for other goods. The canal system provided an inland link to the manufacturing centres of both Lancashire and Yorkshire, to which was added the world's first passenger railway which was opened in 1830. It was at the Rainhill Trials, which had been held to choose the best locomotive for the new line, that Liverpool's MP, William Huskisson was sadly killed. In his eagerness to greet the Duke of Wellington he walked onto the track and was run over by George Stephenson's Rocket.

I turned from the Mersey to look at the impressive Liver building which was glinting white in the bright sunlight, its famous Liver Birds firmly secured by cables. It was erected in 1911 by the Royal Liver Friendly Society, its design is said to have been influenced by the skyscrapers of Chicago. The birds, which are ornately carved cormorants, hold a sprig of laver in their beaks. They are Liverpool's emblem which was derived from the city seal and are said to bring good luck to sailors. Liverpudlians will tell you that the female Liver Bird is facing the sea awaiting the sailors return, while the male bird is looking inland to see if the pubs are open! Like the ravens at the Tower of London, if the Liver Birds fly away then disaster will come to the city.

On this impressive water front I stopped to read two of Liverpool's saddest memorials. Close to Pier Head is recorded on metal plates the names of the 1,930 local men who died at sea in the Battle of the Atlantic. Then adjacent to the Liver Building I looked at a pillar of white granite known as the Memorial to the Engine-Room Workers which remembers the 1300 Liverpool men who died when the *Titanic* sank in 1912. It is also a reminder of the thousands of Lancastrians who for generations sailed from Liverpool in the *Mauretania, Aquitania,* the *Empress of Britain* and many more of our finest liners.

Away from the exposed river I was sheltered from the biting cold wind, and was able to continue my stroll around the city in relative comfort. Here gracious Georgian and Victorian buildings which mingle with the architecture of today, look over the bustle of sophisticated Liverpudlians hurrying to offices and shops. Yet hidden up alleyways and behind ornate frontages lie vestiges of Liverpool's past: warehouses, pubs and houses once known by men who talked of storms in the China Sea, going round the Horn or making a fortune in the Yukon.

Walking along Castle Street I was stopped by a young man from the Bible and Gospel Trust who gave me a pamphlet which proclaimed the Word of God. Of course he would be well received in Liverpool, for it is a city renowned for religious tolerance and unity. This is epitomised by the closeness of the Anglican Bishop Sheppard and Roman Catholic Archbishop Warlock who ceaselessly work together to improve life in the city..

After strolling around the Walker Art Gallery, which houses a breathtaking collection of old masters, I continued my exploration by visiting Liverpool's two contrasting cathedrals. As if to highlight their religious tolerance, I discovered that the Roman Catholic Cathedral had been designed by a Protestant and the Protestant Cathedral designed by a Catholic! Known affectionately as Paddy's Wigwam or the Mersey Funnel, the Metropolitan Cathedral of Christ the King was consecrated in 1967. It was designed by Sir

Frederick Gibberd who won a competition to produce a building which would hold 3,000 people and could be built in ten years. Of an ultra modern design its shape is based on a concrete ribbed cone, surmounted by a cylinder of magnificent stained glass with a filigree of the Crown of Thorns.

The beautiful Anglican Cathedral which stands in splendid contrast, was designed by the twenty-two-year-old Sir Giles Gilbert Scott at the turn of the century and it became his life's work. It is a lofty Gothic building constructed from warm red sandstone with towering arches and delicate stained glass windows. Following the death of Scott in 1960 it was completed by his successor, Frederick Thomas, and opened by the Queen in 1978. It now ranks as the world's fifth largest cathedral and was the first Anglican Cathedral to be built in the north since the Reformation. The huge 321 feet high tower which is one of Liverpool's great landmarks, houses Europe's heaviest set of bells which were bought by Samuel Vestey who founded Dewhurst Butchers. Among its many memorials is one that remembers a recent tragedy, the horrific Hillsborough Football Disaster in which 95 people died in 1989.

Returning once more to the windy waterfront I began my exploration of the restored Albert Dock complex which has become the centre-piece of Liverpool's modern image. Here in elegant splendour, fine shops which sell prints, designer clothes, food, books and a thousand other items to tempt the visitor, line the same stone wharfs at which sailing ships once unloaded their cargoes. These impressive warehouses and docks were designed by Jesse Hartley, the talented Victorian engineer, and opened by Prince Albert in 1846. As well as shops and cafes, the cosmopolitan crowds are drawn to the Maritime Museum, the Tate Gallery and of course The Beatles Story.

Remembering the swinging sixties I half expected to find myself wedged in by a crowd of screaming teenagers when I visited the Beatles gift shop. But of course, those girls who once fainted at the mention of John, Paul, George and Ringo are now, sadly, approaching middle age. So it was a more demure type of visitor than I expected, who was purchasing Beatles rock, Beatles key-rings, Beatles postcards and of course nostalgic CDs of She Loves You and I Wanna Hold Your Hand. But this fine exhibition is a forceful reminder of the four local lads who started playing in the Cavern Club, then in a few short years took the show business world by storm. Of course they had been born into a show-business community, for Liverpool has produced more such talent than any other city. Great names such as Tommy Handley, Arthur Askey, Ken Dodd, Jimmy Tarbuck, and Cilla Black are among the many Liverpudlians that have become show-business superstars.

However, it is football that ranks as the city's biggest attraction for a quarter of all Liverpudlians are football supporters. Everton, which began as St Domingo's Church Sunday School club in 1878, play at Goodison Park. While their rivals, Liverpool FC, who started out as almost entirely a team of Scotsmen, play at legendary Anfield Road. Among the unforgettable characters who are forever associated with these great teams are Liverpool's manager Bill Shankley and one of Everton's finest players, Dixie Dean.

Before leaving the city I decided to find out why the locals are so often referred to as Scousers. It seems that the name is derived from a type of stew which was popular with sailors from Scandinavia. This meal, which was made up of various vegetables and meat, was known as lob-scouse. The seamen from Liverpool became so partial to this dish that it eventually became used as their nickname and is now applied to any Liverpudlian.

## 2

My journey continued inland, following the northern bank of the Mersey past the airport where I caught a glimpse of ancient Speke Hall which lies almost on the runway. This half-timbered Tudor manor house, which was built by the Norris family, has miraculously managed to survive in an expanding city hungry for land. It was constructed around a central courtyard in which grow two magnificent yew trees known as Adam and Eve. This was once a wild and isolated spot which, during penal times, was a perfect hiding place for Roman Catholic priests who had newly arrived in England by boat.

Less than three miles from the airport in a green oasis, I discovered Hale, a delightful village full of thatched cottages in which once lived a giant. In St. Mary's churchyard is the resting place of John Middleton, a man who is reputed to have grown to a height of nine feet and three inches, and whose hands measured seventeen inches across. The cottage where he was born in 1578 still stands and the local pub sign remembers him as the Child of Hale.

A local landowner, Sir Gilbert Ireland, sent him down to London to the court of James I to fight the King's champion. He arrived in the city to the admiration of the gentry, for he was dressed in a fine doublet of white and red, with flowered breeches. However, when he easily beat his opponent this did not go down well, so he was given a £20 prize and sent quickly home. On his way back to Lancashire he was entertained by students from Oxford University who had his portrait painted for their college library. He died in 1623 at the age of 45, but legends about his exploits are still told locally, and a full size painting of him can be seen in Speke Hall.

From the church I wandered down a path to the sandstone banks of the

Mersey, following in the steps of Prince Rupert who led the King's forces during the Civil War. When he came this way in 1644 to ford the river into Cheshire, he must have been in a depressed state of mind. His army had just been defeated at the crucial Battle of Marston Moor, near York, which meant that the Royalist cause in the north had been lost. Earlier in the month a bloody battle had taken place at Liverpool Castle when around 1500 people had been killed. Anyone who wishes to see what this castle looked like can see a replica which was built by the soap magnate, Lord Leverhulme. However, it stands not on Merseyside but in the magnificent countryside of the West Pennine Moors, at Rivington.

Looking across the choppy waters of the river I could see the rooftops of Runcorn on the opposite bank which rise above what is known locally as the Big Ditch, the Manchester Ship Canal. With Victorian enthusiasm this mammoth scheme to allow ships to bring their cargoes direct to Manchester and Salford, was begun in 1887. The first ship passed along this 35 miles long waterway in 1894 and they continued to come in huge numbers until the mid-fifties. Now, most ships only come up to Ellesmere Port and Runcorn, with the upper reaches being developed for leisure activities.

### 3

As I drove through Prescot on my way to St Helens to look at the Church of Three Saints, I began to ponder on the reason behind Lancashire's strong Catholic allegiance. It is said that a quarter of England's four million Catholics live within the old boundary of Lancashire and it can boast seven saints. Of course historical evidence excavated from Manchester's Roman fort has proved that Christianity got a firm foothold in the area at a very early date. A piece of pottery with a Christian cryptogram inscribed upon it was found in 1978. This dates from AD 170 to 175, making it Britain's earliest Christian relic.

So it would seem that Christianity, which had first appeared in Lancashire during the Roman occupation, managed to survive the successive invasions of Saxons and Vikings, and rose to new heights after the Conquest. However, when Henry VIII began to reform the church in the early 16th Century, Lancashire grew to become the centre of Catholic resistance. The Fylde priest, William Allen, who was regarded as a traitor by the authorities, founded a seminary for English priests at Douai. Many of these newly trained priests originated from Lancashire, so the flame of Catholicism was kept burning from abroad until more tolerant times arrived. But it was the massive influx of immigrant workers from Ireland during the last century which boosted the Catholic population to today's large numbers. These families came here to escape from famine and poverty, and their descendants can be found in most Lancashire towns.

It was in the church of St Anne's at Sutton that I discovered yet more evidence of this great Christian tradition. Here, in a quiet chapel lies the body of Father Ignatius Spencer, great-great grand uncle of Lady Diana; Blessed Dominic Barberi, a prospective Patron Saint of England; and Mother Joseph Prout, foundress of the Sisters of the Cross and Passion. This unlikely trio, the aristocrat, the Italian peasant and the Shropshire girl, together represent the re-birth of Christian unity in Britain.

George Spencer, later Ignatius, was born in 1799 in Admiralty House, London. His father was the second Earl Spencer and his grandfather was Earl Lucan. His mother, Lavinia, was regarded as a great beauty of her day, having sat many times as a model for Sir Joshua Reynolds. She was described by a contemporary as 'a charming woman who, with sense and spirit, has the playfulness of a child.'

George, who was the youngest of seven children, grew up at the family estate, Althorp. He took the traditional path by attending Eton and Cambridge, followed by the Grand Tour. Then, as was a common practice at this time for the younger sons of the aristocracy, he entered the Church of England. For the next five years he pursued his religious role, but deep inside he was beginning to have grave doubts about his true vocation. Finally, in 1830, he dropped the bombshell that he intended to become a Roman Catholic. This shocked the English establishment who immediately began to shun him. His aristocratic family were very embarrassed, but they stood by him and were to provide him with financial support for the rest of his life. To escape the limelight he departed for Rome where he began to study for the priesthood, here he came under the influence of the second member of the trio, Dominic Barberi.

In complete contrast to the aristocratic George Spencer, Dominic Barberi was the son of an Italian peasant farmer who had been born in 1792 at Pallanzana, a hamlet near Viterbo. When young he was described as being a plain, uneducated youth who walked and talked in an ungainly fashion. Having no strong religious feelings he was on the point of marrying when he suddenly began to have a series of supernatural experiences. Voices told him that he must go out and preach to many peoples, and at the same time he was filled with an intense love for England, a country he knew nothing about. But this event quickly changed his entire life for he found he now had great academic ability. In a short time he became a brilliant scholar, then he went on to become a Passionist Brother and one of Italy's most imminent professors.

When George Spencer began his training in Rome the brilliant Dominic Barberi was one of his teachers and the pair became great friends. After his ordination in 1832, Spencer returned to England to begin his work among the poor of West Bromwich in the Midlands. Eight years later he was joined by Dominic Barberi, who opened the first Passionist Monastery in Britain. Eventually Spencer decided he too would join the Passionist order, which led to his new name, Ignatius.

The two men worked tirelessly in the squalor of Victorian England, fighting poverty and disease they brought hope to the starving casualties of the Industrial Revolution. By their example, other like-minded people joined them including the third member of the trio, Elizabeth Prout. She left her comfortable Shropshire home to begin work in the terrible slums of Manchester. Other women came to help her, which led to the founding of a new religious order, the Sisters of Cross and Passion. Elizabeth, now known as Mother Mary Joseph, became their leader.

Dominic Barberi, after encountering many initial set-backs in his early years in England, became recognised by his contemporaries as a man of unique compassion and holiness. One of his greatest moments came when he received John Henry (later, Cardinal) Newman into the Catholic church. Following his death in 1849 he was succeeded by Ignatius Spencer as Superior of the Passionist Order, and then later as the director of the newly formed community of nuns. This was a difficult task, reconciling the conflicts of the women, organising financial aid and controlling their work among the poor.

After eventually receiving official approval from Rome, he established the motherhouse here at Sutton and today the community has spread throughout Europe, America and Africa. Ignatius Spencer continued to fight to improve the terrible conditions which prevailed at the time, becoming in great demand as a sincere preacher. He was one of the first holy men to preach the futility of disunity between religious groups, working tirelessly for reconciliation. In October 1864, after completing a mission at Castairs, he suffered a heart attack. The man who had been born an aristocrat died, like many of those to whom he preached, penniless and alone in a roadside ditch.

I stood beside the graves of the three friends who once worked together and are now revered together, for many believe they should be elevated to sainthood. Then before leaving the serenity of this impressive shrine I took a final look at the superb stained glass window which shows Ignatius Spencer with a remarkable Churchillian profile. Of course this should be no surprise, for as well as being related to Princess Diana, he was the great-uncle of Sir Winston Churchill.

## 4

On a cool October morning, under a sky of pale grey, I went to see the place where Manchester began. I stood on the same spot on which the great Roman General, Julius Agricola, once stood around 79 AD as he probably deliberated on which site to choose for his new military station. Here he would have walked along a windswept sandstone ridge, looked down at a small meandering river which we now call the Medlock, then conferred with his officers. Another quick glance around to confirm what his instinct already knew, then pointing to a rounded high-point, he would have perhaps said, "Here, Mamucium", which means 'a breast-shaped hill', and the seed of one of the world's great cities was sown.

What was once the Roman settlement lies adjacent to the White Lion Pub on Liverpool Road at Castlefield, which boasts Britain's first Urban Heritage Park. Here I looked at the foundations which outline Manchester's very first buildings, I walked along green lawns which were once defensive ditches and I saw the impressive North Gate which has been re-built on the original site.

The fort, which was originally constructed of turf and timber, then later re-built in stone, stood at an important crossroads. Chester lay to the west, York to the east, with other links to Ribchester and Buxton. It grew in size until a garrison of 500 soldiers were housed here. An altar found on the site reveals that some of these men came from Austria and that their centurion was named Lucius Senecianius Martius. A civilian settlement, known as a Vicus, also sprang up to supply the needs of the military personnel. This became a large village of around two thousand people and was occupied for some time after the fort was abandoned in 410 AD. However, this Vicus eventually became unoccupied too, and together with the fort it once served, returned its tumbled stones to the earth. But even a millenium later, when the site had become a woodland where deer roamed, it was still remembered as the Castle-in-the-Field.

It was not until the 18th century that Castlefield returned once more to prominence, for here that engineering genius, James Brindley, brought Britain's first canal. It was constructed to carry coal from the Duke of Bridgewater's mines at Worsley, to satisfy the needs of a town which was growing into a city. Nearby, in what is now the splendid Museum of Science and Industry, was built another first, the world's oldest passenger railway station which was opened in 1830. Of course Manchester can boast a host of other 'firsts'. These include the first Rolls Royce car which was produced here in 1903, the first splitting of the atom by Rutherford in 1918, the first non-stop flight across the Atlantic by Alcock and Brown in 1918 and the world's first stored-programme computer which was produced at Manchester University in 1948.

*Castlefield, now in modern Manchester.*

Looking over the renovated canal wharf, in which a brightly painted barge was anchored, I could see the Granada Television Studios in which the ever-popular Lancashire drama, Coronation Street, is produced. This too holds a record as Britain's longest running TV serial, for it began in December 1960.

Before continuing my walk around the city I escaped to the green oasis of what was once St John's church, a building that was taken down in 1931. Here, an inscribed cross remembers William Marsden who lies buried in the graveyard. Although probably unknown to most of us, he deserves our thanks for he was instrumental in bringing about the Saturday half-day holiday, at a time when everyone worked six days each week.

I walked up Quay Street, passing the Opera House at which *The Phantom of the Opera* was appropriately being performed, to reach the bustle of the city centre. Stopping outside the home of the Hallé Orchestra, The Free Trade Hall, I read a plaque which tells how the horrific Peterloo Massacre took place on the site. In August 1819 a large crowd gathered on what at this time was an open field, to discuss parliamentary reform. The meeting was judged to be illegal by the local magistrates, who were watching from a house in Mount Street. They were guarded by 300 special constables, together with several hundred troops who were hidden in nearby streets.

The Reformers had come marching to the meeting place in an orderly and good mannered fashion. There was a carnival air about the event, with bands playing, girls dancing and silk banners fluttering in the breeze. These proclaimed such aims as: No Corn Laws, Annual Parliaments and Vote by Ballot, with others listing the names of participating towns and unions.

At first the magistrates did not know how to cope with the situation, then they decided to act. After obtaining 30 signatures on a paper which stated that the meeting was a danger to the town, they ordered the officer in charge of the troops to disperse the people. Trumpeters sounded the charge and the Hussars began to beat back the crowds, some used the flats of their swords but others began to use the edges. Within ten minutes the field had been swept, what had begun as a peaceful meeting had ended in a massacre. Eleven people lay dead and over six hundred injured, some having been trampled by the horses while other had suffered directly at the hands of the soldiers.

A wave of horror and indignation swept through the country when the details of the event were told, it became known as Peterloo because it was compared to the Battle of Waterloo which at this time was a recent event. After Peterloo the Reformers still continued with their fight, but it was over a century later before they fully achieved their aim. This was in 1928 when the Representation of the Peoples Act was passed, giving each man and woman the right to vote.

Just beyond the Free Trade Hall stands the prestigious Midland Hotel, leading to the stylish curved roof of the exhibition hall known as the G-Mex Centre. In the hotel foyer I read a plaque which has been erected by the Institution of Mechanical Engineers to commemorate a meeting that took place here on May 4th 1904. When the brilliant minds of Charles Stewart Rolls and Frederick Henry Royce came together in this building it led to the creation of the most famous car in the world.

Passing the impressive circular Library in St Peter's Square, which is served by the city's unique Metrolink tram system, I continued along Oxford Street and into Chinatown. Here, in colourful splendour, a breath of the orient has been transported to the north. Bright signs advertise the Chung Yee Academy of Martial Art, Wong Chu Chinese Restaurant, a Chinese Herbal Medicine Centre and others businesses which often have a fiery dragon as their logo. But it is the breathtaking Chinese Arch which spans Faulkner Street that is the symbol of cosmopolitan Manchester. Here I sat on a bench sampling a Chinese pasty which was filled with delicious but unpronounceable vegetables, and admiring this feast of oriental art. Bedecked in an intricate tracery of blue, red and gold this huge structure, in an odd way, provides a perfect contrast with the sturdy Victorian buildings.

"I would like to look at a kimono," said a young girl, in a broad Lancashire accent, to the Indian man who was serving in a Chinese store.

"Certainly, madam," he said with a smile, leading her down a passageway to see the garments.

This store was unlike any other I have ever seen for it specialised in equipment used in Chinese Martial Arts. Leaflets advertised Muay Thai, which means Thai Boxing, Seven Star Kung-Fu, and training in Filipino Weaponry and Grappling. Wooden swords, truncheons, head protection masks and a host of other clothing essential to these activities filled the room. It is the one shop where the customer must always be right!

By-passing the crowds of early Christmas-shoppers who were filling the glitzy departmental stores of Market Street, I crossed Piccadilly into the seclusion of Thomas Street to reach Medieval Manchester. Here I stood on the steps of the elevated Cathedral, looking at the orange double-decker buses and endless streams of cars which were entering the city: a vast, almost overwhelming, conurbation that has grown outwards from what was once a green meadow.

When the Romans withdrew from their garrison at Castlefield after an occupation of over three hundred years, they left a void which was filled by successive invaders. First came the Angles and Saxons followed later by the menace of Viking longboats: this warring race tried to make the north their own. In 923 AD Edward the Elder, who was the son of Alfred the Great, decided to stop this Danish advance by strengthening his forces around the small settlement of Manchester. This was now centred about half a mile from the former Roman garrison, at a spot overlooking the River Irwell. Inside of the cathedral I looked upon the most precious relic of this period, a small piece of Saxon stone that was part of the original church. On it is carved an angel carrying a scroll which bears the message, Into thy hands, O Lord, I commend my spirit.

*The Old Wellington Inn*

After the Conquest much of Lancashire was given to the powerful Roger of Poitou, who in turn granted the Manor of Manchester, which was part of the Salford Hundred, to a knight named Albert Grelley. The Grelley family held the manor for two centuries, and it was from this agricultural estate that the modern city was to grow. In the 13th century, although still only a village by today's standards, it was already gaining a reputation as a place of trade. Two centuries later it was described by Leland as the 'most populous town in Lancastershire.' It was at this time that Manchester's two oldest institutions were established: the grammar school which was founded by Hugh Oldham in 1515 and Chetham's Hospital and Library, founded by Humphrey Chetham in 1656.

But it was business and commerce, spearheaded by the discoveries and inventions of what we now call the Industrial Revolution, which caused the rapid expansion of Manchester. It became a highly progressive town, always open to new ideas and the natural commercial centre for the lucrative textile industry. In 1717 the population was about 10,000 which had risen to 70,000 in 1801, then to an enormous 544,000 in 1901. In a hectic wave of commercial euphoria the 19th century had transformed a semi-rural community of villages and hamlets into a single bustling city. Cows and sheep would never again graze on the once rural pastures of Cheetham, Ardwick, Crumpsall, Didsbury or Moss Side.

I wandered around the inviting alleyways, back-streets and hidden backwaters near to the cathedral looking for clues which might reveal Manchester's fascinating past. I watched young pupils of the music school dashing late for their lessons and I saw business men drinking pints in the Old Wellington Inn; on the face of it an unlikely place for John Byrom to write the hymn *Christians Awake*, but this pub was once his home. In the Royal Exchange Theatre, where 7,000 cotton-men once traded with the world, groups of well-dressed theatre goers were awaiting the start of the matinee. Outside, shoppers were spending their money with dignity in St Ann's Square, while academics were perusing the Books of Hours in the Gothic portals of the John Rylands Library. Prince Albert was looking out over the square which bears his name, as he has done since 1861, while the lovely church of the Hidden Gem was receiving a well-deserved face-lift.

## 5

"Hey look at this picture. It shows a bloke lying on a wall smoking a fag."

Lowry would have smiled at this comment which concisely describes one of his most famous paintings. It came from a ginger haired boy of about ten, he was one of a noisy group of school children who were being introduced to the great man's works at Salford Art Gallery. Here, in a most appropriate setting, is the largest collection in the world of the Match-stick figures and brooding landscapes that made L.S. Lowry Lancashire's most famous artist of this century. At the time of his death in 1976 he had become recognised internationally for his unique interpretation of what, to many of us would be regarded as industrial ugliness.

Laurence Stephen Lowry was born on the 1st November 1887 at Old Trafford, the only child of estate-agent Robert Stephen Lowry and his wife, Elizabeth Hobson. He was a quiet, shy, home-loving boy, attributes which were to remain intrinsic to his character throughout his life. He was at first educated at Victoria Park School, then at the age of sixteen after showing artistic talent, he attended Manchester School of Art. Here he met Adolphe Valette, a painter and teacher who was to become a major influence. He made Lowry aware of the vibrant and colourful artistic world of Paris, leading him to enthusiastically experiment with impressionist themes. Lowry later recalled that the works which he admired most at this time were those of Madox Brown and D.G. Rossetti.

The family moved in 1909 to live in Pendlebury, and this house in Station Road was to be his home until 1948 when he was to move to the quietness of Mottram. At this time the area around Salford, where he now attended art classes, was on the fringe of a grimy industrial landscape that surrounded most of Britain's cities. It was a festering legacy from the exploitation of greedy Victorians men who cared little for the welfare of their workers.

At first he hated the sombre buildings, the smoky grey skies and the mean rows of terraced houses. Then, quite suddenly this all changed, for with his unique foresight he became aware of the hidden beauty of this industrial scene. He later recalled that this happened when he missed a train from Pendlebury Station, which forced him to walk past the Acme Spinning Mill. Hundreds of cotton-workers were leaving for home from the towering building, whose bright yellow lighted windows dominated the grey sky. With wonder he gazed on the outwardly common-place scene, and he then knew that Manchester would be his subject for the rest of his life.

Joining the children, who were looking with inquisitive innocence on Lowry's masterpieces, I wondered what was going through their minds. The mill chimneys, the grim streets and the pale-faced drab workers which are depicted on these canvases have now completely disappeared. Those of us over forty still remember the awfulness of the remnants of this age, but to these young minds it is an era as remote as Tudor England. Lowry was not only painting the complex mixture of bleakness and beauty that was once part of south Lancashire, but he was recording history.

After having a warm drink in the thankfully quiet, coffee shop I went to explore Salford Museum and Art Gallery's other great attraction, Lark Hill Place. Named after a Georgian mansion which once stood on the site, an amazing Victorian street has been created using original features from shops and houses. Stepping back in time I looked into the inviting windows of E. Morand the tobacconist, John Hamer the chemist and druggist, and Mrs Driver who was a bleeder with leeches. This marvellous exhibition, with its cast-iron pillar boxes, boneshaker bicycle and carriages known as Phaetons and Broughams, captures perfectly the warm atmosphere of yesterday's Salford.

Walking back to my car which I had parked beyond the busy crescent which lies at the heart of the Salford, I noticed a plaque on an impressive Georgian house with stands in Acton Square. It states that James Prescot Joule, 1818-1889, Lived and Worked Here. Those like myself, who spent sleepless nights as a student learning the First Law of Thermodynamics forever have the name Joule firmly imprinted on their brain. This great engineer's work led to what is called Joule's Mechanical Equivalent of Heat, and his name was given to a unit of energy measurement.

## 6

The sombre November sky spoke more of winter than of autumn, for the last leaves had now tumbled from the trees. Once this slender covering has disappeared the northern landscape takes on a stark appearance, colours become diffused by a misty greyness and Lancastrians begin to button up their coats. It is a time of preparation, a time to fill the car radiator with anti-freeze, to check that the central heating boiler is working, and to hope that the relative mildness of recent winters continues for another year.

My route now lay to the east, passing through busy Ancoats and Droylsden I reached Ashton-under-Lyne, an ancient town which marks the end of Manchester's sprawling suburbia. Here I stopped to explore the streets around St Peter's church, accompanied by the endless lines of cars and lorries which were scurrying past. I was really undertaking a literary pilgrimage, looking for the birthplace of the celebrated travel writer and journalist, H.V. Morton. But sadly, I discovered that the bulldozers had beaten me, for No 17, Chester Square, the house in which he was born on the 26th July 1892, has now disappeared.

*H.V. Morton: much-loved author of over 40 travel books.*

Henry Vollam Morton's father, Joseph, who had been born in India, worked as a sub-editor at a local newspaper and his devoted mother, Margaret Maclean Ewart, came from a proud Scottish family. Shortly after the birth of his son, Joseph took up a position as editor-in chief of the Pearson's Group of newspapers, so the family then moved to Birmingham. H.V. Morton attended the famous King Edward's School, then following his father's lead, he joined the staff at the Birmingham Gazette and Express.

In 1912 he was made the assistant editor, but hoping for bigger things he then found a job at the Empire Magazine in Fleet Street. Afterwards he worked on several other newspapers, broken by a spell in the Warwickshire Yeomanry during the Great War, before becoming one of Lord Beaverbrook's young men at the Daily Express. These were highly talented reporters who had been hand-picked by the tycoon to ensure his newspaper stayed at the forefront of journalism. Among his colleagues who shared the same office was J.B. Morton, who was to become the famous columnist Beachcomber, and S.P.B. Mais, who was also destined to write travel books.

H.V. Morton's big chance came in 1923 when he was sent out to Egypt to report on the opening of the newly discovered tomb of Tutankhamun. The world was waiting impatiently for news of what turned out to be, the greatest ever find in the history of Egyptology: an astonishing event which had been masterminded by Lord Caernarvon and Howard Carter. Morton sent home his highly descriptive reports, which were circulated to more than a hundred other newspapers, making him a household name.

His fame continued on his return home when he began to write a series of essays about London, which many believe are among the best ever written, for they capture the very soul of the city. These outstanding works were spotted by the chairman of Methuen Publishers, E.V. Lucas, who wanted to publish them as books. In June 1925, *The Heart of London* was published to wide acclaim, then went on to be reprinted countless times over the next thirty years. In response to public demand four other volumes of his writings were published the next year, including the companion volumes, *The Spell of London* and *The Nights of London*.

It was while Morton was on a newspaper assignment in the Middle East that he became ill, thinking at one point that he might die. This suddenly filled him with terrible home-sickness, leading him to make a vow that if he was saved from death he would return to England and undertake a personal journey through his neglected homeland. In 1926, after he had fully recovered, he began his pilgrimage which is recorded in *In Search of England,* a volume now regarded as the classic travel book of this period.

It went on to sell over a million copies and sixty years later it is still available, being frequently reprinted. During this tour he made a fleeting visit to Lancashire, but he paid a much longer visit to the county the following year for his companion volume, The Call of England. This success led to a string of other best-sellers in the *In Search of*... series that made Morton the leading travel writer of his day. He visited every corner of Britain, uniquely capturing with his pen the spirit of the thirties.

During this period he joined the staff of the popular *Daily Herald*, combining journalism with travel writing. His brilliant series of articles in which he visited the terrible slums of our major cities, including Liverpool and Manchester, helped to stir the social conscience of the nation. Soon afterwards, his book about the Holy Land, *In the Steps of the Master*, topped the best-seller list for 1935. For this volume he received an advance of £10,000 with royalties of 33%, which was an unheard of sum at this time. Two years later he completed an equally successful companion volume, *In the Steps of St Paul*, in which he followed the route of the first great missionary journey.

In May 1939 he went on a journey through the southern counties, taking a last look at an England which he knew would soon be at war. Five months later, after war had been declared, he began another tour looking at the British people facing the threat of invasion. This marvellous record of one of the most poignant periods in our history appeared as *I Saw Two Englands*; it was re-published in 1989 on the fiftieth anniversary of the outbreak of war.

During the Second World War both H.V. Morton and adopted Lancastrian, Howard Spring, were asked by the government to take part in a highly secret operation.

"I want you to leave England for three weeks, but I regret to say that I can't tell you where you are going to or what you will see when you get there", was the request put to them by the Minister.

The two men accepted the challenge which was eventually revealed as being the historic meeting between Winston Churchill and President Roosevelt. This took place on board the battleship Prince of Wales which was cruising off the Newfoundland coast. This secret rendezvous led to the signing of the important Atlantic Charter and Morton was able to brilliantly record the whole historic episode which appeared in his book, *Atlantic Meeting* (1943).

Continuing with his writings for the war effort, he completed a small paperback novel, *I, James Blunt*, which sold for just sixpence. This fascinating work of fiction was intended as propaganda to warn people of complacency during the critical days of the war. It was the diary of an Englishman living in 1944 in an England which had been invaded by the Germans.

Shortly after the war he and his family went to live in the beautiful town of Somerset West, which lies on Table Bay in South Africa. This new home was to become the base for all his future writings, but he returned home frequently to England, the country he really loved. His success continued as he wrote about his wanderings in the Middle East, Italy and Spain. His last book, *A Traveller in Southern Italy*, was published in 1969, and he died ten years later at the age of 86.

H.V. Morton was a quiet humble man who brought travel writing to new heights. His works are cherished by book-lovers world-wide, for they remain an unsurpassed record of Britain in the thirties. Perhaps someday he will be given a permanent memorial in the town of his birth.

# CHAPTER EIGHT

# ASHTON-UNDER-LYNE TO HORWICH

I return to the hill country, climb up Blackstone Edge, visit another drowned village then listen to Our Gracie in Rochdale. I eat a Bury black pudding, learn about Sir Robert Peel then visit the regiment which gained six VCs before breakfast. In Bolton I remember a soccer legend, see the grave of Samuel Crompton and the place where the Earl of Derby lost his head, then I end up in Hometown.

## 1

The Pennine hills rise surprisingly close to Manchester's eastern side, they provide a magnificent natural barrier against the spread of suburbia. A person, if so inclined, could eat breakfast in the splendour of the Midland Hotel then half an hour later be alone in a savage landscape of peaty moorland. I followed one of the meandering roads which skirts these uplands alongside the River Tame, the grey outline of houses and factories lay on my left, while on my right the towering splendour of this wild open countryside.

I discovered that many a confused stranger like myself has searched in vain for Saddleworth. For though there is a splendid Saddleworth Museum, a Saddleworth church and an annual Saddleworth Festival there is no Saddleworth village. For this rural haven, where tired Mancunians escape to on summer weekends, is really a district which embraces a series of fiercely independent villages. Uppermill, where I stopped to admire the pleasure boats which sail along the narrow Huddersfield Canal, is the largest of these and the one most frequented by the casual visitor. It lies in the valley bottom, a sturdy unspoilt settlement which dates from the 18th century. Here, in what was once Yorkshire, farmers first began spinning wool as a sideline. Their success led to a number of small friendly mills springing up, but thankfully this industry never destroyed the relaxed feeling of rural peace which still remains.

The other villages of Saddleworth, which hide along narrow lanes or in moorland hollows, are Greenfield, Dobcross, Diggle, Delph, Denshaw, Grasscroft, Lydgate, Scouthead and Friezland. They stand as guardians on this wild border from which tortuous roads wind their way ever upwards, crossing the windswept summits to reach Holmfirth, Huddersfield or Halifax.

It was along the lonely Holmfirth road that a brutal killing took place in 1832, which is still talked about in these parts. Known as the Jack o' Bills Murders, the victims were the landlord of the old Moorcock Inn and his son; the crime still remains unsolved.

Oldham, which lies on the doorstep of this splendid isolation, has created a circular footpath linking some of these villages. The Oldham Way follows the borough boundary for forty miles, passing across some of the most varied countryside in England.

Beyond Milnrow I took a lane which overlooks the banks of choppy Hollingworth Lake. It was here that the athletic Captain Webb trained in the freezing waters before becoming the first man to swim the English Channel. From Littleborough I drove up the road which early travellers feared more than any other in England, Blackstone Edge. This is the most famous of a series of fascinating lonely hilltops which form the border between Greater Manchester, West Yorkshire and the Peak District. It is a unique landscape, a dramatic wilderness of peaty moorland which is capped here and there by impressive gritstone crags which have been carved into weird shapes by wind and rain.

Parking close to the lonely White House Inn I crossed the road to join a moorland pathway which is part of the Pennine Way. William Camden was one of the earliest travellers to record his thoughts on his journey across this hillside. He referred to the local people as 'the Brigantes' when he began his journey with trepidation: 'first into Lancashire which I go unto (God speed me well) after a sort somewhat against my will.'

Towards the end of the 17th century Celia Fiennes, who had travelled widely, found the hill 'a most dismal high precipice with mists and raines almost perpetually'. Daniel Defoe was particularly unfortunate when he followed the same route a few years later for he encountered a snow storm in August. 'It is not easy to express the consternation we were in when we came near the top of the mountain; the wind blew exceedingly hard, and blew the snow directly in our faces, and so thick, that it was impossible to keep our eyes open to see our way. The ground was also covered with snow, we could see no track . . .'

My walk, compared with these early travellers, was much less harrowing, a chill wind being the only obstacle. Soon I reached the two mile long paved road which crosses the moorland and is indicated on the Ordnance Survey map as a Roman Road. It has been described by one historian as the 'best preserved section of Roman Road in Britain', but other experts believe it is not of Roman origin. It has an unusual trough carved down its centre which has led to all kinds of speculation. Some believe it was filled with turf to allow horses to gain a foothold, while others say that it formed part of a winching system for hauling up coaches. This ancient road, however, was certainly part of the packhorse route over which both Celia Fiennes and Daniel Defoe travelled, and it is likely to have its origins in prehistoric times.

I followed it up the hillside to just below the windswept ridge to reach the Aiggin Stone. This, I discovered, is a vertical column of gritstone about two metres high, which is believed to be part of a medieval wayside cross. It was probably used to guide travellers, who may have stopped here to pray for a safe journey. Several guide books to this area, including Wainwright's *Pennine Way Companion,* show the stone toppled almost horizontally as it was for many years, but now it has been restored to its original vertical position.

Turning right I now followed a series of cairns which led me along the isolated ridge to the summit trig-point which was visible on the skyline. I found this high-point of Blackstone Edge to be one of the most dramatic places in Lancashire, a hilltop which exhudes a marvellous feeling of isolation. A jumble of gritstone crags are exposed across the curving hilltop, formed into strange rounded shapes by centuries of merciless Pennine winters. There is no grass around these crags, this has long since disappeared, what remains is a glinting bed of jet-black peat.

The trig-point, which has been secured to the top of a large boulder, provides a magnificent vantage point. To the west the brown moorland plunges downwards to the distant rooftops of Littleborough which shelter in the valley below, then spreads outwards to the suburbs of Rochdale. Beyond, the rounded profile of Brown Wardle Hill dominates the scene leading on to a vast skyline of blue hills. Knowl Hill, always easily identified by its unique sharp profile, led my eyes westwards over the Rossendale Valley. The dark finger of the Peel Monument was visible on the edge of Holcombe Moor and in the far distance the whale-backed Winter Hill crowned with its towering TV mast.

Turning northwards into the wind I could see the snaking contours of the edge which leads to the famous monument which sits high on Stoodley Pike. Here a vast panorama of hills sweep in a dozen shades of blue, deep into Yorkshire. Eastwards the moorland descends away to the horizon, broken only by the grey waters of Green Withins Reservoir and the dark thread which marks the path of the M62 trans-pennine motorway.

Before heading for Rochdale I made a detour to the village of Wardle to look at Watergrove Reservoir, for like Stocks Reservoir, it hides a drowned village. A narrow cobbled lane led me to the picnic site, then I walked up to the eastern side of the reservoir, stopping to view the History Wall. Here are sad reminders of the old village, mullion windows, datestones and even an ancient stone drinking trough.

Watergrove village was a thriving community with a population in excess of two hundred people. It consisted of over forty houses, two mills, a chapel and two pubs. It was in many ways self contained for on its doorstep lay most of the necessities of life. Water from the Wardle and Higher Slack Brooks was used for both drinking and as a power source to drive the mill machinery. Stone was plentiful on the hillside as the raw material for the buildings and these same uplands provided fine grazing for sheep, which in turn provided both meat and wool.

However, the early 1930s was destined to change this harmonious village for ever. Unemployment at nearby Rochdale had brought the worst kind of privation since the time of Victoria, but a temporary solution was possible. Two new reservoirs were desperately needed by the town and such a venture could provide much-needed jobs. Watergrove was identified as an ideal site, so the villagers together with some local farmers were forced to vacate their homes which were quickly demolished.

I wandered along what is known as the Watergrove Trail, a footpath which skirts this former village. Overlooked by a landscape of rising moorland, dominated by the rounded summit of Brown Wardle Hill, the grey waters of Watergrove look as if they have been here forever. But here and there half hidden piles of tumbled stones testify to the moorland community that tragically disappeared.

## 2

Being marooned in my car by a sudden downpour of rain had its advantages: I was able to study in comfort the impressive exterior of Rochdale's finest building, its Victorian Town Hall. Up till 1856 those upright citizens who administered the town, met for their meetings in rather dismal rooms above the fire station. But having just been granted a Royal Charter which made them a Municipal Corporation, they decided a more dignified setting was required. A prize of £100 was offered for the best plan and this was won by a Leeds architect named William Crossland. It was estimated that an initial design would cost £20,000, however, after a number of alterations were approved the final cost soared to £155,000!

John Bright, the town's famous Quaker reformer, laid the foundation stone in 1866 and the lavish new building began to take shape. Built in the Gothic Revival style, with marvellous stained glass windows, ornate carvings in both wood and stone, and decorative tiling, it was a masterpiece. Its dominant feature was a 240 feet high spire which had a gold statue of St George at the top. To enhance it even further, the surrounding land was cleared of old property and a magnificent wide esplanade was constructed.

The Corporation could at last hold its head with pride, but only for twelve years for then disaster struck – dry rot! The spire was found to be riddled with the creeping menace. It was so bad that plans were put forward to dismantle it, but these were overtaken by another event – it caught fire! The blaze was visible from ten miles away and led to the spires complete demolition. But the people of Rochdale refused to accept defeat. A replacement was designed by Alfred Waterhouse, this time a splendid gilt clock tower, which remains the centre piece of this Grade 1 building.

'Can I help you,' said the smiling receptionist in the Tourist Information Office.

At first I thought that I had mis-heard her accent; was this some strange dialect from Littleborough, Heywood or Whitworth? No, it was none of these, but that of New York State! She related how she was Rochdale born and bred, but had lived for many years in the USA and had now returned permanently to her home town. We talked about the history of the town, of John Bright, the Rochdale Pioneers, Sir Cyril Smith and above all about Gracie Fields. She told me how she remembers as a child going into the chip-shop where Gracie had been born, and how a new exhibition had recently been created to commemorate the star. As I left the office I asked her how Rochdale compares with New York State.

"I much prefer it, even on a rainy day."

Rochdale's Wheatsheaf Shopping Centre is one of those amazing places that have sprung up in many Lancashire towns to become the envy of Europe. In this futuristic building of glass and marble the women of Rochdale can spend their money in a warm, bright atmosphere of splendid opulence. Here too they can celebrate the life of Britain's greatest-ever female artiste in an exhibition affectionately called Our Gracie.

I wandered into this marvellous array of memorabilia; newspaper cuttings, photographs, and record-sleeves line every wall, highlighting the most spectacular rags-to riches story of all. In a small cinema I sat and watched Gracie's antics in a comedy film of the thirties, on another screen I saw her returning to a civic reception in her home town, then in a booth I heard her sing Sally and Little old Lady; she was indeed our very first superstar.

*Gracie Fields*

Grace Stansfield was born in a room above a chip shop in Molesworth Street, Rochdale, on the 9th January 1898. It was the home of her grandmother who was known locally as Chip Sarah. Her father, Fred, was an engineering worker and her mother, Jenny, at only 19 years old helped to pay the households bills by working in a mill and by taking in washing. Gracie's family grew over the next few years by the addition of her two sisters, Betty and Edith, followed by a brother, Tommy. Her mother, who possessed a fine singing voice, had once had aspirations to become a performer but these faded as family responsibilities grew. However, Grace had inherited her talent and she saw that perhaps her show-business dreams might come true through her children.

At the age of seven, Grace was given the only singing lesson she was ever to receive, from a former music hall singer named Lily Turner. She then took part in a singing contest at the Rochdale Hippodrome where she tied for first place to win 10s 6d. Spurred on by her mother's determination to forge a theatrical career, three years later she joined a juvenile troupe named Clara Coverdale's Boys and Girls. This proved to be a non-starter, for the other girls, who were much older than Grace, were jealous. Under the pretext of teaching her acrobatic dancing they ensured she could not perform, for the robust exercise strained the ligaments of her legs. However, shortly afterwards she joined the Haley Garden of Girls which led to her first tour. But this ended even more disastrously, for the loose morals of the troupe led to her almost being raped. The shock on the young child brought on St Vitus Dance which resulted in her being taken to a convalescent home in St Anne's to aid her recovery.

Returning home to Rochdale she started work as a half-time, cotton winder in a mill. But her fine singing voice together with her warm, humorous personality, ensured that this low-paid job would only be temporary. Her break came when a performer at the Rochdale Hippodrome was suddenly taken ill and a replacement was urgently required. Grace was given the job at short notice, for which she received thirty-five shillings a week. Billed as 'Young Grace Stansfield, Rochdale's Own Girl Vocalist', the audience gave her act a rousing cheer of approval. The theatre manager was well pleased with her performance, but her name was too long to put up in lights. After much deliberation it was eventually changed to Gracie Fields – Our Gracie, at the tender age of only thirteen, had arrived.

The next year she joined a juvenile troupe named Chatburn's Young Stars which led to her first performance at the north's show-business capital of Blackpool, which she loved. She later went on to Oldham, then reluctantly to

St Annes to join Cousin Freddy and his Pierrot Show. Here she performed at the Cosy Corner, which was a wooden hut on the sands, considered by young Gracie to be beneath her. However, it proved to be an important stage in her career for old-time comedian, Fred Hutchins, recognised her natural talent. He taught her the importance of timing, then helped her to develop her act into one of partial comedy.

A Manchester theatrical agent, Percy Hall, had seen Gracie perform at Chesterfield and he offered her a five year contract for a salary of five pounds a week, which her mother signed. She then went on to an audition for the revue, *Yes, I Think So,* at which her comedy routine was poorly received, but led to her engagement because of her marvellous singing voice. Here she met a small, thin cockney comedian named Archie Pitt, who at first she disliked. He appeared arrogant, telling her where her act was weakest, which she resented. But he was persistent for he had seen the possibility of stardom for the naive sixteen-year-old Lancashire lass, a possibility which he was determined to exploit.

Archie Pitt kept on telling Gracie that she was going to be a star and that he would like her to appear in a show of his own. Eventually after he was able to persuade her that he was serious, he managed to buy her contract from Percy Hall and with loans, set about putting on his own show. In 1917 *It's A Bargain* began its first run at the Tivoli in Manchester, then took to the road. The show, although far from being a success, managed to survive. Gracie's mother then put pressure on Gracie to try to find a place for her sister Betty in the show. Eventually both her sisters and her brother were to join the company.

But it was Archie Pitt's next show, *Mr Tower Of London,* which was to soar Gracie to stardom. Its first performance in Nottingham proved far from successful for all manner of things seemed to go wrong. These initial problems, however, were soon ironed out and the show went on tour. It was received in an atmosphere of elation following the ending of the First World War, and proved to be a tremendous success. But Gracie's world was now confined to just a small group of people who were in the cast, she inwardly still lacked confidence for she had never had a boyfriend. Archie was the only man who had ever taken care of her, so although she never really loved him, the couple drifted into marriage in April 1923. The next year saw the show in its first West End run at the prestigious Alhambra Theatre in Leicester Square. Gracie Fields received rave reviews from the critics, what Rochdale had known a decade ago was now discovered by London.

Her success was phenomenal, offers came from the greatest names in show-business. She took the stage with Gerald du Maurier in his play S.O.S. in 1924, and at the same time sang in night clubs and music halls, earning an incredible £700 a week. She cut her first gramophone record and in 1928 she made the first, of what was destined to be ten, Royal Variety Show appearances which would span half a century. But sadly, her married life was proving to be far from happy. Archie was revelling in their success and wealth, he had purchased a huge mansion in Hampstead filled with rich furnishings, looked after by a host of servants. Gracie hated the house, she also suspected that Archie was having an affair; sadly, she knew in her heart that their marriage was beginning to fall apart.

It was at this time that she was introduced to a handsome Irish painter named John Flanagan. He was a gentle carefree man who appealed to Gracie's homely character, the two quickly became friends. Their friendship was to later develop into a love-affair on the beautiful Isle of Capri, which was eventually to become her home. But this new-found happiness was not destined to continue, with his creative talents came bouts of depression; he was a man who loathed money and possessions, and had to keep moving on. But they were to remain close friends.

Following her continuing success in *The Show's the Thing* (1929) and *Walk This Way* (1931), she went on to star in her first and most famous film, *Sally In Our Alley* (1931). She was to complete eleven films in the thirties, including the ever popular *Sing As We Go* which was written by J.B. Priestley, making her Britain's biggest female film star. In 1935 her sister Betty introduced her to Monty Banks, an Italian film director who had once been one of the original Keystone Cops. He became her adviser, he introduced her to Hollywood, and after her divorce from Archie in 1940, he became her second husband. At this time she was recovering from a major operation, which only in later years was revealed to have been cancer.

As well as enduring the after effects of her illness she now faced a new crisis, a hostile National Press. Monty was an Italian citizen so when Italy declared war he risked being interned in Britain as an enemy, so they both left for the USA. She had also been advised by Winston Churchill that the best way she could help the country was by earning dollars abroad. So she continued her wartime work by entertaining troops and factory workers both in America and Canada, with many return trips to Britain. But the criticism continued for many years, some national newspapers even accused her of deserting Britain in its darkest hour.

However, after the war had ended the public found they could no longer resist the charm and charisma of Our Gracie. Her life began to improve:

Rochdale had given her the Freedom of the Town in 1938 and they still loved her, she was living back in sunny Capri and she had the thrill of starting a new restaurant on the island. But sadly her happiness was to be short lived. In January 1950 Monty was suddenly taken ill as they travelled on the Orient Express to Venice. He was taken to hospital near Lake Maggiore, but he died soon afterwards.

With Lancastrian tenacity she slowly began to pick up the threads of her life, making guest appearances in London, making more records and looking after her restaurant which had become a great success. Then in 1952 she announced she was to be married once more. She had fallen in love with Boris Alperovici, a radio engineer and inventor who was part of the elite group of artists, writers and scientists who had made Capri their home.

Although Gracie had been threatening to retire for years working was her life. She continued making concert tours, appearing on television and making charity appearances to the end of her life. When she was eighty she returned to Rochdale to open The Gracie Fields Theatre, then in November 1978 she appeared for the last time at the Royal Variety Show. She died in her sleep in September 1979 and was buried in a small graveyard on the Isle of Capri.

Gracie Fields was unique, her magnetic personality and vitality made her the most loved entertainer of her day. Only one other person approached her popularity during the thirties and forties, this was fellow Lancastrian George Formby. Honours were poured on her, she was made a Dame Commander of the British Empire and she had a rose, a ship and even a cocktail named after her. But in spite of all these accolades she never forgot the people of Rochdale and her humble birthplace above a chip shop.

Not far from the modern shops of Rochdale I found a survival from the 18th century with the splendid name of Toad Lane. Visitors from all over the world come to look at this street, for here is the first shop from which the vast International Co-operative Movement was to grow. I entered the building, which is now a museum, to find a young woman explaining to two students the history of how it all began. I was allowed to quietly wander around, looking at the display of original documents and a host of fascinating items that reminded me of the time when every village in Lancashire had its own Co-op shop.

It was here in December 1844 that a group of working men, who had formed the Rochdale Equitable Pioneers Society, opened their store. They were trying to break the existing system by which private shopkeepers could exploit people by charging excessive prices for shoddy goods. Each member of the group paid a weekly subscription of 2d (two old pence; about one new penny) to raise capital to rent the premises and buy goods. At first these were restricted to basic commodities such as sugar, butter, flour, oatmeal and candles. But the venture proved to be an immediate success, leading to the stocking of a larger variety of products and even paying out a dividend to its members.

At first they traded under a legal disadvantage, but in 1872 this was overcome when they won the right to sell to non-members. In 1863 the movement had become known as the familiar Co-operative Wholesale Society, and within ten years they had opened three of their own factories. At this time they had 7,639 members and a capital in excess of £192,000. This incredible growth continued, the CWS bought farms in Britain, tea-plantations in Ceylon and purchased goods world-wide. Today it remains one of this country's leading consumer-goods organisations.

Before leaving the little shop in Toad Lane, I glanced at a photograph of thirteen of the original members. With Victorian solemnity they look down, perhaps in total bewilderment at the almost unbelievable success of their venture.

In a shower of rain I climbed the steep steps of Sparrow Hill for a final look at the grey rooftops of the town. I wandered around the Norman church of St Chad where on the 2nd February 1898 a baby was baptised Grace Stansfield. Then I looked at the churchyard where the dialect poet John Collier, known as Lancashire's Hogarth, shares a resting place with Hamlet Nicholson who invented the compound cricket bat. Yes, Rochdale remains a town of diverse and incredible talent.

## 3

"Would you like some mustard?" asked the smartly dressed assistant at Chadwick's famous Black Pudding stall on Bury Market.

I told her that I did not, so smiling, she handed me the neatly wrapped bag which contained the piping hot, jet-black, Lancashire delicacy. In the privacy of my car I began to feast on the mixture of herbs, fat, flour, oats, dried pig's blood and those other closely guarded secret ingredients which make every pudding maker's recipe unique. I found the mild herby taste richly delicious, it was also a welcome 'warmer up' against the cold November wind which was blowing across the market and along The Rock.

Bury is a lively town of just the right size to have a host of modern facilities yet to still be able to retain an intimate friendliness. When the Romans built their road which ran from Manchester to Ribchester it skirted what is now the town, but it was the Saxons who gave it the name which means a stronghold. A castle, which has sadly disappeared was built here by Thomas Pilkington in 1465, but its permanent historic links were forged during the Industrial Revolution. New found wealth created fine Georgian town houses, inns where stage coaches brought merchants from Manchester to make business deals, and was the environment which bred talented men who helped to shape the country.

I returned to the busy outdoor market which was overflowing with visitors who were intent on getting a bargain. Books, clothes, fruit, food, pictures, and a thousand other commodities which we regard as the necessities of life, were piled high. The indoor market reverberated with the voices of competing stall holders, over shouting each other to gain the elusive customer.

" Wild river salmon, should be seven pound fifty for two, but I'm letting them go for a fiver. I'm giving them away."

The stall was piled high with an enormous mixture of game and fish. Chickens, turkeys, pheasants, rabbits, widgeon, and venison steaks lay side by side with trout, salmon, hake, cod, sole and herrings. This market is a gourmet's delight.

I joined a group of people who had gathered outside the splendid new Mill Gate shopping centre. They were listening to two men who were dressed in the Lincoln green garb of Robin Hood. Perched alongside was a fluffy, wide-eyed tawny owl together with two young kestrels who were squawking ferociously.

"Please don't stroke him luv, he gets upset," said the older man to a young child of about ten who found the owl irresistible.

He then went on to tell us that he was collecting money for a sanctuary at Didsbury which looks after these birds. Some were casualties of accidents while others had been taken by children from their nests. The people of Bury gave generously.

The Victorians seemed to have been less sceptical about their politicians than we are today, and this is particularly true of Bury. Sir Robert Peel, who was born in the Irwell Valley in 1788 and rose to become Prime Minister, is still regarded as a local hero. As I stood sheltering from the wind beneath the sturdy dark walls of the Parish Church I could see the slim profile of the Peel Tower, standing dominant and windswept on the moorland edge above Holcombe village. This monument was erected in 1852, two years after his tragic death which had resulted from a horse riding accident. It cost a thousand pounds which was raised by public subscription, but inside is a clue to why he was so well thought of by the working class people. Carved on a marble tablet is an extract from his famous resignation speech of 1846:

> *'It may be that I shall leave a name sometimes remembered with expressions of goodwill in the abode of those whose lot it is to labour and earn their daily bread by the sweat of their brow – when they shall recruit their exhausted strength with abundant and untaxed food the sweeter because it is no longer leavened by a sense of injustice'.*

What he was referring to was his part in the repeal of the Corn Laws, which were as popular in their day as our recent Poll Tax proved to be. During Britain's wars with France (1793 to 1815) and later with the USA (1812 to 1815) our imported food supplies became disrupted. British farmers tried desperately to fill this shortfall by growing more corn, which led to larger farms with more farm hands. However, with the end of the war came the prospect of loss of finance for these farmers, for the imported grain was once more available. To protect them the price of corn was held artificially high by the introduction of the Corn Laws of 1815. Food was much more expensive that it needed to be, yet the agricultural workers still lost their jobs, only the farmers and landowners gained. So when this very unpopular law was finally removed from the stature book in 1846 it was a time for general rejoicing.

I gazed upon the handsome profile of Peel which is carved in a fine stone statue which overlooks the Market Place. This gifted man, who gained a double first at Oxford, then went on to form the Metropolitan Police Force before giving us cheaper food, deserves to be remembered.

Bury has also bred many other great personalities who have risen to become household names. Adjacent to the Bus Station, in a small green oasis known as Kay Gardens, I read another memorial plaque. It told me what every student of social history should know, that 'John Kay of Bury, whose invention in 1733 of the Fly Shuttle quadrupled human potential in weaving'. Sadly, like so many other talented inventors of his day, he ended his life in poverty, he now lies in an unknown grave in France.

American visitors to the town will be interested to learn that the first president of Harvard University, Henry Dunster, was born here. Others, like myself, who giggled in childhood to the antics of Just William on the radio will forever remember Bury's best-selling authoress, Richmal Crompton. Born in 1890 she was the daughter of the Rev. Edward Lamburn, who taught at Bury Grammar School. Her inspiration for the young William is said to have come from the escapades of her brother and her nephew.

Another of Lancashire's gems which deserves to be better known I discovered at the Wellington Barracks on Bolton Road. For fifty pence I was allowed to look at an astonishing array of historical memorabilia in this marvellous regimental museum of the Lancashire Fusiliers. I was greeted by a smiling faced boy of seventeen, who told me he was a volunteer worker who came from Heywood. With quiet diplomacy he allowed me to freely wander around the cases of exhibits which link Lancashire with some of the world's most renowned military campaigns.

I was surprised to discover that the famous Lancashire Fusiliers began not in Lancashire, but in Devon! When William of Orange landed in Torbay in 1688 he met a number of English noblemen who were commissioned to raise regiments for him. One of these, a Regiment of Foot, was raised by Sir Robert Peyton by recruiting men from the Exeter area. It was initially known as Peyton's Own, then more correctly in 1782 as the East Devon Regiment of Foot. After a highly successful recruiting campaign in the Bury area last century it was renamed The Lancashire Fusiliers and Wellington Barracks became the headquarters; a more recent change, which occurred in 1968, has made it the Lancashire Headquarters of The Royal Regiment of Fusiliers.

Ironically, this Regiment which first saw service in Northern Ireland which led to King James II being deposed, is still in the province today. During the 18th century it fought at Dettingen and Fontenoy, which were concerned with the Austrian succession, followed by the bloody Battle of Culloden. It's soldiers fought so gallantly at the Battle of Minden during the Seven Years War that it was honoured by having a Laurel Wreath added to its colours. Among its distinguished commanders of this period was Major-General James Wolfe, who later became the celebrated victor of Quebec.

After taking part in the Napoleonic Wars the regiment guarded Napoleon during his captivity in St Helena. In the museum I was fascinated at the many souvenirs from this period. They include a button from Napoleon's tunic, grass from his grave and a detailed autopsy which was carried out on him by British surgeons.

Men from Lancashire were present at the Crimean War (1854-55), the Indian Mutiny (1857), the Relief of Khartoum (1898), the Relief of Ladysmith and Spion Kop (1901). But it was during the Great War that they gained their greatest accolade when they won 'six VCS before breakfast' at what became known as the Lancashire Landing. In total they won 18 Victoria Crosses during this terrible war, which was more than any other regiment in the British Army. During the Second World War they fought at Dunkirk, Malta, Italy, North Africa and Burma, then continued in the post war years fighting the terrorist campaigns in Kenya, Cyprus, and Egpyt.

I wandered for an hour looking at the remarkable array of exhibits which have been collected by these Lancashire soldiers as they travelled around the world. Uniforms, weapons, medals, colours, and a thousand small intimate objects – such as Field Marshal Rommel's orderly bell – chart some of the most momentous landmarks in British history.

As I left the museum I spotted a leaflet which advertises the Gallipoli Association; as the campaign took place in 1915 I wonder how many veteran members it now boasts ?

## 4

"That's Bruce Rioch over there. I expect he's talking about tactics for tomorrow's match. He's done very well, you know, taking the Wanderers to promotion in his first season as manager."

A small, talkative man of about sixty was pointing across the plush dining room of the executive club at Bolton Wanderers. He was one of a group of visitors who had come for a tour around the famous football ground. Fortunately I was saved from his endless chatter by the appearance of our guide, a dark haired young man named Peter.

We followed Peter down the stairs then continued through a tunnel which has a large, old notice painted above it, proudly announcing This is Burnden Park. It was no doubt intended to put fear into the visiting team at the time when Bolton Wanderers had the best players in England.

Our tour began in the Trophy Room, looking at walls filled with cups, medals, shields and photographs which chart the high points of the teams fascinating history which began in 1874. At this early period they were named Christ Church, one of a number of local teams who had 'a kick around' on Saturday afternoons on any field which was available. But this fledgling team began to produce good results which led to them becoming more ambitious. They had felt inhibited at their headquarters in Christ Church School, for the vicar had insisted on being present at all their meetings.

By 1877 they had moved their HQ to a local pub and changed their name to Bolton Wanderers. This new name is said to have resulted from their wanderings from one ground to another, it also led to their nickname, The Trotters. But by now they had found their first permanent ground which was situated at Pike's Lane, which is now Wigan Road. Football was rapidly growing in popularity, the FA Cup competition had been inaugurated in 1871 and Bolton Wanderers were now taking part. On the 8th September 1888 a new landmark was reached for the club when they played their first Football

League match in the town, drawing in a crowd of around 5,000. But the record attendance at Pike's Lane occurred in 1894 when 20,000 spectators saw Bolton defeat Liverpool in the FA Cup semi-final. However, the hilly ground was far from ideal, so they began to wander yet again.

"The club moved here to Burnden Park in 1895 and it has been their home ever since," our guide explained. He then showed us a photograph of Bolton's 1923 FA Cup winning squad who were the heroes of the very first Cup Final to be held in Wembley Stadium. About 126,000 people passed through the turnstiles and up to another 100,000 managed to gain admission by pushing through the barriers, with an estimated half a million supporters waiting outside. It is known in football history as the White Horse Final because a policeman on a white horse tried gallantly to control the huge crowds. Among the team 'greats' who took part in this memorable match were the legendary Pym and Vizard.

But, of course, there is just one name which will forever be associated with Bolton Wanderers, Nat Lofthouse. With Sir Stanley Matthews and Tom Finney, this local lad ranks among the all-time greats of football. He joined the ground staff at the club in 1939 at the age of only fourteen and today he still remains here as the president. In 21 years as a player at the club he took part in an amazing 505 games, scoring 285 goals. He also won 33 caps as an England International player, being remembered in soccer history for his marvellous performance against Austria in 1952 when he scored twice, this earned him the title Lion of Vienna. He is now regarded as the town's finest ambassador, having just received a long overdue OBE. But this much-loved soccer star who believes " ..nowhere compares with Bolton," has already received the town's supreme honour by having a pub named after him!

As we looked in awe at Nat's England strip which is preserved in a case, a young boy of about twelve stepped forward. We watched in silence as he gazed at a photograph of the triumphant team of the fifties which brought fame once more to the club.

'This is my grand-dad, Stan Hanson', he said proudly.

Our tour continued around the unusually quiet ground of Burnden Park. We saw the spartan changing rooms and Edwardian baths which have been known to generations of our greatest soccer stars; we looked on the emerald green turf which hides an underground heating system with computerised sprinklers; we saw the artificial turf training pitch and the gymnasium where the young athletes build up their stamina; and we stood in the chill wind reading the plaque which remembers the Wanderer's saddest moment. For here in 1946 thirty three supporters tragically died when a huge crowd tumbled through the barriers.

*Nat Lofthouse*

# 5

I sat in the corner of Bolton's oldest inn, drinking a half pint of bitter and thinking of the last moments of James, the 7th Earl of Derby. For it was here at the Old Man and Scythe in 1651, that he spent his final hour on earth before being taken outside into Churchgate to face the executioner's axe. Amazingly, the chair in which he sat just prior to his execution is still preserved inside this half timbered building, whose history goes back to 1251.

At the end of the 16th century Bolton-le-Moors, as the town was then known, was a centre for Puritanism being nicknamed The Geneva of the North. So when the Civil War erupted, unlike many other Lancashire towns, it declared an allegiance to Parliament. This led in 1644, to its 3,000 troops being attacked by a Royalist army of 11,000 ending in what has become known as the Bolton Massacre. The streets of the town ran red with the blood of 1,200 people, and the slaughter continued in the surrounding countryside, added to by rape and plunder.

But the Royalist triumph later turned to despair following their defeat at the Battle of Worcester. The Earl of Derby, who was regarded by many as being responsible for the Bolton Massacre, although he denied this, was captured. After a swift trial at Chester at which he was sentenced to death, it was thought appropriate that he should die in Bolton. Symbolically, the scaffold on which he died was constructed from the timber of Lathom House and the executioner who wielded the axe was one of those whose families had been murdered during the massacre.

I wandered from the inn into Churchgate which is the oldest part of Bolton. I read the plaque on the Market Cross which lists landmarks in the history of the town; I looked at the building in which the inventor of the Water Frame, Richard Arkwright, once practised as a barber; then I went to the Olde Pastie Shop to sample one of their famous delicacies which are sent all over the world.

In the graveyard of the impressive Parish Church I stood on the green lawn beside the tomb of a another famous Boltonian, Samuel Crompton. The town has, quite rightly, ensured that the man who invented the highly ingenious Spinning Mule, will never be forgotten. His birthplace, a thatched house at picturesque Firwood Fold can still be seen; Hall'ith'Wood where he perfected his machine is now a museum; a modern shopping area is named Crompton Place and a highway Crompton Way. But his statue which looks thoughtfully out over Bradshawgate, seems full of regrets. He is perhaps thinking, "If only

I had patented my machine". For unwisely he trusted in the goodwill of men who made a fortune out of his idea, leaving him to die penniless in 1827.

One of the lesser known Boltonians who would have witnessed the struggles of Crompton, was John Albinson, who was described in a directory of 1832 as a land-agent and surveyor. But only when this eccentric character died in 1854 was his true worth revealed. He occupied a complete row of cottages in Chapel Alley, which were all inter-connected to allow him to house his incredible collection of paintings and books. Over 25,000 rare volumes were uncovered, together with piles of highly valuable manuscripts, documents and bric-a-brac. Rows of old masters lined every wall, many never having been dusted for twenty years. These included the works of Rembrandt, Velasquez, Hogarth and Turner, which would be valued at millions of pounds at the present day. His collection was so massive that it was split into 357 lots and the sale lasted for nine days!

Another eccentric character who early this century roamed the streets of the town, then unwittingly started a show-business legend, was Robert Thomas. He worked as a refuse collector in the town, becoming well known for his strange clothes and odd behaviour. He wore a jacket which was cut short, a bowler hat, very large trousers and big black boots, which led to him becoming known as the Bradshawgate Masher. His antics of drinking other people's ale in pubs, occasionally singing in a refined light baritone voice and raising his hat to every policeman he met, was accepted with good humour.

At this period The Grand Theatre in Bolton attracted many top music hall stars, including the famous Fred Karno's Company. On one visit to the town Charlie Chaplin was among this group, appearing in a play called Mumming Birds. It is said that he was introduced to the Bradshawgate Masher and seeing the humour of this Boltonian, he copied both his mannerisms and eccentric clothes for his next act. The audience immediately loved this new character which Chaplin further developed to become his world famous tramp.

I wandered down Bradshawgate in the footsteps of the Masher, looking at the statue of Crompton and the adjacent Pack Horse Hotel where the annual Best Black Pudding in Great Britain Contest is held. Turning down cobbled Wood Street I stopped outside a row of attractive Georgian houses to read a plaque which stated that William Hesketh Lever was born here on the 19th September 1851. Ironically, this building in which one of England's wealthiest capitalists was born, is now the headquarters of the local socialists.

William Lever, who was the son of a grocer, started out as a traveller working for his father then went on to create a vast soap empire. He chose the name Sunlight for his product, he built the village of Port Sunlight for his workers and he took the title of Lord Leverhulme. But the high moral values that were inspired by his Non-conformist background never left him, he became a generous philanthropist who gave much to the people of Lancashire, including the freedom to roam through lovely Lever Park at Rivington. Perhaps his spirit still keeps a friendly eye on the local people for his birthplace is reputedly haunted by a man in Victorian clothes.

I continued my walk, looking now at the face of modern Bolton which is centred around the architectural glory of its splendid Victorian Town Hall, which is one of the finest civic buildings in Britain. It is built in an attractive classical style, with Corinthian pillars and stone lions which stands elevated above a spacious square, surrounded by the sweep of an elegant crescent. Here I walked among the bustle of the visitors who come to shop in the city atmosphere of the Market Place or to watch a play at the famous Octagon Theatre.

*Rivington: the lovely gateway to the West Pennine Moors.*

It is perhaps appropriate that Bolton has become a centre for drama for this corner of Lancashire has bred a host of actors, writers, and show business stars. These include Sir Ian McKellen, Frank Finlay, Bryan Pringle, Shirley Anne Field, Hylda Baker, band leaders Alyn Ainsworth and Jack Hylton, Bill

Naughton who wrote Alfie, Jonathan Gash who created the character Lovejoy and travel writer Geoffrey Moorhouse. Others who have their names carved on Bolton's wall of fame are steeplejack Fred Dibnah, Lord Haslam who headed the Coal Board, Ray Horrocks who was a former boss of British Leyland and little-known Robert Whitehead who in 1823 invented the torpedo . . . this list of famous Boltonians is endless.

## *6*

Lying five miles to the north west of Bolton, surrounded by the wild splendour of Rivington Moor, lies the small, highly independent town of Horwich. When it was convenient to label each place in Lancashire by the main product it produced Horwich was known as a Railway Town. The last locomotive built here has long since steamed away but for me Horwich will always have its own special label of Hometown, for it was here that I was born and grew up in the forties and fifties.

Each one of us has our own personal Hometown and when we return we experience the same feelings. Locked firmly in our memory are half-forgotten scenes from childhood which, prompted by a once familiar landscape, come flowing back. Buildings and streets which have now vanished are miraculously rebuilt in our mind, departed relatives and friends are remembered and both the pain and joy of our past is temporarily revived. This nostalgia is of course nothing new, for the good old days have always been with us. No doubt the Edwardians looked back in this same way to their Victorian childhood and Shakespeare thought of the good times when the young Elizabeth was on the throne.

There was a hint of rain in the leaden sky when I walked down Winter Hey Lane thinking of the time when Norman knights chased wild boar in what was then Horwich Forest. It remained a small, isolated community up till the 16th century when the infant textile industry was born. Two centuries later the Ridgeway family built their bleach works overlooking the village which brought further prosperity, but it was the coming of the railway works which transformed Horwich from a village into a town.

The Lancashire and Yorkshire Railway began digging out the foundations of their new works at Horwich in 1885. Four years later, on the 20th February 1889, the first locomotive to be built here, L & Y 1008, began trials. But this was more than just a remarkable engineering feat, for it had also created a new town. The population of Horwich had risen from 3,761 in 1881 to 12,850 in 1991, the largest percentage increase of any town in England. It had also become uniquely cosmopolitan, for workers had been brought in from every part of Britain and Ireland. This is reflected in today's community for only a handful of Horwichites can trace their local ancestry back beyond this period.

For over half a century the Loco-works dominated both the educational and social life of the town. Whole families were employed there, sons following their father and often their grandfather. The Mechanics Institute became renowned for its engineering training and the streets of the town were proudly named after great engineers. But sadly this all came to an end, in 1964 the last steam locomotive was repaired and a gradual decline followed until the works finally closed. However the town has now successfully completed its transition, the former Loco-works has become the base for scores of small businesses.

But my childhood memories of post-war Horwich is of a town at the beginning of this transition. Even then the influence of the Loco-works was declining as smiling men, bronzed by the desert sun, returned home with their kit-bags to build a new Britain. The huge trams with hard wooden seats which for half a century had glided to Bolton were now being replaced by buses and the first bananas that us former war-babies had ever seen, came at last to the shops. But the town, in spite of its industrial base, had a rural atmosphere which is still apparent. Overlooked by the moors and with the beauty of Rivington as its back-yard it possesses the tranquillity of a village. Up till the fifties milk was delivered by horse and cart, and there were few cars. People either walked or travelled by bus, fostering a community spirit that had been an essential feature of the war years.

Young boys at this time played with Meccano-sets and Dinky cars, avidly read Beano and Dandy, and spent their Saturday afternoons at the Picture House watching Roy Rogers and Hoppalong Cassidy. When Silcock's Fair came we excitedly collected empty bottles which we returned to patient shop-keepers for a penny refund. This money allowed us a couple of enchanting hours riding in Dodgem cars, shooting with air-rifles at tin ducks, or gazing with wonder at Siamese-twins and bearded-ladies. When Good Friday arrived we proudly joined crowds of fellow Lancastrians from other towns who converged on Horwich to climb to the top of the Pike, which we jealously regarded as our own. In a carnival atmosphere, but formally dressed in their Sunday clothes, the crowds bought bottles of pop and toffee apples, and laughed with their friends.

But inevitably this age of relative innocence was soon to be swept away forever. The Swinging Sixties, the influence of television, widespread car ownership and foreign travel has created a new 'good old days' for our children and grandchildren to feel nostalgic about!

# *CHAPTER NINE*

# *HORWICH TO DUNSOP BRIDGE*

I reach Rivington, attend a Remembrance service on Anglezarke Moor, then visit a pagan hilltop. In Blackburn I learn about Kathleen Ferrier, in Accrington I remember the 'Pals', then I warm up with a glass of black beer in Rossendale. I see the snow fall in Burnley, make a pilgrimage up Pendle Hill then I return to Dunsop Bridge in time for Christmas.

## *1*

I entered the West Pennine Moors by its loveliest and most popular gateway: Rivington. Here, where the harsh brown moorland tumbles down to the green of the valley hides some of Lancashire's most attractive countryside. It is an ancient landscape that man has transformed and miraculously enhanced. A place of woods and lakes, of stone cottages and old churches, where bluebells and celandines grow in early springtime. Here the elderly and very young stroll serenely on sunny days, while athletic hill-walkers and fell-runners test their muscles on steep slopes.

On a mild November day I parked my car at the Great House Barn which lies close to Rivington village. My stroll began along the wooded banks of the Lower Rivington Reservoir, following a path which gave me a marvellous view of the rounded summit of Rivington Pike. Crowned with its square stone tower it is one of Lancashire's best known landmarks, dominating the skyline for miles around. On its lower flank lies the remains of Lord Leverhulme's Rivington estate, now known as the Terraced Gardens. Here the Soap King spent some of his large fortune by purchasing the Manor of Rivington, this included Rivington Hall and Barns, together with a number of farms. In 1902 he built a large timber bungalow in which he lived, but this was destroyed in 1913 by a fire that had been started by a suffragette. Shortly afterwards it was replaced by an impressive stone residence, but after his death this fell into disrepair and was eventually demolished.

Continuing along the flat path I came to the recently restored ruined castle. This was also constructed by Lord Leverhulme as a replica of Liverpool Castle, it has now become popular with visiting Liverpudlians who see it as part of their heritage. It is believed that he intended it to be used as an open-air, french-style cafe, but any such plans were abandoned after his death. Nearby a farmer was busy at work hedging and ditching, one of those tasks left for the bleak days of winter. He was being watched by a field full of magpies who had discovered that the food which had been placed out for the sheep makes an easy picking.

My walk continued in a large circle through the wooded fringes of Lever Park, returning through pretty Rivington village, which has a green complete with stocks, a church, but sadly no inn. I ended my stroll, like most visitors to Rivington do, in the cafe at Great House Barn. This impressive building, with its massive 400-year-old, oak cruck-framework has a design based on that of an upturned Viking long-boat. As well as being a cafe it also houses a small information centre with permanent displays concerning the history and wildlife of the West Pennine Moors.

The magnificent moorland of Anglezarke, which stretches in wild splendour towards Winter Hill, was suddenly coming alive. Walkers, shielded from the cold November wind by multi-coloured anoraks of purple and green, could be seen ascending the narrow pathways that lead to Lead Mines Clough. Some had walked from Rivington, some from Belmont, and others from Chorley, while those less able through age had parked their cars at Jepson's Gate and made the easiest approach along a wide track. But there was a common aim among all of these four hundred men and women who had trekked to this wild place on Armistice Day: to remember the crew of a Wellington Bomber who died here half a century ago.

As I joined the crowd which was beginning to form around the weathered stone memorial that looks out over the rising hills, I began to speculate on the fate of Zulu 8799. The bomber had taken off on the 16th November 1943 from Wymeswold in Leicestershire on a training flight. Its pilot was Flight Sergeant Joseph B Timperon who came from Alice Springs in Australia, he was attached to the RAF from the Royal Australian Air Force. The five other members of the crew were Sergeants Eric Barnes, Joseph B Hayton, Robert S Jackson, Matthew Mouncy and George E Murray.

As the plane reached this part of upland Lancashire it began to get into difficulties, local people are reported to have heard the engines screeching. It then tore into the remote peaty summit of Hurst Hill, scattering wreckage over a wide area and killing all of the crew. The results of an investigation by the RAF concluded that it was probably caused by a 'loss of control in cloud, possibly due to icing' which may have led to structural failure as it went into a high speed dive.

*Anglezarke Moor: walkers gather on Armistice Day to remember the crew of Zulu 8799.*

This emotional anniversary ceremony, which had been organised by Eric Unsworth and Fred Jolly of the West Lancashire Long Distance Walkers Association, had stimulated great interest. As well as representatives of the Adlington British Legion, Horwich Rotary Club and the RAF, English relatives of the pilot had travelled down from Carlisle.

As eleven o'clock approached we were linked by radio to the service that was taking place at the Cenotaph in Whitehall, allowing us to share directly the poignant two-minutes silence. Prayers were then said to remember 'those who perished on this spot so far from home', which was followed by the hymn O Valiant Hearts. Tears were shed by many at the words of the Commemoration Act, which were being spoken at this time in every corner of England:

*They shall grow not old as we that are left grow old:*
*Age shall not weary them, nor the years condemn.*
*At the going down of the sun and in the morning*
*We will remember them.*

The British Legion Flag was lowered and the bugler played the Last Post, the plaintive sound echoing over Anglezarke's sunlit hills. After more prayers and the hymn, *The Day Thou Gavest*, there followed the laying of wreaths.

Squadron Leader Steven Haves, in the smart blue uniform of the Royal Australian Air Force, saluted his dead comrades then placed his wreath of poppies against the memorial. Others followed, until the blackened stone pillar was a blaze of red: wreaths, crosses and single flowers remembering the young lives that were lost in the fight for freedom, on this lonely Lancashire moorland.

The unique ceremony ended with the playing of the National Anthem, then the quiet crowd of walkers began to quickly disperse. The hillside was once more empty of people, the memory of these heroes having been duly honoured.

## 2

The road which links the villages of Rivington and Belmont is one of the most spectacular in Lancashire. It ascends quickly from a green wooded valley to reveal a panorama of magnificent moorland which stretches in every direction, ending only at the skyline. Overlooked by the savage grandeur of Winter Hill, the rolling grassland of Anglezarke Moor gives an impression of wild tranquillity. However, this is not the whole story, for I discovered that this ancient landscape hides secrets of our pagan past which go back to the hazy reaches of time.

I left my car at the high point of this road, looking northwards I could see a small, yet strangely significant mound on the skyline. This is Round Loaf, a man-made hillock which is marked as a Tumulus on the Ordnance Survey map. It is believed to be a place of ritual burial, the largest and most intriguing site of its type in the north-west, dating back 3500 years.

To reach the site involved me in a long trek across boggy, tussocky grass for it stands in the centre of the moorland. Those who choose a route from the Limestone Clough, which is to the east, can approach the mound up a deep gulley, appropriately named Devil's Ditch. The boggy walk, however, was more than worthwhile for the mound which is one of Lancashire's most ancient monuments, exudes an hushed atmosphere of mysticism. It was easy to imagine that I was standing on a giant outdoor altar, for the site is encompassed by a magic circle of wild hills. What strange pagan rites have been carried out on this lonely spot can only be guessed at for archaeologists have little evidence. The earlier stone circles are believed by some experts to have been associated with a goddess of fertility and in some cases with human sacrifice.

Round Loaf is a Bronze Age burial mound known as a Round Barrow which probably contains the cremated remains of the leader of the settlement. However, it is likely to be more than a mere grave, as its size and prominent position suggests. It is possible that rituals combining both fertility rites and the worship of dead ancestors took place on the spot. Due to its isolated location no official excavations have yet taken place, but sadly, over the years vandals have dug into the mound which may have destroyed valuable historical evidence.

It is said that Round Loaf is still regarded as a sacred site by members of modern witchcraft covens who meet here in secret. Symbolically placed stones, the macabre dismembered body of a bird and the ritualistic display of a sheep's skull discovered by hikers, bear testimony to their presence..

Of the people who built this mound we have little knowledge, although it is believed that they were immigrants who originated from the eastern Mediterranean. Human remains which have been discovered in other areas suggest that they were a strong people with generally robust features, unlike the earlier neolithic tribes who were slightly built. Their culture in some ways was like that of the ancient Egyptians, great emphasis being placed on the tombs of their leaders; Round Loaf being a Lancashire equivalent of the Pyramids.

Just over two miles to the south of Round Loaf stands Noon Hill, a high-point on the side of Rivington Moor which also has a mystical reputation. Excavations which took place in 1958 revealed an unusual form of burial mound which dated from 1100 BC. Cremated human remains were uncovered in a broken urn, which was later reconstructed and can now be seen in Bolton Museum. This spot, like Round Loaf, has always been regarded as being of special significance by the local people and has a reputation for being haunted. During the 17th century it was chosen as a secret meeting place by the Protestant martyr, George Marsh, and later by Non-conformists. Half a mile east of Noon Hill another mound was excavated in 1957, this too was identified as a burial site from 1500 BC, but it had been previously opened.

Rivington Pike is also steeped in legend and folklore. The crowds which climb to the summit each Good Friday are carrying on a tradition whose origins stretch back many thousands of years. It was once customary to ascend the hill on the first Sunday in May to greet the sunrise. This probably has its roots in Floralia, a Roman festival concerned with Flora, the goddess of spring and flowers. But flint chippings which have been discovered on the summit reveal that the site is much older. The hill is also reputed to be haunted by a Spectre Horseman, who rides across the site on St. Bartholomew's Eve, which suggests a Celtic connection.

A mile from Rivington Pike, on Wilder's Moor, stands Two Lads Hill which traditionally marks the burial place of two Saxon children who died on the moor in a snow storm. But a twin cairn, excavated two centuries ago was probably of Bronze Age origin and the site was later used as a hill fort.

Evidence in the form of place names and words commonly used in local speech suggest that the Rivington area has strong Norse connections. It is likely that the Vikings settled here during the early 9th century, probably arriving from Ireland. Their inheritance was the wild windswept uplands together with the magical sites of an earlier people, which they no doubt viewed with trepidation. They named their settlement Anglezarke, which some experts believe means Anlaf's-argh, or Anlaf's heathen temple. Could this perhaps refer to mysterious Round Loaf which was at the centre of their territory and did they use this ancient site as a place to worship their own Norse gods?

The name Rivington too has Norse origins which may well have links with the supernatural history of the area. It is said to be derived from Rowan-ton meaning the village of the mountain ash. This tree, with its bright red berries which appear in August, was of great significance to the Vikings. They believed its branches were a protection against evil spirits and witchcraft, and that a weapon made from its wood could ward off the Devil. The local rituals connected with these beliefs, perhaps intended to fight off the demons of the surrounding moorland, may have given the village its name.

Lying to the east of Round Loaf and linking the high points of Great Hill and Winter Hill is the impressive moorland ridge known as Spitlers Edge along which I returned to my car. This name is a reminder of the influence that the powerful order of the Knights Hospitallers of St John of Jerusalem, had on Anglezarke. They are reputed to have ridden along this route to supervise their holdings in the area, which included some moorland mines. They had claimed exclusive privileges in Britain, which had been granted by King Henry III. It does seem appropriate, that this order which became involved with the search for the Holy Grail together with many other strange events, should have associations with mysterious Anglezarke.

In recent years the puzzle of these moorlands has been added to by the reported sightings of UfOs. Representatives from a group of Lancashire UFO enthusiasts come regularly to the area, armed with cameras, binoculars and Geiger counters to watch for any strange happenings. Cigar shaped objects and odd flashing lights have been reported over the years adding fuel to the theory that Anglezarke Moor is also a UFO landing ground.

In spite of its rich reputation for supernatural activity this unspoilt corner of the West Pennine Moors continues to attract thousands of visitors each year. Sceptics may say that the UfOs are really satellites, that the witchcraft symbols on Round Loaf were placed there by practical jokers and that the ghostly horseman is just a legend. However, many locals are not too sure. They have a healthy regard for these sacred places of the past and they take particular care to avoid the summit of Rivington Pike on St. Bartholomew's Eve – just in case!

## 3

A gale force wind was driving the icy rain across Turton Moor and into the streets of Darwen. Window frames were rattling, fallen leaves were being tossed into neat piles in sheltered corners and small boys were finding out if their shoes were really waterproof by paddling in roadside pools.

This turnpike road along which I was travelling was built in 1797 to link Bolton to Blackburn, but it also transformed Darwen from a moorland village in to a small but prosperous manufacturing town. I stopped my car on the roadside so that I could admire the landmark which symbolises the confidence of Victorian Darwen, the India Mill chimney. This remarkable structure towers to a height of 300 feet, its ornate design being based on that of the Campanile in Venice. The top is crowned with two wide platforms and a cast iron cap which weighs almost forty tons. It is said to have taken fourteen years to complete, using tens of thousands of hand built bricks. As I gazed up at its windswept ledges I remembered the man who fearlessly climbs his red painted ladders to maintain such structures, Bolton's famous steeplejack, Fred Dibnah.

As I approached Blackburn the clouds had now lifted from the top of Darwen Hill revealing the dark outline of the Jubilee Tower. This is the landmark seen by thousands of football fans from all over England as they converge on Ewood Park to watch the Rovers. Thanks to the cheque-book of one of Britain's wealthiest men, steel magnate Jack Walker, Blackburn Rovers have risen to become one of the top sides in the Premier League. This team, which in 1888 was one of the founder members of the Football League, now has legendary manager Kenny Dalglish at its helm. Around £14 million pounds has already been spent attracting high-calibre players such as Alan Shearer and another £12 million is financing a reconstructed stadium. But even these huge sums are small fry to the man who is determined to make the Rovers the best in the world, for his personal fortune is estimated to be £320 million!

Despite having to dodge between showers of torrential rain I had a splendid afternoon exploring Blackburn's impressive town centre. I gazed into its modern shop windows, bought oranges from its famous market, looked at the treasures in its Anglican Cathedral, admired the architecture of St. George's Hall then I discovered a gem of a museum. For here under one roof are examples of the fascinating, Heath-Robinson type machines which began a revolution that shook the world.

It would seem that in every gloomy attic and every dank cellar of 18th century Lancashire young men suddenly became obsessed with inventing. Everyone wanted fine clothes, we now had imported cotton as a marvellous raw-material, but we lacked the machines capable of producing the quantity and quality required. It became apparent that fortunes could be made by those who could solve this problem; the race was on.

In this small yet fascinating exhibition in the Lewis Textile Museum I looked at the winners of this race, names that children learn to pass exams without perhaps realising their true significance. John Kay of Bury who in 1733 invented his Flying Shuttle; the local man from Blackburn, James Hargreaves, who developed his attractively named Spinning Jenny; Richard Arkwright the barber from Preston, who with his Water Frame and business acumen gained a knighthood; and Samuel Crompton of Bolton whose Spinning Mule made many a millionaire but left him penniless.

However, these wooden beams and clever hand forged mechanisms which turned pieces of fluffy cotton into lengths of fine cloth, were more that mere textile machines . They were the seeds which inspired other great and often uneducated, engineers to experiment. This led to steam engines, electrical power, and eventually cars, aircraft and the computers which have changed the world.

"We have a new Kathleen Ferrier exhibition in the museum around the corner which is really worth seeing."

I decided to take the museum assistant's advice.

Of all the talented people that the town has produced, Kathleen Ferrier is the one Blackburnians have taken closest to their heart. For as well as being, to quote the words of Bruno Walter, 'one of the greatest singers of all time', she had that marvellous indefinable quality which we call charisma. The temporary exhibition which I wandered around, had been arranged to coincide with the anniversary of her tragically early death in 1953 at the age of only forty one. Cancer had cruelly robbed us of one of our most cherished stars, but forty years on our memory of her is as alive as ever and a new Kathleen Ferrier Society has been formed in the town.

*Kathleen Ferrier*

It was in the village of Higher Walton that Kathleen Ferrier was born on the 22 April 1912. When she was eighteen months old the family moved to Blackburn where her father, a school teacher, took up a new position as a Headmaster. As both her parents were singers and Blackburn was a musical town, this proved an ideal environment to develop her natural aptitude for music which was apparent from early childhood.

She learned to play both the violin and the piano, and also sang with local choral groups. Under the tuition of her highly talented piano teacher, Frances

Walker, she quickly developed her skill. She became a brilliant young pianist with the ability of not only being able to read music at a glance, but to know how it would actually sound.

At the age of sixteen, with her sights set on becoming a piano teacher, she entered a competition which was sponsored by the *Daily Express*, and won herself a Crammer upright piano. At this time she was working as a telephone operator in Blackburn, a job which she held for seven years, but her real ambition still lay in the world of music. In 1934 she was transferred by the post office to work in Blackpool. There she lived in digs, making the trip home each weekend on a bike which she was paying for at half a crown a week.

In 1935, at the age of twenty three, she married bank clerk Bert Wilson and they set up their new home at Warton. Both Kathleen and her new husband joined the Lytham Vocal Society, but the next year they had to move again for he was transferred to a bank at Silloth near Carlisle. In 1937 Bert bet her a shilling that she dare not enter both the piano and singing competitions at the Carlisle Festival. She rose to the occasion, and to her surprise she won both contests.

This success led to her being offered a number of engagements in the Lake District, and at one of these she was seen by BBC producer, Cecil McGivern. This led to her first broadcast in February 1939 from the Newcastle studio, in which she included the ever popular Curly Headed Babby. Two months later she again took part in the Carlisle Festival where her potential was immediately realised by adjudicator, Dr. J.E. Hutchington. He said that 'the beauty of her voice stood out like a beacon' and he offered her voice training lessons.

In 1940 Bert joined the army and Kathleen moved to Carlisle where her services as a singer became in great demand. But it was in June 1941 that her professional career really began, having now decided to revert to her maiden name. She toured with CEMA (Council for the Encouragement of Music and the Arts) and was later heard in Manchester by the celebrated conductor, Sir Malcolm Sargent. He told her he believed she had a great future, but to succeed she would need to live in London. Following his advice she auditioned at the Wigmore Hall for Ibbs and Tillett, the famous concert agency, who accepted her as a client.

At first she continued her concert tours mainly in the north, but as her experience and reputation grew she became in great demand throughout the country. After the war she was the first British singer to take part in the Salzburg Festival, then in 1946 she made her operatic debut in the premier of Benjamin Britten's Rape of Lucretia at Glynebourne. Rapidly she now became an international celebrity, making concert tours throughout America and

Europe, making gramophone recordings and occasionally appearing in private performances before the Royal Family. Sadly, her short career came to an end in February 1953 when she made her final appearance at Convent Garden as Orfeo under Sir John Barbirolli. Her terrible illness forced her to cancel two performances, then she spent the next few months in hospital where she died on October 8th 1953.

Those that come to this exhibition expecting to look on the personal effects of the stereotyped, highly serious opera singer, will no doubt be pleasantly surprised. The letters, postcards and cheeky poems which she wrote to her sister Winifred from all parts of the world, reveal her to be a marvellously warm person. Her down to earth Lancashire wit and sunny personality shine through; this great and much-loved singer refused to be changed by fame.

## 4

I left Blackburn by the Accrington road, but after a couple of miles I stopped my car near the brow of a hill. On the wall of a cosy terraced house, No 331 Audley Range, I read the words : The Birthplace of Alfred Wainwright, Author and Fell Walker (1907-1991). Here, the man whose books had guided me to the summits of Gragareth and Blackstone Edge, was born into the poverty of Edwardian Blackburn. But, it was with north country tenacity that he fought his way first to a good job at the local Town Hall, then later to the council offices at Kendal.

As soon as he was established in his beloved Lakeland he was then filled with an irresistible urge to explore every facet of the mountains. Each weekend for ten years he wandered up every valley, climbed every summit and walked around every tarn. Having now acquired a unique knowledge, he became intent on passing this on to other mountain lovers. With remarkable artistic skill and dedication he began to produce his classic, hand written, series of guide books that have become the bible of all who walk in the Lake District.

It was raining with grim determination in Accrington and I had arrived at the wrong time for it was Wednesday, which means half day closing. Dodging the showers I wandered along Warner Street, admired the marvellous Victorian Arcade and the recently restored Town Hall, I bought a postcard from the Tourist Information Office, then I went on a pilgrimage to see England's saddest memorial.

*Alfred Wainwright*

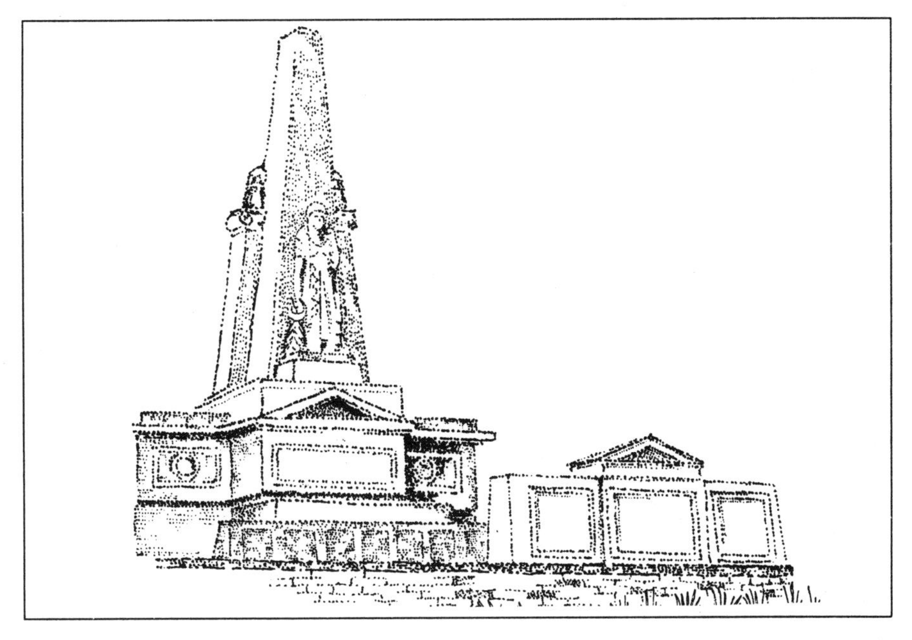

*The memorial to the Accrington Pals overlooking Accrington.*

On a green hilltop in Oakhill Park I stood alone in the rain looking up at a magnificent stone obelisk which towers into the grey sky. At its base is carved the poignant female figure of Maternity, forever mourning her lost children. Below I read the names of some of these children, row upon row, a seemingly endless list. These were the young men who left this corner of Lancashire then died in the fields of the Somme, remembered forever as the Accrington Pals.

At the outbreak of the war against Germany in 1914 a large scale recruitment campaign began, epitomised by the portrait of Lord Kitchener with the 'Your Country Needs You' slogan. It was decided that if men who were friends or neighbours, could be certain of serving together then they would be more likely to enlist. Known as the Pals Battalions, these were raised in many towns in England.

Recruitment offices were opened in Accrington, Chorley and Burnley, together with a number of other small towns in this area. Within ten days the 11th (Service) Battalion (Accrington) East Lancashire Regiment or the Accrington Pals had been raised. It was made up of 1,076 men and thirty six officers, who for five months were billeted at home and carried out their training wearing civilian clothes. When their uniforms finally arrived they were made from a blue material as no Khaki coloured cloth was available.

The Pals departed from Accrington in February 1915, amidst a large cheering crowd. After training in various camps in Britain for most of the year they then sailed for Egypt to guard the Suez Canal. But in March 1916 they were moved again, this time to France, for the large offensive against the German positions known as the Big Push, was underway.

The terrible Battle of the Somme began on a fine sunny morning on July 1st 1916. As the British Artillery had been blasting the German trenches almost non-stop for a week, it was believed that they could now offer no resistance. The orders to advance were given to the 100,000 British troops who stretched along a fifteen mile front. But the strength of the enemy had been mis-judged, for their deep trenches had been largely unaffected by the shelling. The unprotected British troops were quickly mowed down by machine guns in the worst defeat the army has ever known. The Accrington Pals sent 700 men in the advance, of these 235 were killed and 350 were wounded; in total there were 60,000 British casualties.

This terrible slaughter of innocent young men devastated this part of Lancashire, in just twenty minutes a whole generation had been wiped out. The Pals are remembered today by a Memorial Chapel in St John-the-Evangelist Church in Accrington and by a recent memorial on the Somme Battlefield which has been built, appropriately, of Accrington Brick. A play, which has also been written about this tragedy by Peter Whelan, is regularly performed throughout Britain.

## 5

The first snow of winter had arrived in Rossendale. The wild moorland summits of Whittle Hill, Bull Hill and Cribden had vanished under a ghostly veil of white cloud. Only the lower slopes of these towering hills were visible, transformed from the mahogany tints of autumn to a soft glinting silver. In the sweeping valleys, which criss cross this pennine landscape like the strands of a spiders web, the hawthorn hedgerows were bare and stark. The only hint of colour came from solitary holly trees hidden in sheltered cloughs, their prickly leaves and vivid red berries speaking of the approach of Christmas.

As I descended through Haslingden I could see to the south the path of the Irwell as it meanders in twists and turns towards Bury then on to Manchester. Some say the Industrial Revolution began here when it was known as the Golden Valley, yet if this is so it has hardly touched the countryside. The residents of Ramsbottom, Edenfield and Helmshore can walk from their homes and within ten minutes be in rural tranquillity. C.E. Montague was quite right when he wrote about 'the factory hooter waking the grouse on the moors'.

I parked my car in Rawtenstall then I asked a pale faced old man, who was obviously hating the cold weather, if he could direct me to the Herbal Shop. On reflection, he seemed to be the last person to ask such a question for he hardly looked a picture of good health. However he knew the place, even if he had never tried its products, so in two minutes I was entering Britain's Last Temperance Bar.

This remarkable shop has somehow managed to escape the passing of time, its interior remains splendidly Victorian. If Dickens' ghost was to visit this valley where he discovered the Cheeryble Brothers, in this shop he would feel most at home. An ancient copper boiler was steaming cheerfully on the counter, while on the wall was a list of drinks available. These included Sarsaparilla, Black Beer, Cream Soda, Ginger Beer and Blood Tonic. After much indecision I asked the woman who is the fortunate owner of this unique Temperance Bar for a glass of Black Beer and Orange, which I had served hot.

Sitting in a quiet corner of the shop I was able to sip my warming and hopefully, health giving drink while observing the customers. Children on their way home from school asked for glasses of warm sarsaparilla, a young man wanted a large supply of cod-liver oil tablets, while a girl was given a bag full of herbs whose name I was unable to hear. It could have been any of about sixty types which I could see carefully labelled in glass jars. It was perhaps Scullcap, or maybe Marshmallow, Periwinkle, Wormwood, Valerian, Yarrow . . .

In this atmosphere of natural remedies I began to wonder if I ought to buy some Rutin Tablets which a notice said would 'guard against blood-pressure and thrombosis'. Maybe I was in desperate need of some Garlic Capsules or Ginseng or Devil's Claw. Was that a twinge of rheumatics I could feel in my right knee?

I decided to leave for Bacup – time might be running out!

## 6

I followed the deep-cut Rossendale Valley in which stone built cottages and small mills cling precariously to narrow strips of flat land, secured two centuries ago from the steeply rising hillside. In this unchanging landscape where generations of Lancastrian craftsmen have fashioned slippers and shoes, the moors sweep down to the doorsteps. I drove slowly through

Newchurch, Waterfoot and Stacksteads, reaching the crossroads at Bacup in a flurry of snow.

The cold wind was blowing hard up Yorkshire Street forcing the few hardy shoppers to seek refuge in sheltered places. With my anorak hood securely fastened I wandered along the sturdy streets and peered into unspoilt alleyways of what is said by the experts to be 'the best preserved cotton town in Britain'. It was here in 1879 that my own grandfather was born, his parents having been forced to leave rural Norfolk by a decline in agriculture. Victorian Lancashire held hope for tens of thousands of such families; here in the workshop of the world jobs and housing were plentiful in a new community which attracted people from all corners of Britain.

It is said that men who came here from Cornwall to work in the quarries started the famous Brittania Coconut Dancers. Each Easter Sunday they begin their strange rituals around the town, starting at 9.0 am their performance continues throughout the day. With blackened faces and highly polished clogs, the eleven colourful dancers in the best Morris dancing tradition, skip their way to every pub. Dressed in black, with a skirt of red and white they carry half-hoop garlands and are accompanied by music from a concertina. Known affectionately as the Nutters, their ritual is believed to have been derived from a tribal dance. This was brought by Africans who came working in the Cornish tin mines during the 17th century.

Surrounded by snow laden hills whose summits had vanished into a cold white mist, I drove through Broad Clough and Weir village, then past the remote Deerplay Pub which lies on the slopes of Thieveley Pike. In recent years these moors, which link Bacup, Burnley and Todmorden, have become named The Bacup Triangle by journalists. This results from the many reports of UFO sightings made in the area. A coalman from Crawshawbooth is reported to have actually seen aliens dressed in silver suits whose featureless heads were covered by helmets. Two teenagers from Newchurch came face to face with a strange figure who was dressed in a shining black gown, who they say had a large forehead. Scores of other independent reports which are on the files of the Defence Ministry tell of hovering circular spacecraft and unexplained piercing bright lights which move at high speeds through the night sky.

In spite of the snow, the golfers of Burnley were still playing their morning round as I drove through the park to Towneley Hall. I parked my car facing the front of this lovely historic house, then as I began to eat a sandwich the wily birds of Towneley appeared as if by magic. A robin, its blood-red breast contrasting vividly with the newly fallen snow, was the first to beg a crust.

Seeing his success a huge speckled-breasted mistle thrush thought he too would try, soon to be joined by a wild-eyed blackbird and two magpies. Not to be outdone a grey squirrel bounced like an acrobat from the branches of an oak on to the lawn, so together they shared my lunch!

The people of Burnley are particularly fortunate in having one of England's most splendid buildings on their doorstep which has become their local Art Gallery and Museum. This ancient land was first granted by the powerful Roger de Lacy to his daughter in 1200, when she married the Dean of Whalley. Their descendants became the Towneley family, who for 800 years played a major role in the shaping of the country. At the turn of this century, Lady O'Hagan, the last of the Towneley family to be associated with Burnley, offered the Hall and park to the town at a fraction of its real value. Here I walked along the impressive Long Gallery, looked at magnificent paintings and porcelain, saw military displays, learned about eccentric members of the Towneley family, admired the ornately carved altarpiece; and wished that I had a week to saunter through this Lancashire treasure-house.

*Burnley: the canal lies frozen and a bitter wind blows across the Weaver's Triangle, once the heart of the town's industrial life.*

Burnley town centre was quiet, which was no surprise for a bitter wind was sweeping along the valley bringing with it large flakes of snow. I wandered along its impressive precinct, explored its fascinating alleyways, and then read a notice outside a methodist church which announced: God. Never lets us down. Never lets us go. Never lets us off. Trying to unravel the deeper meaning of this message I took refuge in the Mechanics, where I was saved from hypothermia by two cups of piping hot coffee.

The accent of the girl who served me in the cafe seemed strangely familiar, yet it was far removed from this part of Lancashire. When she told me that, "I come from Sydney, I'm over here for two years,' I suddenly realised that it was in an Australian soap opera on TV that I had last heard a similar voice. She went on to tell me how her mother had emigrated from Burnley over forty years ago after paying just ten pounds and had never been back. Having had the urge to return to her roots this young Aussie was now stopping with a relative and "Yes, she had grown to love the town".

I asked the smartly uniformed receptionist who was standing behind the Tourist Information desk in the Mechanics if she could direct me to the Weavers' Triangle.

"Just turn right up Manchester Road," came her reply, but her eyes added, "you would be crazy to go there in a snowstorm in December."

The Weavers' Triangle, which I am quite sure is a splendid place to visit in springtime, looked like a scene from an Antarctic travelogue. The canal was frozen, the Wharfemaster's house and the Toll Office were enveloped in snow, and a blood-freezing wind was blowing from the hills. Yet in an odd way this severe weather marvellously captured the austerity of what was the centre of Burnley's Victorian industrial life. Here, generations of workers spent their days in weaving sheds, spinning mills and in the intolerable atmosphere of heat and smoke at the foundry hammer. For by this time, the little settlement that had begun in 800 AD on the banks of the Brun and the Calder, had grown to become the world's leading producer of cotton cloth.

## 7

The east of Burnley is dominated by brooding moorland which stretches unbroken into West Yorkshire. This curving border links the lonely summits of Black Hameldon Hill and Boulsworth Hill; wild Pennine country where small moorland villages and isolated farms nestle in secluded hollows. Such places as Hurstwood, the birthplace of the Elizabethan poet Edmund Spenser; Briercliffe, once the home of Bronze Age Man; and haunted Wycoller, whose ruined hall was transformed by Charlotte Brontë into Ferndean Manor when she wrote Jane Eyre. It is a place where curlews and red grouse nest on heathery hilltops, kestrels and stoats cruelly hunt for food, and solitary walkers follow in the steps of the Brigantes. But this harsh landscape becomes tempered in early springtime, its lower slopes clothed in the yellow of celandine, the rich purple of dog violet and the fragile white of wood sorrel.

I took the road northwards, passing through Brierfield and Nelson, then from Barrowford I turned up a narrow lane which climbed a gentle hillside to lead me to the west. After stopping my car on the brow of a hill beyond Newchurch, I walked towards a farm gate to be rewarded by one of the most spectacular views in all of England. Framed by the gateposts I looked upon a series of rolling green fields which dipped steeply downwards towards the valley in which hides lovely Barley village. My eyes were led at first along the line of two converging drystone walls which curve across this marshy pastureland. Here sheep were feeding with timid determination, their grey wool highlighted by the dilute wintry sunshine. Here and there, joined by the thin dark lines of narrow tracks, I could see the glinting white of remote farmhouses. But this was only a rich foreground, for beyond, soaring into the December sky was the magnificent bulk of Pendle Hill. From the angled profile of the Big End it rises majestically to its high summit, then filling the landscape, its savage outline gradually declines towards Whalley. Its elevated slopes appeared the colour of velvet, merging on their descent with the dull orange of dead bracken. Pencilled in shadow, I could see to the right an ascending pathway up which I would soon be climbing to reach the top of this mysterious hillside.

From the car park in Barley I followed the yellow and black witch signs towards the village centre, firmly ignoring the inviting Pendle Inn. Turning left just before the village post office my path continued alongside a stream leading at first, to gently rising pastureland. But I found that the really steep climb begins beyond Ing's Farm, for here a groove worn by generations of walkers has now been transformed into a stepped track. It ascends diagonally towards the Big End, a quick but stamina-testing ascent. I inwardly reassured myself that the half dozen stops I made were not taken to gain my breath, but of course to enjoy the view!

The summit of Pendle Hill lies about 400 metres from the Big End. It consists of a trig-point which stands on a slightly elevated mound 1827 feet (557m) above sea level, amidst a boggy plateau of tussocky peat. Walking to the edge of the hill I now got the real feeling of height, for from here it tumbles almost vertically to the valley below. My view over the rooftops of Barley was restricted by winter gloom, but on a bright day a magnificent panorama is unveiled. This sweeps from the brown uplands of Lancashire to the limestone peaks of Yorkshire, and so I am told, with the occasional glimpse of York Minster.

As I stood on this wild summit with the eerie white mist swirling around me I began to ponder on its strange history, for it is only rivalled by Glastonbury Tor for the title of England's Most Mysterious Hill. Measuring some seven miles long and varying between one and three miles wide, it was known by the Celts simply as The Hill. The Big End which lies to the north-east, is the most impressive side, for the opposite approach from the south-west is surprisingly gradual up a sloping plateau of moorland. It has been revealed by geologists that this outward covering of peat lies on top of a layer of millstone grit, which in turn lies on a bed of white limestone. One of the odd phenomena which occasionally occurs here is known as a water-brast, when for no apparent reason a powerful torrent of water erupts from the hillside, often resulting in local flooding.

Lying on the boundary of the ancient Saxon kingdoms of Mercia and Northumbria the hill has always been regarded as special; a place of romance and mystery. This supernatural atmosphere in which it is shrouded is perhaps why it was once regarded as being one of England's highest mountains. It was said:

*'Pendle Hill, Ingleborough and Penyghent,*
*Highest hills between Scotland and Trent.'*

In 1652 George Fox, the founder of the Quaker Movement, ascended to the top of the hill where he had a great vision. Many local folk became converted to the Quaker faith and today the hill has become a place of pilgrimage for Quakers world-wide.

But for many people the name Pendle Hill is synonymous not with Christianity, but with Witchcraft. It was early in 1612 that the rest of England first heard of the diabolical discovery of two families of witches who were living in the shadow of this hill. The king sent his witch-finder, Thomas Potts to investigate the strange affair, aided by a local Justice of the Peace, Roger Nowell. Accusations and confessions came fast and furious, with a widow known as Owd Demdike being identified as their leader and a gentlewoman, Alice Nutter of Roughlee Hall being also implicated. Soon the dungeons of Lancaster Castle were filled with the accused, nine of whom paid with their lives, but Owd Demdike cheated the executioner by dying while in custody.

The romance of Pendle has attracted many writers to come here over the years with the intention of capturing, with their pen, this atmosphere of mystery. Thomas Potts recorded a contemporary account of the witch trials in his *Wonderful Discoverie of Witches* in 1612. But it was Victorian writer Harrison Ainsworth, who popularised the tale when he wrote *Lancashire Witches* in 1848, for which he received a handsome fee of £1000 from the Sunday Times. In 1928 the great travel writer, H.V. Morton, ascended the hill which he describes in *The Call of England*, then Robert Neill followed in 1951 when he wrote his best selling novel, Mist Over *Pendle*, which still remains in print.

# 8

My mood was of elation tinged with sadness when I drove through lovely Downham village to reach the Ribble Valley, for I was approaching the end of my journey. In the half-light of a December afternoon I began the ascent of the tortuous road which climbs between Waddington and Easington Fells. As I passed the lonely Moorcock Inn visitors, protected from the cold by sheep-skin coats and fur hats, were dashing from their cars. With hardly a glance at the brightly-lit Christmas Tree, which on this remote fellside I thought was particularly welcoming, they escaped into the warmth of the inn.

Soon I was above the snow line, the bronze coloured moorland which stretches unbroken on each side of this road had suddenly been transformed into a misty carpet of white. On the roadside I caught a quick glance of the ice cold water of Walloper Well, where Gypsies and travellers once stopped to drink, then I was descending towards the Hodder. Here I was greeted by the breathtaking panorama of the Bowland Hills, towering upwards from the subdued green of the valley. But what a startling difference between this winter landscape and that of the hot splendour of June when my journey began. This jumble of wild fells was now showing its savage face. Craggy gulleys and once inviting summits appeared bleak and menacing, deep windswept snow which began on the lower slopes, ended in a trail of ghostly cloud. In this harsh winter landscape only the tough Lancashire farmers and shepherds who have lived here for generations, really feel at home.

I dipped down to Newton, where fat pheasants stood feeding unmolested on the riverside and Christmas wreaths lay upon cottage doors. Melting snow, which had turned some low lying fields into watery quagmires, had also provided mallards with new pools to explore. At last, along the quiet lane which overlooks the Hodder I came upon the sign Dunsop Bridge, which meant my journey through Lancashire had come to an end. The village was quiet, I was now alone in the Centre of Britain. With hail blowing in my face I walked over the bridge to the war memorial that in summer had been festooned with flowers but now had only the forlorn poppies of Remembrance Sunday. I gazed upon the bleak heights of Mellor Knoll and Totridge Fell, I looked in vain for salmon in the gushing waters of the river, then I bought a Christmas card from the village shop which had Greetings from Dunsop Bridge printed upon it.

In the marvellous festive atmosphere of a roaring open fire at the Inn at Whitewell, I was joined by my wife, Wynne, in a drink to celebrate the end of my journey. Here we talked of rocking-horses on Whalley Nab, of hidden shrines and skulls, of llamas in the Lune Valley and of witches at Pendle Hill. I spoke of the incredible diversity of the Lancashire countryside which I had seen, from the wild mountain summit of Gragareth to the fertile flatness of the Fylde and Martin Mere. I remembered those odd half-forgotten places which I had explored, Sambo's Grave at Sunderland Point, Cromwell's Stone at Lathom and the eerie pagan site of Round Loaf on Anglezarke Moor. Then in contrast I talked of the cities, the astonishing waterfront at Liverpool, the Roman Fort where Manchester began and the hundreds of fascinating historic links to be found in every town. Preston with its elk, Wigan with its Pier, Rochdale with its first Co-op shop and Bolton with its Spinning Mule. But perhaps, more than anything, it is the bewildering talent of Lancastrians which has made the county unique. People like Kathleen Ferrier, Alfred Wainwright, George Formby, Gracie Fields, Nat Lofthouse, H.V. Morton, The Beatles, Thora Hird, Morecambe and Wise, L.S. Lowry . . . and a thousand more.

# Index

## D



## F



## G



## H



## I



## K



## L



## M